PARENTING

GUIDE TO
YOUR BABY'S
FIRST YEAR

PARENTING
GUIDE TO YOUR BABY'S FIRST YEAR

Anne Krueger
with the Editors of PARENTING Magazine

BALLANTINE BOOKS
NEW YORK

A Ballantine Book
Published by The Ballantine Publishing Group

Copyright © 1999 by Parenting Magazine

All rights reserved under International and Pan-American Copyright Conventions. Published in the United States by The Ballantine Publishing Group, a division of Random House, Inc., New York, and simultaneously in Canada by Random House of Canada Limited, Toronto.

Ballantine and colophon are registered trademarks of Random House, Inc.

http://www.randomhouse.com/BB/

Library of Congress Cataloging-in-Publication Data
Krueger, Anne.
    Parenting guide to your baby's first year / Anne Krueger with the editors of Parenting magazine.—1st ed.
       p.   cm.
    ISBN 0-345-41180-3 (alk. paper)
    1. Infants. 2. Infants—Care. 3. Infants—Development. 4. Child rearing.
5. Parenting. 6. Parent and infant. I. Parenting (San Francisco, Calif.) II. Title.
HQ774.K78   1999
649'.122—dc21   98-21987
                                                                                                          CIP

Text design by Michaelis/Carpelis Design Associates
Cover design by Dreu Pennington McNeil
Cover photo © Joe Polollio/Tony Stone Images

Manufactured in the United States of America

First Edition: March 1999

10   9   8   7   6   5   4   3   2   1

For my mother, Jean Kemp Krueger

CONTENTS

FOREWORD

From PARENTING's Editor in Chief

As new moms and dads quickly discover, parenting is unpredictable, challenging, joyful, humbling, exhilarating, exhausting, and immensely satisfying—sometimes all those things in a single day, or hour!

Especially during the first weeks and months of your baby's life, adjusting to things that you'd expected to be simple, such as routine feedings (that are anything but routine), or sleep schedules (your infant's *and* yours), can seem overwhelming. When my son, Jack, was born, I remember feeling that as soon as I was getting a grasp on mothering, something new would crop up. After he started eating solid food, for instance, he seemed interested only in orange foods—strained carrots, squash, sweet potatoes. As soon as we stocked up on those, his interests turned elsewhere in the color spectrum.

Adjusting to the realities and mysteries of caring for a baby is probably more demanding than anything else in life. The good news, of course, is that it's one of the most rewarding things we'll ever do. And the whole adjustment process can be much smoother if you have a helpful guide to turn to—for advice, to know that you're not alone, to see that there's an answer to whatever surprise your infant throws your way.

That's where PARENTING *Guide to Your Baby's First Year* comes in. Just like PARENTING magazine, it's a clear, warm, easily accessible resource, with facts from experts as well as reality-tested advice from moms and dads around the country. Armed with essential information that's both practical and authoritative, you'll find life with your baby—from birth to the first birthday—all the more gratifying. Welcome to parenting!

Janet Chan
Editor in Chief
PARENTING

ACKNOWLEDGMENTS

As with so many of the most rewarding things we do, this book was a group effort. I'd like to thank PARENTING magazine, especially editorial director Janet Chan, for supporting this project. PARENTING franchise development editor Bruce Raskin deserves special thanks for his skilled and insightful editing and for his unflagging enthusiasm and friendship. It was Bruce who kept me on track and on time. This book is as much his as mine.

Thanks also to Ballantine editor Elisa Wares, who—literally—had life with baby on her mind during this project; she delivered her second child in the midst of Chapter 3.

It's thanks to the efforts of Mary James, Renée Swanson, Heidi Kotansky, Julia Bourland, Nicole Balin, Anna David, and Kristen Bruno that this book is peppered with interesting experiences of new parents from across the country. Mary James's skillful interviewing and reporting capture the excitement of everything from the delivery room to the classic first-birthday celebration. Valerie Fahey's top-notch fact-checking kept me honest. Kathy Gunst, PARENTING's cooking guru, contributed the excellent recipes. And Lisa Hilgers's photo selection and editing make the book come alive. Thank you to them all.

Heartfelt thanks go to our tireless advisory board. Their expertise and integrity greatly enhance the book. Thanks, too, to the New Mother's Club in Knoxville: Bett McLean, Nancy Reding, and Vicki Seebeck. I couldn't have made it through my own first year of life with baby without them, or without our smart, funny pediatrician, Dr. Joseph Peeden.

And most of all, a very special thank-you to my daughters Halley Rose and Emily Grace, who continue to think that mommy can leap tall buildings, and to my husband, Tony Corapi, who knows I can't but has faith in me anyway. Without them, none of this would have been possible.

A.K.

The Medical Advisory Board for Parenting *Guide to Your Baby's First Year*

Anne Krueger and the editors of Parenting wish to thank the UCLA Center for Healthier Children, Families, and Communities and its affiliated faculty for carefully reviewing the manuscript of this book.

Neal Halfon, MD, MPH, Professor in Pediatrics and Public Health, University of California at Los Angeles Schools of Medicine and Public Health; codirector, UCLA Center for Healthier Children, Families, and Communities

Claire Kopp, PhD, Professor in Psychology and Applied Developmental Psychology, Claremont Graduate University

Neal Kaufman, MD, MPH, Director, Division of Academic Primary Care, Pediatrics, Cedars-Sinai Medical Center

Michael Regalado, MD, Director of Developmental and Behavioral Pediatrics, Children's Hospital, Los Angeles; Associate Clinical Professor of Pediatrics, School of Medicine, University of Southern California

Wendy Slusser, MD, MS, Assistant Clinical Professor, Department of Pediatrics, UCLA; Director, UCLA Breastfeeding Program, Center for Healthier Children, Families, and Communities

Jill Hoube, MD, Robert Wood Johnson Clinical Scholar, UCLA

INTRODUCTION

When I was pregnant with my first daughter, I was lucky enough to know three other women at my office who were expecting around the same time. We picked out baby clothes together, shared fast-food cravings, and talked, talked, talked. We discussed baby names, the size of our bellies, our worries about labor, and our excitement about motherhood.

After our babies (two girls, two boys) were born, the new mothers' club really took off. We exchanged dinners plus a great deal of advice and loving support. I received near-hysterical calls in the middle of the night and did my share of crying on friends' shoulders. What made us weep? Happiness, fatigue, worry . . . well, who could understand better than another new mother that sometimes you don't have a clue why you're feeling the way you do? The emotions, challenges, and joys of the first year of life with baby aren't always easily explained. But they certainly are a lot more manageable—even fun—when you can share them with folks who are in the same boat.

As a former editor-in-chief of PARENTING magazine, I have been reminded again and again of this power of shared experiences. PARENTING's readers have always turned to the magazine for the authoritative advice for which it is known, but they love the magazine for the honesty of the voices and experiences of real parents presented in its pages. It is that combination of expertise and accessibility that the editors of PARENTING and I had in mind when we conceived this *Guide to Your Baby's First Year*. We'd love it if you thought of this book as your own new mothers' club, a place where you can turn for practical, timely information, side by side with the experiences of many new mothers and new fathers, too; a club where you can find inspiration, reassurance, and answers to your questions; a club, in fact, with an index.

To deliver answers to your questions as easily as possible, PARENTING *Guide to Your Baby's First Year* is organized chronologically. Information is served up when you really need it—whether you're in the throes of baby's first bout of colic or in the thrall of his first word. You don't have to slog through a whole year's worth of baby's social development, for instance, when all you really want to know about is that belly laugh you just heard bursting from your 4-month-old.

After a chapter on newborns, all the information in the book—from baby-care basics (care and feeding, sleeping, health and safety) to baby's development (physical, mental, social, and language)—is packaged into four chapters, one for each quarter of a baby's first year. This ensures that age-appropriate information is easy to find and puts the emphasis on development where it should be—that is, that each baby has his or her own timetable of development and that there is a wide range of normal development. Since months are grouped together, the subject of walking, for instance, can be covered in the 10- to 12-month chapter instead of being arbitrarily dropped into a section on 11-month-olds—a much more realistic way of presenting how babies develop.

Each chapter also includes a section specifically about Mom and Dad's development as parents. The transition to parenthood, while exhilarating, can also be rocky. One of the hottest topics of conversation in my new moms' club was how motherhood changed us, scared us, delighted us—far more than we had ever expected.

Before I was a mom, for instance, would I have ever dreamed that I'd keep my daughter's nasal aspirators as keepsakes (the rubber bulbs used to suck out a baby's nose and mouth when she's born)? Would I have been able to guess the identity of the little raisinlike thing in the memory box (an umbilical cord stump)? Would I have imagined that I'd let my own mother take a Polaroid of my engorged breasts? That I could happily watch a sleeping baby for hours? That I'd cry when the baby was born, cry when I went back to work, cry when she turned 1?

No, no, no, no, and no. There's just no imagining all the delicious details of what your new life with Baby will be like. Your first year with your infant will be a unique journey, just as your pregnancy or adoption was. It is our hope that with PARENTING *Guide to Your Baby's First Year* at your side, your trip will be enlightened and enjoyable. And that you'll know you're not traveling alone.

Anne Krueger

PARENTING
GUIDE TO
YOUR BABY'S
FIRST YEAR

Affectionately yours: It's never too early to begin lavishing attention on your baby.

YOUR BABY IS BORN

There will be a thousand memorable moments during your baby's first year of life. But for many parents, it's the time during and right after birth that is the most unforgettable—those first Technicolor minutes, hours, and days when your world revolves around your tiny bundle of joy and time seems to stand still. New parents often describe this special period as "intense," "awesome," "overwhelming," and "unreal." How could it be anything but, when life as you know it is about to change so dramatically?

THE FIRST MINUTES

The minutes leading up to the birth of a baby are often fraught with equal parts excitement and fear. After the birth, these emotions sometimes take a backseat to a potent mix of euphoria and exhaustion. So, get ready: the more you know about labor and delivery, and about your baby's first minutes of life, the better you'll be able to handle the physical challenges and the emotional roller coaster that is part and parcel of new parenthood.

In the Delivery Room

About 30 minutes before the birth of my first child, a wonderful labor nurse named Mary rolled in a full-length wardrobe mirror. For a second I worried that in addition to pushing I'd be asked to try on bathing suits or get my pants shortened.

"It's to watch the baby come out," Mary said as my husband and I stared blankly at the mirror.

Ah, the *baby*. After eight and a half hours of labor, the last one spent in what seemed like totally fruitless pushing, I had forgotten all about the baby.

"See, see there," Mary said, pointing to the mirror. "Every time you push I can see a tiny bit of your baby's head."

3

My baby's head? In that moment, it finally sank in: I was going to be a mom. Soon. Today. But not before I experienced 30 of the most intense minutes imaginable.

Having a baby is like that: surreal moments when time seems to stretch out forever followed by flurries of activity when you feel as if someone hit the fast-forward button when you weren't looking. What exactly is going on in those final 30 minutes?

- You are pushing—and pushing. And if it's your first baby, you're probably pushing some more. Your labor attendants will be giving you lots of encouragement—from kind words and progress reports, to bringing in that mirror so you can take an inspiring look at the action.
- The baby makes her way down the birth canal and the crown of her head begins to stretch the perineum (the area between the vagina and the anus) in preparation for birth (typically, the baby's chin is down on her chest and she's facing Mom's back). The practitioner gets in position to help the baby out. (Sometimes your partner is allowed to help "catch" the baby.)
- The staff prepares the equipment that's needed to perform an episiotomy, cut the baby's cord, and examine her once she's born. A bassinet with

DEFINITION

Episiotomy

An episiotomy is a surgical incision in the perineum (the area between the vagina and the anus), made during a vaginal birth. Doctors typically numb the area with an injection of anesthetic and then make a small vertical cut.

The incision is repaired with a few stitches, which dissolve by themselves within a week or two. Mothers who don't have an episiotomy may still need stitches if their perineum tears during delivery; even perineums that don't tear may feel bruised and sore.

Although episiotomies are performed in 90 percent of first births and 50 percent of second births, the common practice has been coming under intense scrutiny. Some experts say there's no proof that the surgery speeds up delivery, or that a surgical cut is easier to suture and more likely to heal well than a tear. Some studies indicate that an episiotomy requires just as many or more stitches, and that it makes a woman more likely to tear.

If you haven't delivered yet and want to try to avoid an episiotomy, discuss it with your practitioner and put it in your birth plan. Massaging the perineum in the months before labor may make it more resilient, and some labor-preparation classes teach gentle second-stage breathing techniques that help the mom-to-be push the baby out with less strain on her bottom.

ANATOMY OF

Baby's First Breath

In one short, miraculous instant, a newborn begins to breathe on his own. Here's what's happening:

1. Until birth, a baby's lungs are collapsed and aren't being used. Instead, he gets all the oxygen he needs from blood that's pumped through the placenta, where it's oxygenated.
2. When a newborn's head first pops out, even before the rest of his body is delivered, his nose and mouth are usually suctioned out with a nasal aspirator (a blue bulb syringe) in preparation for his first breath.
3. Once out, the baby takes a breath, which expands his lungs. (Doctors today don't hang a baby upside down or swat his bottom to facilitate the first breath.)
4. When the lungs fill with air, the body signals to valves in and near the heart to shut off permanently.
5. Blood now passes directly to the lungs for oxygenation (instead of through the placenta). Baby is breathing on her own!

Hospital staff give a baby an initial exam and use the Apgar score (see page 11) to assess how well he's breathing. If he's having respiratory trouble, he may be given oxygen via a face mask or, in more serious instances, through a tube inserted into the windpipe (see "When Baby Has Complications," page 54).

warming lights is usually set up nearby.

- If it looks as if your perineum is going to tear and you and your doctor have decided on an episiotomy, the surgical cut is made right as the baby's head crowns; given the circumstances, you probably won't even notice the incision (until later).
- As the baby's head crowns, you may feel the sting of the episiotomy and a release of pressure as the baby's head and shoulders are eased out, followed by the rest of her body. Your baby is born! If you hadn't already learned the sex of your child, this is when you'll hear the news.

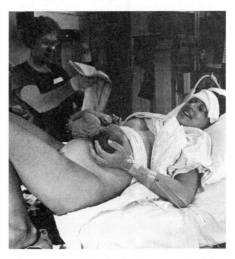

After a vaginal birth, the first wonderful skin-to-skin contact often occurs when Baby is put on Mom's tummy.

A Father's View

"My Big Moment"

Jon Stein has never liked gory movies. He's not fond of real-life blood and guts, either. "I get faint at the sight of my own blood," the Chicagoan admits. So when the subject of cutting his baby-to-be's umbilical cord came up, he was willing to consider it, but he was hardly enthusiastic.

"I knew my wife, Cathy, would be doing all the work, so I thought I should do something," says Jon. "But I had heard umbilical cord stories ranging from 'It's a simple snip' to 'It's a bloody mess.'" He decided to take a wait-and-see attitude.

Jon was surprised by his fortitude during the delivery. "I thought if things got hairy, I would bow out," he recalls, "but the truth is, I didn't leave."

The defining moment for Jon's active participation in the birth process came and passed quickly. "Some blood squirted out, but my mind was on little Bennett emerging," Jon says of cutting the cord. "So I didn't have time to get grossed out." Holding his wife's hand and comforting her during the labor, he believes, contributed far more than his deft handling of the scissors.

And any emotions generated by the cord cutting were quickly eclipsed when Jon held his son a few minutes later. "What I remember best was holding Bennett for the first time—sitting down and watching his eyes open up and look at me."

Jon's advice for the faint of heart:

- **Don't obsess over what's the right or wrong way to help out during the labor and delivery.** Just being there will be a great comfort to your partner.
- **Try not to let fears about blood build up, Jon says.** "It will probably be less gory than you think, and you can always leave," or stay up by the mother's head away from all the action.
- **Do cut the cord if you get the chance, Jon says.** "It's one of those things you may regret afterwards if you don't." Plus, he says, it takes only about two seconds.

After Baby's umbilical cord is cut, a clamp is attached. A nurse will show you how to care for the stump.

- Your newborn's nose and mouth will be suctioned out with a nasal aspirator (see "Anatomy of: Baby's First Breath," page 5) and she may be put on your belly while her umbilical is clamped and cut (often by her delighted daddy).

How Baby Looks

Many parents find they can't keep their eyes off their beautiful new baby. Of course, beauty is in the eye of the beholder. Most babies are beautiful in that scrunched-up, wrinkly, newborn sort of way, which can be quite a shock to new parents. My daughter, for example, was blue. And she bore a close resemblance to a miniature pugilist with balled-up fists and a cross look on her little face. She seemed to be all head and belly and mouth. And she had definitely been shortchanged in the neck department. But to me, she was perfect and all I could think was: my baby, my baby, my baby. In an instant, my world had both grown to make room for this precious new life and shrunk to focus only on her—a state of maternal insanity experienced by many new moms.

Baby's First Physical

After your baby's nose and mouth are cleared and her cord is clamped and cut, she'll be examined from head to toe and given a number of tests—a process that's quite routine but can seem alarming to new parents.

All this prodding and poking will help doctors determine your newborn's general health

DEFINITION
Fontanels

Some of the bones in a newborn's skull are not yet fully joined. The spaces between these bones are called fontanels, or soft spots. One fontanel is in the middle of baby's head above the brow (anterior). The other is near the crown of the head (posterior). These spots are nature's way of helping a baby's skull safely compress as it's being pushed through the narrow birth canal.

Your baby has two soft spots called fontanels (one above her brow, the other near the crown of her head) where her skull is not yet fully joined. Covered with a thick membrane, the fontanels disappear by the time a child is two years old

Don't be alarmed if you see the baby's pulse beating in the soft spots; that's normal. And it's OK to touch the fontanels or to brush baby's hair (if she has any); the spots are covered by a tough membrane. By the time your child is 2 years old the skull bones will have hardened and fused and the soft spots will have disappeared.

Call the doctor if . . . the fontanels seem unusually sunken (a sign of dehydration) or appear to be bulging (a sign of serious illness).

ANATOMY OF A NEWBORN

Weight and length
The average newborn weighs between 6 and 8 pounds and measures between 18 and 22 inches.

Head A newborn's noggin usually accounts for about one-fourth of the baby's total size, with an average head circumference of 13.8 inches.

Eyes The eyes of babies born vaginally are often squinty, swollen, and bloodshot, thanks to the pressures of traveling through the birth canal. C-section babies' eyes are usually less puffy. Babies don't get that wide-eyed look for several days. Caucasian newborns' eyes look dark blue or gray; Asian and black babies are typically born with brown eyes. True eye color can't be determined until a baby is at least six months old and sometimes older.

Genitals For boys and girls, genitals are often swollen, due to Mom's elevated hormone levels before birth. The swelling subsides within the first week or two.

Hands Newborns often keep their fists tightly closed.

Skin Newborn skin is often thin and dry—so thin that you can sometimes see a spider web of veins beneath it, and so dry that the top layer often peels off of baby's hands and feet.

Umbilical cord It will be several months before parents will know whether their baby's belly button is an inny or an outie.

Legs After nine months of being curled up, a baby's legs are in no hurry to unfold. They're short in proportion to the abdomen, head, and arms, and often look bowed.

Feet Baby's wrinkly foot, with its loose skin and amazing little toes, is made up of just one bone (the heel) and lots of cartilage. Over time, the cartilage will form into bones.

so that she can get speedy treatment if there's a problem, and get right to the business of being cuddled and cooed over if there's not. Which tests are administered depends on the baby's condition, your medical history, and state and hospital regulations. Throughout these examinations, your newborn may be quiet and alert, seemingly as spellbound with it all as you are with her.

If you're lucky, most of these procedures will take place in your room with the baby by your side; many of today's birthing rooms are set up so moms can labor, deliver, and recover in the same room. My daughter was placed in a bedside bassinet with warming lights where I could reach out and hold her little hands while she was being examined.

NOT TO WORRY

My Baby Is Covered with Goo!

Many a parent takes a first look at her long-awaited arrival and thinks, "Euwww, what *is* that stuff all over my baby?!" Typically, that stuff is:

› **Blood and amniotic fluid** picked up in the uterus or from the trip through the birth canal or cesarean incision.
› **Vernix caseosa,** a cheesy, white coating that protected the fetus from getting water-logged while it was in the uterus. A nurse may wash off the slippery vernix during baby's first hours.
› **Lanugo,** a fine, downy hair that may be all over a newborn's shoulders and back, even on his forehead and temples (and that is particularly common among premature babies). Don't worry, your little Mr. or Ms. Hyde will lose that hair within a few weeks, and it has no connection to future hairiness (or lack thereof).

If you've delivered in one room and are moved to another for recovery, or if you had a cesarean, your baby may not stay in the room for his checkups. If you're going to be separated, just make sure you and your newborn have been given your matching identification bracelets. The procedures may also vary somewhat if you've delivered at home or in a birthing center.

The Apgar Test. Named after anesthesiologist Virginia Apgar, who developed it, the Apgar test is the most common way doctors assess a newborn's overall condition. Given at one minute after birth and again five minutes later, the test measures appearance (skin color), pulse, grimace, activity (muscle tone), reflex response, and respiration. (For nonwhite babies, doctors examine the color of the inside of their mouths, or the palms of their hands or soles of their feet, to determine whether their skin color is blue or pink.)

A score of 0 to 2 is given for each of the five categories, with 10 being the maximum score possible. The results, which are tallied right on the spot, are

⌒ A Mother's View ⌒

"I Had My Baby at Home"

"**G**iving birth is a powerful bonding experience that should be the foundation of family life," says Robin Gaura, who chose to deliver her third baby at her home in Santa Cruz, California. During Robin's previous two hospital deliveries, she had a hard time concentrating on her labor with doctors and nurses walking in and out of her room all of the time. "Every time I moaned I felt like I had to apologize," she recalled.

Not so the third time. Robin delivered Lily Rose in her bedroom with just her partner, Jack Feldman, and a nurse-midwife and assistant present. The midwife had cared for Robin throughout her pregnancy, performing the usual prenatal visits, as well as advising Robin on how to deal with the changes her growing family was experiencing. "Midwives are such wonderful educators," says Robin. "My visits felt more like counseling sessions than medical appointments." Before agreeing to perform a home birth, the midwife had thoroughly questioned Robin about her suitability, ruled out any hesitations or medical problems that put Robin in a high-risk category, and cautioned her about what could go wrong. Next, she had her sign forms taking responsibility for the outcome and agreeing to move to a hospital emergency room if necessary.

On the big day, the midwife arrived when Robin was 6 centimeters dilated. An hour later, Robin's water broke and she was 8 centimeters dilated. From then on, the midwife periodically applied hot compresses to Robin's perineal area to reduce the possibility of tearing.

When labor seemed to stall, Robin and Jack roamed the house and spent some time alone together. As the urge to push became stronger, she called the midwife into her bedroom. After 14 minutes of pushing, the baby girl was born and Jack cut the cord. Lily was cleaned and given Apgar tests and Robin was checked.

Robin's tips for those considering a home birth:

- **Find a midwife with whom you have a good rapport.** You're going to need to be able to discuss your feelings and fears with her and trust her completely.
- **Make sure you're sure about a home birth, and that your partner is, too.** "Don't do it if you are feeling doubtful about it," says Robin.
- **Read the right stuff.** Focus on books about how birth is a healthy, normal process, not just a medical condition.

used only to determine baby's current health and measure stress during delivery, not to predict future development.

Most babies score between 7 and 9, which is considered normal (few score 10). Those who score between 4 and 6 may need a little extra help—some oxygen, for instance—to help regulate their breathing. The majority of these babies improve markedly by the second test. A baby with a total score lower than 4 will receive immediate resuscitation and life-saving attention (see "When Baby Has Complications," page 54).

Apgar Scores			
SIGN	**POINTS**		
	0	**1**	**2**
Appearance/ (skin color) * *Indicates how well lungs are working*	blue, very pale	blue extremities, pink body	pink all over
Pulse (heart rate) *Indicates strength/regularity of heartbeat*	none	below 100	above 100
Reflex response *Indicates alertness/reaction to stimuli*	none	grimace	cry
Activity **(muscle tone)** *Indicates health of muscles*	no or weak activity	some movement	very active
Respiration *Indicates health of lungs*	none	slow, irregular	good

*For nonwhite babies, doctors examine the color of the inside of their mouths, or the palms of their hands or soles of their feet.

☙ A MOTHER'S VIEW ❧

"My Birth-Center Birth"

*I*f there were decisions to be made during her labor and delivery, Mary Lou Kopas wanted to be the one making them. "You can lose control of your birth in a hospital," says the Arlington, Massachusetts, mother of two. "By contrast, a midwife expects a pregnant woman to be in charge of her own birth process."

At each prenatal visit, Mary Lou weighed herself, checked her urine, and then entered the results in her medical chart before meeting with the midwife. Each visit reinforced for Mary Lou the sense that she was managing her own pregnancy.

When her labor began, she waited until the contractions were five minutes apart before leaving for the birthing center. Mary Lou soon realized she was a little further along than she had planned: "As soon as I got in the car, I started feeling the urge to push," she recalls. Once at the center, the midwife massaged the little bit of remaining cervix out of the way. And then it was time to push.

Forty minutes later, baby Dexter was snuggled up on Mary Lou's tummy. A few hours later, she bathed and dressed the baby and had dinner with her husband, friend, and older son—all in the homey birthing center cottage.

"I felt like I got a gift," Mary Lou says. "It was wonderful having an unmedicated experience, the kind of birth I really wanted." Mary Lou's advice on planning a birth experience:

- **Interview prospective obstetricians or midwives.** Find out their philosophy on medical intervention. An obstetrician should be able to tell you her rate of C-section deliveries and her attitude about episiotomy.
- **Surround yourself with like-minded people.** Hang with folks who have confidence in the power of a woman's body and tend to believe that your body knows what to do in order to deliver a baby without lots of intervention.
- **Realize that even the best-laid plans go awry.** "In labor, you get what nature deals you," says Mary Lou. Her first labor was so drawn out that she ended up moving to a hospital for an epidural. Although medical intervention was never her first choice, Mary Lou acknowledges it isn't always a bad choice. "I slept for three hours after I got the epidural and that's what I needed to do then."

Temperature. Your baby's temperature will be monitored with a thermometer placed in his armpit or with a probe attached to his body. Warming lights are sometimes kept on during these examinations so your baby won't get chilled. (Remember that the climate out in the real world is quite different from the cozy confines of your womb, and newborns have a difficult time regulating their body temperature.)

Physical Check. The initial physical examination also includes checking your newborn's hips for dislocation, feeling the abdomen for abnormalities, ruling out any visible birth defects, counting his fingers and toes, and listening to his heart for murmurs—checkups that your baby's own pediatrician will repeat the next day. The doctor or nurse will also assess your newborn's gestational age (how long your pregnancy lasted) and test his reflexes (see "Baby's Amazing Reflexes," page 22).

Measurements and Identification. Your infant's measurements will be taken: weight, length, head size, and sometimes her abdomen. Don't be surprised if your baby is bigger or smaller than you thought she would be; even doctors aren't so good at the prediction business.

The day before my second daughter was born, the obstetrician said, "Oh, she's about normal size, seven and a half pounds I'd say." At birth, the nurses weighed her once, twice, then a third time on a different scale borrowed from the room next door. No one (except me and my bottom) could believe she weighed in at a whopping 9 pounds, 6 ounces.

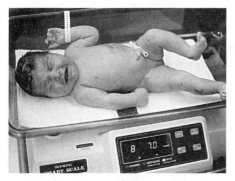

Your baby will be weighed during the first minutes of life. The average newborn weighs between 6 and 8 pounds. A full-term baby weighing less than 5 pounds, 8 ounces is considered underweight.

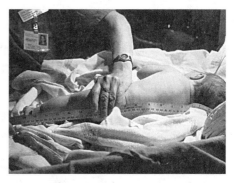

Most newborns are between 18 and 22 inches long.

Don't be surprised, either, if during his next-day checkup, your baby's weight, length, and head measurements may have already changed. It's difficult even for the pros to accurately measure a curled-up, wiggly newborn, and your baby's head may have rounded out overnight, changing its circumference.

Footprints (and sometimes fingerprints) are taken right after birth. These measurements and prints are often put on a card that's attached to Baby's bassinet (ask for a copy as a keepsake).

Preventive Measures. It's standard practice for newborns to get a vitamin K shot, since they are born with low levels of this vitamin, which is needed to help blood clot. In rare instances, lack of vitamin K could cause dangerous bleeding. The staff will also administer eyedrops or ointment to prevent any infection that may have been picked up during passage through the birth canal.

Blood Tests. Depending upon which state you live in and your hospital's operating procedures, blood will be drawn from your newborn's heel (your baby's first bandage will be applied) and screened for phenylketonuria (PKU). This is the inability to metabolize (break down) the protein phenylalanine. A buildup of protein in the bloodstream can affect brain development and result in serious retardation. The metabolic disorder is fairly rare in this country, occurring in about 1 in 14,000 births. If PKU is found, it's likely that treatment will be a special diet.

An anemia screen, which checks your newborn's red blood cell count, is sometimes done. If your baby has lost a lot of blood from the umbilical cord or placenta during delivery, he may need iron supplements to increase the number of red blood cells. Severe anemia (which is very uncommon) is treated with blood transfusions. Anemia (Rh-negative) can also be caused by a reaction between the baby's and the mother's blood.

Your baby's blood will also be tested for hypothyroidism, which occurs when a baby's thyroid gland (which controls her metabolic rate) doesn't function correctly. The condition can be treated with the thyroid hormone; left untreated, it may cause several abnormalities, including retardation.

If you are Rh-negative, the *Coombs test* may be performed to determine whether Rh antibodies have formed in your baby's blood (the antibodies may have passed through the placenta). For this test, blood is taken from the umbilical cord. Rh-negative antibodies in an Rh-positive baby may cause serious anemia. If the condition is present, your baby may need jaundice treatments or blood transfusions.

Some hospitals also give babies the *Brazelton Neonatal Behavioral Assessment Scale*, a 30-minute test created by Dr. T. Berry Brazelton. The test, which shows how your infant reacts to his environment, is sometimes given to low birth-weight babies or newborns with suspected neurological problems. It usually isn't given for days or sometimes weeks after the birth, however.

The Labor Continues . . .

Believe it or not, while your baby is being examined from head to toe, you're still in labor. Yes, you've delivered the baby but—sorry, Mom!—your job isn't done: now you have to deliver the placenta. The contractions you're still feeling are nature's way of helping you expel the 1-pound organ that nourished your baby those long nine months. You may be given a shot or IV drip of oxytocin to help the uterus cramp down, and an attendant may massage your abdomen in an effort to help you push out the placenta. (If you're breastfeeding, oxytocin is being released naturally to help this process along.) This process can take just a few minutes or as much as an hour. The organ will be examined to make sure it's intact; any pieces left inside could cause abnormal bleeding or infection.

Once the placenta is delivered, the doctor will stitch up your episiotomy or any perineal tears you may have experienced. The nurses will explain how to care for your sore bottom (see "I Wish I'd Known . . . How Much My Bottom Would Hurt," page 33).

The C-Section Experience

The last minutes of a planned C-section are not unlike that of a vaginal birth: there's great anticipation in the air and everything has been prepped for the baby's arrival. In most hospitals, your partner is allowed to attend the birth and will be able to hold the baby and show her to you soon after she's born.

If your cesarean is unplanned—owing to complications during delivery (the baby has his umbilical cord wrapped around his neck, for instance)

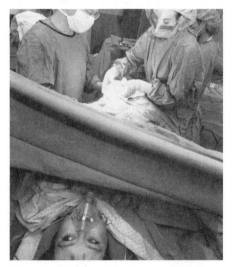

During a birth by C-section, a mom's view of the proceedings is usually blocked. She'll get to see her baby just as soon as he's made his entrance and been examined.

⸎ A MOTHER'S VIEW ⸎

"Unexpected C-Section"

Barbara Gottlieb thought she was having a textbook labor: She waited until her contractions went from 10 minutes to 7 minutes apart before she called her husband to come home from work. He helped her breathe and walk through the pain until they left for the hospital when the contractions were 5 minutes apart.

"I was surprised when the doctor told me my blood pressure was elevated and that they were worried that the baby had meconium in her lungs," says Barbara. "My doctor recommended a C-section."

Like most mothers-to-be, Barbara had been prepared for the possibility of having a nonvaginal birth by her ob-gyn at one of her regular checkups. But she didn't think it would happen to her.

"My husband and I really wanted to deliver the baby naturally," she says. "But we soon realized the baby's safety was more important than anything else."

An hour and a half after she arrived at the hospital, Barbara gave birth to daughter Bradie Ann via C-section. "Immediately they gave her to my husband to hold. She came out beautifully and healthy! Right then I realized that having a C-section was no big deal. It was the best thing for the baby, and I haven't felt bad about it since." Barbara's advice for dealing with an unexpected C-section:

- **Be positive from the start.** "I felt good about having a C-section because my primary concern was for the baby's health." Don't let anybody else make you feel guilty.
- **Think positively.** Don't assume that your future deliveries will have to be cesareans. "I was pleased when my doctor told me that I had a good chance of having my next child vaginally," Barbara says.
- **Let the hospital staff help you find a comfortable nursing position.** "I was really sore from the incision and couldn't use the cradle position, but the nurses showed me the football hold, which works fine. I also found that nursing in bed was a real lifesaver."
- **Baby yourself.** "I didn't realize the pain in my stomach would slow me down so much. It hurt to get up off the couch. I had to learn to ask for help."
- **Be clear with relatives about your needs.** "We had a hard time telling people that what we really needed help with was cleaning, preparing meals, and doing laundry so that we could take care of the baby ourselves."

Something Goes Wrong? If your doctor suspects your baby has a problem, she may be quickly taken to a special examining room. This may be in a neonatal intensive care unit, if your hospital has one (see "ANATOMY OF: A Neonatal Intensive Care Unit," page 52). It can be incredibly frightening for parents to watch their newborn being whisked away, but understand that your baby needs to get the best care, and that may not be possible in the delivery room. Your partner should accompany the baby if that's allowed and if it makes you feel better. Your partner and the nurses will be able to give you updates on the baby's condition as soon as the doctors can determine the nature and extent of the problem.

Once your baby has stabilized, you'll be able to visit her or she'll be brought back to you.

---

or as the result of a labor that failed to progress (your cervix won't dilate, the baby won't move down the birth canal or can't fit through your pelvis)—your fetus may be in distress and require a quick delivery.

In an emergency, your partner may not be allowed to be with you in the delivery room, and you are sometimes anesthetized for the procedure. Even if your partner is present and you're awake during your cesarean, it may be a while before you get to see or hold your newborn. If your C-section was performed because the cord was wrapped around your baby's neck or because of meconium in the amniotic fluid, for example, your baby may have respiratory difficulties that need immediate attention. The staff will get your baby to you just as soon as it's safely possible.

Because the mother who has a C-section has had major surgery, she's likely to have a longer recovery period, requiring a few more days in the hospital and some special care (see "CHECKLIST: C-Section Do's and Don'ts," page 44).

DEFINITION

Meconium

Meconium is a thick, greenish black stool made up of amniotic fluid and mucus. A baby's first meconium stool typically occurs within 24 hours of birth, but sometimes a baby will pass this stool while still in the uterus. She may be "breathing" this substance in and out of her lungs while in utero. This often happens when a baby is experiencing a stressful delivery. Or, during her first breath outside of the womb, she may inhale some of this meconium in the amniotic fluid that's still inside her lungs. This can cause respiratory difficulties (see "When Baby Has Complications," page 54).

Newborn Care 101: Swaddling

Bundling up your little one in a soft blankie can help him feel cozy and secure. The hospital bassinet offers a safe flat surface for practicing the art of swaddling.

Don't swaddle if . . . Your baby doesn't seem to like being confined (she fusses or kicks) or after she is a few months old (she needs room to move her arms and legs to develop motor skills). Always use a light blanket to avoid overheating.

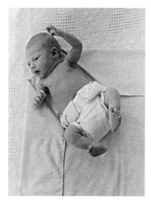

1. Spread out a lightweight blanket on a large, flat surface and fold down one corner. Position the baby on the blanket diagonally so that her neck is on the fold.

2. Scoot her right arm close to her body and fold the right side of the blanket over her body.

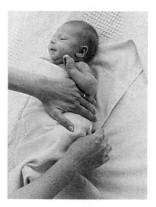

3. Tuck the edge of the blanket under her.

4. Fold up the bottom of the blanket, covering her legs and lower body.

5. Hold her left arm close to her body and fold the left side of the blanket over her.

6. Tuck the edge of the blanket under her. Make sure the blanket doesn't cover any part of her face or prevent her from moving her head.

THE FIRST HOUR AFTER DELIVERY

During the first 60 minutes after birth, you may be pumped up, exhausted, thrilled, relieved. You may also be starving, freezing, sore, and still numb from an epidural or C-section. Some women get uncontrollable shakes. Some weep with happiness, some with unexplained sadness. These are all normal emotional and physical reactions to the hard work you've just done and to the miracle of birth. Your baby is going through his own multitude of adjustments; he may be mesmerized by the new sights and sounds or too pooped to pay any attention at all.

How Mom Is Doing

For the first couple of days, at least, you'll be almost as big a star as the new baby. And you'll get just as much attention from the staff at the hospital. In fact, you may be surprised at how often during the next 24 hours a nurse will come in to take your blood pressure, pulse, and temperature and to check on the state of your bottom or your cesarean incision.

It becomes almost second nature to lift up your sheet and have someone massage your abdomen or comment on your stitches, hemorrhoids, discharge, and so on. (Although it can be annoying if they say "Oh my *goodness!*" every time they look at you.) Modesty probably flew out the window months ago at your umpteenth pregnancy exam, but you may want to draw the line if your nurse suggests she hold up a mirror so you can see what's going on down there. You don't really need to know how many stitches you had or how impressive your hemorrhoids are; you've had enough stress for one day. This is one of those rare instances where ignorance may be bliss.

If you had a normal vaginal delivery, it won't be long before your nurses suggest you shuffle over to the bathroom. So much for being Queen for the Day. Recovery no longer means bedrest and the bedpan thing. These are the get-up-and-get-going-to-feel-better days. Take it slow, however, and tell the staff if you feel too fatigued or light-headed to make the trek. They'll be glad to give you a hand.

Tell them, too, if you're in pain. A rush of natural adrenaline may have wiped out your memory of labor contractions (nature's way of convincing you to have another baby someday), but don't count on it to soothe your sore bottom. For that, feel free to accept a painkiller from the nurse. Acetaminophen (Tylenol) with codeine is one of the most commonly prescribed postpartum painkillers to relieve incision discomfort (episiotomy or C-section), but there's a whole range of medications to choose from, including ibuprofen (Motrin), which, because it doesn't have codeine, won't make your breastfeeding baby sleepy.

When it's time for you to get some sleep, you can usually choose to have your baby room-in with you or be sent to the nursery. Don't think that you'll get more sleep one way or the other. If you room-in, an attendant will still come in to check on you and your baby regularly, and you'll be in charge of responding to your baby's cries.

If your baby goes to the nursery, you'll still be examined regularly and a nurse will bring your bundle back to nurse every so often. If you're breastfeeding, you should know that rooming-in has been found to improve breastfeeding success.

Many hospitals allow the new daddy to room-in, too; he'll probably be the only one who can sleep through all the commotion, a trait that will become less charming as time goes on.

How Baby Looks and Acts

After you've had a little time to recover and your baby's examinations are finished, you'll be able to get to know your newborn with fewer interruptions. This is your chance to take a breath and marvel once more over Baby's pointy head and little fingers and toes.

If you had an epidural or painkiller, your baby may need a little time to work the effects of the drugs out of his system. If no drugs were used, your newborn is likely to be very alert and ready to feed. Take advantage of this period before the trauma and excitement of the birth catch up with both of you, especially if you're breastfeeding. After the first burst of energy, your newborn may be tuckered out for

NOT TO WORRY
About a Conehead

Parents call it conehead, peanut head, or pointy head, but to doctors a newborn's misshapen skull is simply the result of molding during a vaginal delivery—and it's nothing to worry about.

In fact, your baby's skull is built for labor and delivery, with bones that move and compress on their way through the birth canal (see "DEFINITION: Fontanels," page 7). The bones begin to realign right after birth, and by 1 month old your little pointyhead will definitely be a roundhead.

A conehead isn't unusual in a baby who's been born vaginally. Don't worry: Her head will round out in a couple of days.

HOW TO

Use an Aspirator

After the birth of my first daughter, a baby-blue bulb was handed to me almost ceremoniously, as if the nurse was saying this was all I needed to get started as a new parent. Once I got the hang of it—suctioning mucus out of my baby's nose—the aspirator did come in very handy, especially after the pediatrician told me it would be several years before my child would be able to blow her nose on her own. The directions that follow may sound remedial, but take it from someone who blew air into her baby's nose the first three tries: It's not as easy as it looks. Here's how to do it right:

1. Squeeze the bulb of the aspirator.
2. Insert the small point into the infant's nostril.
3. Slowly release pressure from the bulb.
4. Remove bulb from nose.
5. Squeeze the bulb and wipe gunk that was sucked out onto a tissue.
6. Repeat for the other nostril.
7. Clean the aspirator with warm, soapy water.

When using a nasal aspirator, keep the bulb depressed until the tip is in Baby's nostril.

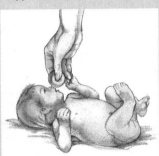

Release the bulb and gently remove the aspirator. Depress the bulb again to blow the contents onto a tissue. Clean with soapy water.

a while. Rest assured, most babies tend to grow more and more alert as the days pass.

When they snooze, newborns are notorious for snuffling, sneezing, and snorting, and for scaring their parents to death with their loud or irregular breathing. Not to worry. Remember, your baby has been breathing on her own for only an hour. However, before you're left alone with your baby, a nurse should show you how to suction out her nose or throat with the aspirator that was used when she was born (see "HOW TO: Use an Aspirator," above). And if you're truly alarmed by your baby's funny breathing, don't hesitate to ring for help. The staff will certainly be accustomed to new-parent worries and should be able to give you as many hands-on demonstrations as you need, answer all your questions, and generally ease your fears. Take advantage of their expertise.

Baby's Amazing Reflexes. Many parents are surprised by how their newborn jerks and startles. These sudden and sometimes bizarre-looking movements are just a baby's natural instinctive responses to some sort of stimulus. In fact, a newborn is a bundle of impressive reflexes, and at his initial examination he was tested by the hospital staff on a few of them. Here's a sampling of your baby's natural tricks:

• **Rooting reflex.** Stroke your baby's cheek and she'll turn in the direction of your touch with her mouth open, ready to suck. This reflex comes in handy when your baby is learning how to feed. You can direct her to breast or bottle with a simple light touch. (Breastfeeding experts suggest that you touch her lower lip with your nipple to elicit this response.) The rooting reflex usually disappears around the fourth month; by then feeding will be well established and she'll no longer need the reflex to help her meet her basic need for food.

Baby's amazing grip is actually a reflex. Touch her palm and she'll respond by grasping your finger.

Hold your baby upright with her feet just touching a flat surface and she'll surprise you by "walking." This is called the stepping reflex.

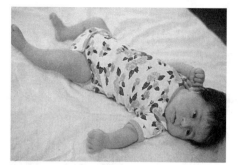

The tonic neck reflex occurs when you place Baby on her back. She'll turn her head to one side and extend the arm and leg on that same side.

• **Grasping reflex.** New parents are often amazed at how strong their baby's grip is. The grasping reflex is really the source of all this awe. Touch a baby's fingers and palm and he'll respond by gripping your finger. This was a never-ending source of glee for my oldest daughter, Halley Rose, who chose to view the reflex as her new sister's way of saying hello. To be able to elicit such a response from one so young does seem miraculous. This reflex is strongest in the first two months of life and usually disappears by the fifth month.

• **Moro (or startle) reflex.** The Moro reflex is your baby's reaction to a loud or sudden noise, or to being moved too abruptly. The baby actually acts startled, as if you've snuck up on her and said "Boo!" She arches her back, throws open her arms and legs, cries (sometimes), and then pulls her limbs back—all in a matter of seconds. This reflex can be pretty startling to parents, too, and the best way to avoid it is to move your infant slowly and gently and to keep her room as quiet as possible. When she does startle, hold her close and soothe her. By the fourth month, this reflex is gone.

• **Stepping reflex.** When you hold your baby upright, with his feet just touching a flat surface, he'll take alternating steps. This "stepping" reflex also occurs when baby is put on his tummy: He'll try to scoot, crawl, or "swim" his way forward. This reflex subsides around the second month.

• **Tonic neck reflex.** This reflex is also called "the fencing position" because the baby looks like a junior Musketeer. When she's placed on her back, she'll turn her head to one side and will extend the arm and leg on that same side. She'll flex the opposite arm and leg and look as if she's ready to say "en garde!" This reflex disappears at about 6 months.

Understanding Birthmarks. As parents spend more time with their baby, they may notice some unusual blotches or marks on her face or body. These, most likely, are birthmarks. Although birthmarks range from endearing to disfiguring, most are nothing more than broken blood vessels under the skin. Many birthmarks fade or disappear before your child is 5 years old and almost all are harmless.

• **Salmon patches.** The most common spot for these pinkish, irregular-shaped patches (also called stork bites) is at the nape of the neck, although they also can appear on the face. Each of my daughters still has a splotchy stork bite on the back of her neck that turns fiery red when she cries, but I'm told that the bites will get fainter each year.

• **Strawberry hemangioma.** Another very common birthmark (1 in 10 babies have one), this one is bright red, as its name implies, and may be present at birth but is most likely to show up when a baby is 2 to 5 weeks old. Typically it's raised and has a soft texture; it may be smaller than a pea or larger than a soft-ball. Although strawberry marks can grow, most disappear between ages 5 and 10. Treatment isn't usually recommended unless the mark is close to the eye, where it might interfere with vision. If this is the case with your baby, see an opthamologist.

• **Cavernous hemangioma.** This birthmark is similar to its strawberry cousin (and sometimes appears with it) but involves deeper layers of the skin and is much less common (about 2 babies in 100 will have one). The mark may grow quite a bit in the first year and be reddish or bluish red in color and have a lumpy texture. As quickly as it grew, it may begin to shrink; half of all marks are gone by the time a child is 5 years old, and almost all disappear by age 12. If the mark is particularly unsightly or worries you, talk to your pediatrician about possible treatments.

• **Mongolian spots.** Most common in babies who are black, Asian, Indian, or Mediterranean, these bruiselike splotches typically show up on a baby's bottom or back. They usually fade during the first year.

• **Café au lait marks.** These permanent tan-colored patches appear at birth or in the first two years of life. They range from very pale to cocoa colored and can be anywhere on a baby's body. It's not uncommon for a baby to have more than one of these marks; if he has six or more, let the doctor know: There is a link between a high number of café marks and certain neurological disorders.

• **Port-wine stain.** This birthmark gets its name from its purplish red color. Port-wine stains typically don't fade much and are considered permanent. Con-cealing creams will cover up the mark, or laser surgery is an option when the child is older. In rare cases, port-wine marks on the face have been associated with brain abnormalities.

• **Spider nevi.** A collection of thin dilated blood vessels that sometimes resembles a cobweb shape (thus the name), spider nevi typically fade during the first year.

• **Congenital pigmented nevi.** Also known as the common mole, congenital pigmented nevi come in a variety of colors, from tan to black, and in a full range of sizes. Some have hair growing from them. Removal is usually recommended for large pigmented nevi, which are relatively rare but sometimes become malig-nant. Small moles, like the one sported by supermodel Cindy Crawford, are fairly common and usually don't need any treatment. If your baby's mole bleeds, or changes color, size, or shape, let the doctor know.

Breastfeeding Basics

It's no secret that breast milk is the perfect food for newborns. Its benefits range from providing a baby with protective antibodies to being easy to digest and encouraging mother-baby bonding. And, recently, studies show that breast milk may contain ingredients that may protect breastfed girls against breast cancer later in life. But the so-called natural act of breastfeeding can feel very unnatural at first. Both moms and babies have to learn how to do it, so the earlier you start, the better.

During the first hour after birth, gently put your baby to your breast (see "HOW TO: Help Baby Latch On," page 26). Some newborns are active nursers and happily suck for hours right away; others are tuckered out from the labor and delivery and fall asleep with barely a nibble. In fact, the first breastfeeding difficulty most moms face is simply keeping their baby awake long enough to make an attempt at nursing.

Getting Baby Interested. If you have an uninterested baby, it's still important to try to nurse her every couple of hours (at least eight times in 24 hours). Your milk won't come in for two to four days, but your baby will benefit greatly from the colostrum produced by your breasts, and the close body contact will delight both of you. To wake up a sleepy baby, try:

- Gently jiggling her and talking to her
- Tickling or rubbing her toes
- Stroking her cheek with your finger or nipple
- Undressing her
- Dripping some colostrum into her mouth

Colostrum is all your newborn needs in the first days of life, so even if you're not planning to nurse when your milk comes in, it's worth letting her suckle for the few days before your milk comes in. There's no need for breastfed

DEFINITION

Colostrum

This watery, yellowish precursor to mature breast milk contains protein, sugar, vitamins, minerals, and antibodies thought to protect your newborn against infectious diseases and to boost his immune system. Colostrum also has a laxative effect that helps Baby have more bowel movements, thereby excreting excess bilirubin (which causes jaundice).

During the two to four days before your mature breast milk comes in, colostrum is the perfect first food for your baby.

Some women find that they produce a little colostrum as early as their sixth month of pregnancy; this early production is just your body's way of preparing for breastfeeding.

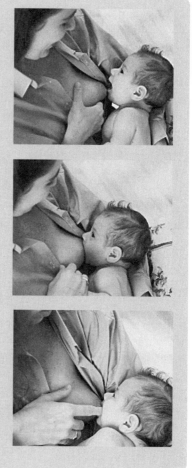

HOW TO

Help Baby Latch On

The key to comfortable and effective breast-feeding is to get your baby to put the entire nipple into her mouth. If she sucks on just the tip of the nipple, she won't get enough milk and your nipples will suffer. To avoid stress on your back, always try to bring Baby to the breast, not vice versa.

1. Support your breast with your hand, thumb on top and fingers underneath. To encourage your baby to open her mouth, stroke her cheek (which stimulates the rooting reflex) or tickle her lips with your nipple.

2. When her mouth opens, pull her close to you so that her nose and chin touch your breast and her lips surround the nipple and part of the darker area around it (areola). If her nose is blocked by your breast, she'll let you know by pulling away or snorting. Tuck her lower body closer to your chest or use your free hand to position the breast so she has breathing space. Baby's lips should cover not just the tip of the nipple, but the areola around it.

3. When she's finished, break the suction by gently inserting your index finger or pinkie in her mouth. Never try to pull Baby off of your breast without breaking the suction.

newborns to have formula, water, or sugar water; if they're getting colostrum they don't need any supplementation, and many parents and professionals believe that introducing a variety of nipples to your newborn can sabotage your efforts to nurse (see DEFINITION: "Nipple Confusion," page 27).

The Right Nursing Hold. You'll be doing a lot of nursing in the first weeks of your baby's life, at all hours of the day, so your mutual comfort is critical. When sitting, try different arrangements with pillows and a stool to find the position that works well for you. If you find a hold that you and your baby both like, it's fine to stick with it; if your nipples get sore, though, consider changing the hold to see if a different position helps him latch on better. And remember these pointers:

Q & A

Does my baby need sugar water?

If your baby is nursing, she's getting all the nutrients and fluids she needs from colostrum. Unless there's some sort of problem (dehydration or hypoglycemia; both are rare), she doesn't need glucose water or any water at all.

Will drinking sugar water actually harm your baby? Probably not, but if she finds it easier to suckle from the bottle nipple (see "DEFINITION: Nipple Confusion," below), prefers the sugary water to the taste of your breast milk, or falls asleep after a few sips of breast milk because she's already full of sugar water, breastfeeding may be more difficult to establish and to continue.

In fact, the practice of offering newborns sugar water is a sore spot with many breastfeeding advocates who claim that it's done for the benefit of the hospital staff, not the new mother or baby. If your newborn is crying, for instance, it may be easier for the nurse to give him sugar water in a bottle than it is to roll the baby back to your room for a feeding. The problem is this: If your newborn is satiated from sugar water and doesn't want to nurse, your breasts won't get the stimulation they need to produce an adequate supply of milk, and breastfeeding may be sabotaged before it's even begun.

Best bets for a good start on breastfeeding: Keep your baby with you in your room and tell the hospital staff that you don't want him to be given sugar water, bottles, or pacifiers.

DEFINITION

Nipple Confusion

You'd be surprised how fickle a newborn can be when it comes to nipples. Although the breast nipple is perfectly designed for nursing, sometimes after a newborn samples a bottle or pacifier nipple, he may decide that your breast is not best. Some newborns prefer the artificial nipples because they may be stiffer, easier to latch on to, and provide more immediate gratification.

To avoid jeopardizing your breastfeeding efforts, experts suggest that you don't introduce a pacifier or bottle for four to six weeks, until breastfeeding is well established.

- Bring your baby to you; don't slouch over to reach her with your nipple.
- Baby should be facing the breast (so she doesn't have to turn her head to reach it) with her body in a straight line (not all twisted up).
- Your baby's mouth needs to be as wide open as possible when you bring her to the nipple, so she can cover it completely (including the areola) with her

mouth. If she sucks on just the end of the nipple, you're going to become very sore. (If this happens, get help right away. Repositioning may be all you need to eliminate the soreness.)

The best nursing position is the one that feels natural for you and your newborn. Some women find that one position is a definite favorite; others vary the hold depending upon the time of day or their baby's mood. Here are three of the most common breastfeeding holds:

• **The cradle hold.** Sit in an upright chair with a pillow on your lap. Cradle your baby in your arms with her head in the crook of one arm. Her body will be lying across you horizontally and her head should be facing your breast. Bring her mouth to your nipple and position the pillow to help keep her as close to you as possible and to hold some of her weight. It's important to relax your shoulders (don't hunch them up!) and to have enough pillow support so that your arms aren't bearing all the weight of the baby.
• **The football hold.** In this popular position, your baby is perpendicular to your body and actually tucked in under your arm a bit (thus the name). Sit in an upright chair, with a pillow on your lap. The lower part of the baby's head is supported by your fingers, her upper back is supported by the lower part of your forearm, and her legs are tucked back in between your elbow and your

The cradle hold is one of the most popular and comfortable ways to breastfeed. Hint: Relax your shoulders and use a pillow on your lap to help support Baby's weight.

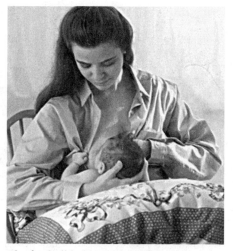

The football hold is an excellent alternative for mothers who've delivered by C-section. Resting the baby on a pillow on your lap also helps protect a sore abdomen.

For More Help: Breastfeeding

Organizations
- **The International Lactation Consultant Association**
  919-787-5181

- **La Leche League International**
  800-525-3243
  900-448-7475 extension 26 (hot line is $1.99/minute)
  847-519-7730 to talk to a live person

- **Medela's Breastfeeding National Network**
  800-835-5968

Books and Other Resources
- *The Breastfeeding Answer Book* by Nancy Mohrbacher, La Leche League International

- *Breastfeeding Pure and Simple* by Gwen Gotsh, La Leche League International

---

body. When you bring her mouth to your nipple, move the pillow under your arm so that it helps support baby's weight. Delivery nurses often recommend this position to cesarean moms who need to protect their sore tummies, but it's also very good for women who're having a hard time getting their baby to latch on to the whole nipple and part of the areola, not just the tip.

• **Lying-down hold.** I've heard new mothers say that this nursing hold is the only thing that got them through the first days of breastfeeding. Many women use the lying-down position at night and find that they catch a few more zzzs while they're feeding. Lie down next to your baby, facing each other. It may take some experimenting to come up with the most comfortable arrangement that allows baby's mouth to be directly in front of your breast. Tuck her body in close and rest her head on the bed or on your arm—whichever works best. Baby's body should be straight and parallel to yours and she should have a rolled-up blanket or towel behind her so she can't roll off. If you can't fall asleep at night because you're worried about smothering your baby (and this is a rare possibility if you're an especially wild or deep sleeper), then this hold is probably not for you.

Practice does make perfect, so let your newborn suckle as much as she wants. The more you nurse, the more confident you'll become and the more comfortable both of you will feel together. There's no such thing as getting too much colostrum, and feeding on demand won't wear out your nipples (as one nurse incorrectly told me); your nipples may get a little sore, but that's the result of improper latching on or some other problem, not from overuse.

Don't hesitate to ask the nursing staff for help. Many nurses are wonderful cheerleaders, welcome your questions, and are pros at helping new moms try different holds and positions. If yours are not particularly helpful, call in a lactation consultant or someone from your local La Leche League.

Bottle-Feeding Basics

If you're planning to bottle-feed your baby, you may be surprised at how little he eats during his first days. Rest assured, however, that he's getting enough. Don't expect him to drink all of a 4-ounce bottle. Newborns don't need much.

More important than the quantity of the formula he's being fed is the quality of the experience:

- Find a comfortable position in which to feed your baby, where you can have as much eye-to-eye and skin-to-skin contact as possible. Stroke his cheek to get him to turn toward the bottle.
- Make sure your little one isn't swallowing a lot of air with his formula. When you tip the nipple into his mouth, look at it closely to make sure it's filled with milk (not air).
- Burp your baby after every feeding. Because formula-fed babies find it easier to latch on to an artificial nipple and are likely to get more at each feeding, they're also more likely to be gassy. Gently rub your baby's back while he's on your shoulder or over your knee until he belches.
- Be the main bottle-feeder for the first couple of days so that you and your baby get to know each other.

What kind of formula, bottle, and nipple you choose for your baby should be discussed with your doctor. Unless you give other instructions, during your hospital stay your bottle-fed baby will probably be given a formula sample from a major manufacturer.

What You Need to Know About . . . Hospital Security

In spite of the numerous book and movie plots about babies being mixed up at birth or kidnapped, these events rarely happen. Security has been heightened at most hospitals and birthing centers; however, it can't hurt to take some simple precautions.

- Every time your baby is taken from your room, have the hospital staff show you their identification and tell you why and where they're taking your newborn. Make sure that the matching identification tags or bracelets haven't fallen off you or your baby.
- Keep the baby's bassinet on the side of your bed that's away from the door. When I had my first baby, the nurses wanted the rolling bassinets on the door side for easier access. Two years later, at the birth of my second child, they were adamant about parking the bassinet away from the door.
- Use the bathroom or take a shower when your partner or a trusted visitor is around to watch the baby. If you're alone, ask that your baby be taken to the nursery.

Newborn Care 101: Picking Up Baby

Your baby will startle easily and has absolutely no control of his big wobbly head. That's why picking up this precious little cargo can seem so scary to new parents. To increase his sense of security (and your own confidence), always lean over with your chest as close as possible to your baby before picking him up. Follow these steps to get the hang of it.

1. Slide one hand under the baby's head and neck, and cup his head in your open fingers.
2. Slide the other hand under his hips and bottom, also with fingers spread.
3. Lean over toward baby.
4. Slowly bring him to your chest, *then* carefully straighten up your body.
5. Cradle the back of your baby's neck with one hand, her bottom with your other.

(Reverse the steps to put baby down.)

The best way to pick up Baby? Bend over face to face and slide one hand with spread fingers under his bottom, the other hand under his head and neck. Straighten up slowly.

THE FIRST DAY

By the end of the first 24 hours of life with Baby, the fun of new parenthood may be tempered with exhaustion. And why not? The day is likely to have been filled with relatives, well-wishers, doctor visits, checkups, a variety of aches and pains, and big decisions. If you're lucky, you fit a hot shower in there somewhere. Your love affair with Baby is off to a healthy start, but are you? It's time to take care of yourself, too.

How Mom Is Doing

Sometime during the first day after the birth, your midwife or ob-gyn (or a partner, if it's an office that splits the hospital rounds) will come around to check on you. She'll review your labor and delivery, and check your charts and vital signs and your bottom.

It may feel at first that your intense nine-month (or more) relationship with this doctor is ending, but it's really not. Your ob-gyn will be very interested in how you're healing, how breastfeeding is progressing, and how you're feeling about new motherhood. Your next appointment with her won't be until the standard six-week postpartum checkup, but you should be encouraged to call her office before the appointment if you're feeling unwell or depressed, or if you have concerns about your incision or breastfeeding. Your doctor may remind you about the importance of taking care of yourself as well as the baby. The number-one regret I hear expressed by new moms is that they didn't use their limited time in the hospital to rest up or prepare for the days and weeks ahead. Some commonsense advice:

• **Take it easy.** Although you may be feeling buoyed by a stream of well-wishers and the sight of your baby's sweet face, it won't be long before fatigue sets in. Try to control how many visitors you see, and limit how long they stay or you'll wear yourself out before you even get home.

• **Eat well.** Drink lots of water and eat as healthfully as possible. If you're not

---

DEFINITION

Lochia

Even women who are prepared for bleeding after childbirth are sometimes shocked at how much they bleed and for how long. The vaginal discharge, called lochia, starts out red but changes color—pink, tannish brown, yellowish white—as healing progresses. Whether you've had a vaginal birth or C-section, you can expect the discharge to last from three to six weeks. Use sanitary napkins, not tampons. And call your doctor if the discharge:

› Is foul-smelling or unusually copious
› Stops and then starts up again
› Lasts longer than six weeks or is brownish for more than three weeks (a sign of possible infection)

getting enough fresh vegetables and fruit at the hospital ("lime Jell-O jewels" don't count), ask one of those many visitors to bring a fruit basket instead of flowers. But if what you really want is a totally decadent double cheeseburger, go for it. You've earned it.

• **Take a shower.** Nothing is as luxurious as taking a shower after having had a baby. The warm water coursing over your body can be both relaxing and invigorating and make you feel that all is well with the world (even if you've had only 90 minutes of sleep in 24 hours). Many hospital bathrooms are equipped with sit-down showers, which is a brilliant idea. If yours does, take advantage of it. Make sure the nurse knows when you're going in to take a shower, however; falling is a potential hazard when you feel weak or light-headed. If you do feel

I WISH I'D KNOWN
How Much My Bottom Would Hurt

Even if you had the easiest labor on earth, your bottom is bound to hurt. Here's why:

Stitches tend to tingle, sting, and pull, especially if you move or pee. Since you can't go long without doing either, your best bet is to:

- Use a plastic squeeze bottle (often provided by the hospital) to splash your bottom with cool water while you urinate.
- Take as many sitz baths as possible. Typically the hospital will send you home with a dishpan-size sitz bath in which to soak your sore bottom.
- Ask your nurse for some Dermaplast or another topical anesthetic that numbs the pain. (Go home with a good supply.)
- Use ice-filled sanitary napkins designed to soothe and reduce swelling.
- Take a painkiller.
- Don't leave for home without your "donut," an inflatable seat cushion.

Hemorrhoids plague some women throughout their entire pregnancies; others find themselves with a postpartum batch after hours of pushing out the baby. In either case, the swelling around the rectum can be painful and itchy. Try:

- Ice packs for the puffiness and itching.
- Preparation-H or Anusol to numb the pain.

A bruised tailbone (coccyx) is another condition that's guaranteed to make you wince every time you sit down or shift your weight. To relieve the pain:

- Sit on the donut.
- Ask for a painkiller.

faint, get a nurse to help you bathe, or wait until you feel stronger.

• **Get drugs.** If you hurt, don't hesitate to ask for medication. You can't rest if you're in pain. You may be experiencing afterpains, which is nature's way of helping your uterus contract back to its original size, and your bottom may be throbbing and sore (see "I Wish I'd Known . . . How Much My Bottom Would Hurt," page 33). If you've had a C-section, your tummy may feel (rightly so) as if all of your organs have been rearranged, and your incision may ache.

• **Take a nap.** Send your baby to the nursery or have your partner or parents or friend spend time with him while you doze. Sleep at every opportunity.

• **Ask for hands-on demonstrations.** Your nurses will be skilled in everything you want to know: bathing, diapering, burping, swaddling, feeding, circumcision, and umbilical-stump care. You name it, they can probably show you how to do it. If you're having difficulty breastfeeding and need extra help, they can help you find a lactation consultant; many hospitals now have a breastfeeding expert on staff. Even if breastfeeding is going along fine, you may want to chat with this knowledgeable, sympathetic professional before you leave the hospital. You may learn some helpful nursing tricks, especially if you've had a C-section and need help finding a comfortable position.

Baby's First Checkup

If you missed out on most of the details of your baby's checkup right after birth, make sure to be there for her first hospital visit with her new pediatrician. Now that you've been a mom for a day, you may have lots of questions.

Many doctors will examine your newborn right at your bedside, talking to you as he works. One of my fondest memories of my first daughter's birth was chatting with the pediatrician as he gently checked her out. He called her a "peach" and described everything he was doing to her. The examination typically includes:

• Looking at your baby's eyes, nose, and ears.
• Examining her mouth to rule out cleft palate and early teeth.
• Feeling his neck for unusual lumps, cysts, or swelling.
• Checking the shape of the skull bones and size and condition of the fontanels.
• Taking her pulse on each leg.
• Checking clavicles for fractures and arms for symmetrical movement.
• Turning him over to examine the spine.
• Looking at fingers and palms (most babies have two big creases across each palm).
• Checking her arms and legs for movement, strength, and abnormalities; mak-

⌁ A MOTHER'S VIEW ⌁

"My High-Risk Pregnancy"

When Valerie Gallup was diagnosed with diabetes at the age of 3, her mother was told that Valerie wouldn't be able to have children.

"The thinking has changed," says Valerie, now 28. "Over the years it's become easier to control diabetes, and the risks have become smaller."

When Valerie became pregnant, the Blue Springs, Missouri, mother-to-be was excited but afraid that she wasn't healthy enough. "I was overjoyed, then scared to death," she recalls. "I was worried that the baby would be born too early, or be too big, or wouldn't have kidneys, or would be blind." For a diabetic mom-to-be, the key to a healthy baby is controlling her blood sugar. "During my pregnancy I took up to seven shots of insulin a day and did more frequent blood testing," says Valerie. "And I had to go to the doctor twice as frequently as other pregnant women."

Throughout those nine months, Valerie's obstetrician was in close conference with her endocrinologist. "They advised me to make a more in-depth birth plan, stating what should happen if I started to crash during a contraction, for instance, and listing the signs that I needed insulin."

Valerie's diabetes caught up with her at 34 weeks, when she developed preeclampsia (high blood pressure and swelling) and had very low blood sugar. Her daughter was delivered by C-section, four and a half weeks early.

"I was happy to get it all over with," says Valerie. "I felt peaceful. And I couldn't believe that I was a mommy of a very healthy baby! Emily was 8 pounds, 11 ounces, and scored a 9 on her Apgar test."

Valerie's advice for women experiencing a high-risk pregnancy:

- **Don't compare your pregnancy to others'.** "Yours isn't going to be like other pregnancies. Maybe you'll have a more difficult pregnancy but an easier labor than others. Everyone is different," Valerie says.
- **Think positively.** "I tried to remember that even when I was feeling terrible, most likely the baby was feeling fine."
- **Get support.** "Hearing stories about other diabetic moms helped reassure me," says Valerie. "Ask your doctor to refer you to other women who've had similar experiences."

DEFINITION

Jaundice

More than half of all newborns develop this yellowish skin discoloration, which usually appears three to five days after birth. It typically shows up first in a baby's face (even the whites of her eyes may turn yellow) and spreads to the rest of her body. Although mild jaundice is usually harmless, it's best to alert your doctor.

Jaundice is caused by too much bilirubin, a chemical produced during the normal breakdown of blood cells. We all have some bilirubin, but during the first week after birth a newborn's liver enzymes that are responsible for metabolizing old red blood cells aren't in full production. (Before birth, the infant's blood was cleaned by the placenta.) So the excess bilirubin isn't being excreted fast enough.

Newborn jaundice often goes away within a week without any treatment, but the doctor may give your baby another blood test to measure bilirubin levels or try phototherapy (exposure to ultraviolet lights, called bili lights) to help speed her recovery. (How well and often your baby is feeding can also have an effect on her bilirubin levels. Since bilirubin is excreted in feces, the more bowel movements your baby is having, the better.)

If bilirubin levels remain high, the doctor may also want to rule out other kinds of jaundice and other illnesses, such as hepatitis.

ing sure the legs and feet are the same length.

- Testing his hips for displacement by holding both thighs flexed and then rotating them outward at the hip. This doesn't usually hurt but your baby may not like being restricted in this way.
- Feeling the abdomen to check the size, shape, and position of the liver and spleen.
- Explaining the signs of jaundice and what causes the condition (see "DEFINITION: Jaundice," above).
- Examining the genitals for abnormalities. In a boy, he'll want to ensure that the testes have descended and that the opening of the penis is in the correct position; in a girl, he'll check that the lips of the labia aren't joined and that the clitoris is a normal size. In both sexes, he'll check the anus to make sure it's open.
- Testing your newborn's reflexes and putting her through a range of movements.
- Using a stethoscope to check on his heart and lungs.

One of the scariest moments of my daughter's hospital stay was when her doctor listened long and hard to her heart and decided at the end of the exam that she needed an EKG because he heard a "click." Heart murmurs aren't at all unusual in newborns, because it takes a while for all the fetal circulation bypass valves to permanently close. The EKG was just a precaution.

What You Need to Know About . . . Circumcision

If you've just delivered a boy, one of your first decisions as a parent will be whether or not to have him circumcised. You may have discussed circumcision before the birth and already made up your mind; if you haven't, you need to think pretty fast: the minor surgery is usually performed by an obstetrician or pediatrician before you go home from the hospital. (Some Jewish parents choose to have the procedure done at home in a traditional religious ceremony on the eighth day after the baby's birth.)

The debate over whether or not to circumcise a newborn boy is relatively new. Thirty years ago in the United States, new parents didn't agonize over the circumcision decision: More than 90 percent of newborn boys were circumcised. By the mid-1990s, however, the circumcision rate had fallen to 62 percent, and today parents and doctors continue to question whether the surgical procedure, which removes the foreskin from the tip of the penis, provides any real preventive healthcare benefits.

Based on studies and reports from around the world, it was once thought

PRO/CON

Circumcision

"We spent a long time discussing whether or not to circumcise our son. I read the arguments, pro and con, in all the books I could find. Ultimately, we decided that it would be less confusing for him to grow up looking like his father, who is circumcised. We also weren't sure exactly what was involved with cleaning an uncircumcised penis, and we were afraid we wouldn't do it properly or be able to show Connor how to clean himself correctly. We didn't want to put our son at greater risk of developing health problems."

—*Pilar and Shawn Shepard*

"Joan and I had never really discussed circumcision until she became pregnant. Neither of us liked the idea of putting our newborn through surgery. Before the birth, we read all the material we could find and looked for any sort of health benefit, but nothing convinced us the surgery was necessary. When Daniel is older, he'll be able to understand why his penis looks different from his dad's."

—*David and Joan Barnes*

that circumcision helped prevent urinary tract infections, the spread of sexually transmitted diseases, and even penile cancer. Now, members of the American Academy of Pediatrics (AAP) don't agree on the validity of the reports, and although the association's official position is that circumcision isn't "medically necessary," many pediatricians still think the procedure can't hurt. In the absence of proven medical benefits, however, a growing number of parents are reluctant to put their sons through a procedure that apparently does hurt.

So how can a parent decide? Your best bet is to find out everything you can about circumcision, talk to your baby's doctor and your family and friends, and then go with your gut. Here's what you may be worried about:

• **That it will be awkward if a son's penis doesn't match Dad's.** This is a big issue since most of today's fathers *are* circumcised. If you're comfortable with your decision and feel you can eventually talk matter-of-factly about how some penises are circumcised and some aren't, your son will be comfortable, too. If the fact that your son's penis won't look like Dad's really bothers *you*, then it's likely that it'll also bother your son.

• **That an uncircumcised penis is difficult to clean.** A baby's uncircumcised penis doesn't need special care. Just wipe it after each diaper change as usual. Since the foreskin doesn't separate from the head of the penis until a boy is 3 or 4, it's not necessary to pull it back for cleaning. Once your child is old enough, he can be taught to gently retract the foreskin to wash his penis. Careful cleaning is important as your son grows.

• **That circumcision hurts.** How much the minor surgery hurts and how long the pain lasts is another hot-button issue. There's no doubt that a baby feels pain during the incision—studies indicate that infants show changes in their crying patterns, hormones, and cardiovascular systems throughout the procedure. But some research suggests that circumcision somehow changes or heightens a baby's pain responses for a much longer time. In one study, circumcised babies cried longer than uncircumcised babies during routine vaccinations four to six months after birth. Other doctors pooh-pooh the whole pain business, believing that circumcision is no more painful than a routine blood test.

If you choose circumcision, ask your doctor how he plans to make your baby as comfortable as possible during the procedure. Will a local anesthetic be injected at the base of the baby's penis to numb the pain, or will he be given a sugar-coated pacifier to distract him? Some doctors now use a topical anesthetic cream that numbs the site of the incision; is that an option for your son? And will he be given acetaminophen before or after the surgery? Ask what, if any, risks are associated with the local anesthetic during circumcision. The more you know, the more comfortable you'll be with your decision.

• **That caring for a circumcised penis will make you cringe.** A circumcised penis will look red and sore for a few days, and may even bleed or ooze a little. If there's more than a few drops of blood, tell your baby's doctor. Each time you

ANATOMY OF

A Circumcision

A hospital circumcision takes less than 10 minutes. During the procedure, the baby is swaddled tightly or bound to a board with Velcro straps on his arms and legs, and is given an injected or topical anesthesia.

The two most common circumcision techniques use either the PlastiBell, a bell-shaped instrument that protects the head of the penis during surgery, or the Gomco clamp, a metal clamp and cap combo that helps reduce bleeding. The PlastiBell technique is illustrated here.

1. At birth, a newborn's foreskin covers the head of the penis, called the glans.

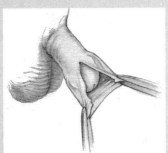

2. The foreskin is separated from the glans and a small vertical slit is made.

3. A PlastiBell device is fitted over the head of the penis.

4. The foreskin is tied with a string or ligature, and the foreskin below the string is snipped off. The doctor breaks off the handle of the PlastiBell, leaving the rim.

5. The rim of the PlastiBell falls off within five to 10 days.

change your son's diaper, dab some petroleum jelly on a clean gauze pad and place it on the end of the penis. This will facilitate healing and help prevent the penis from sticking to the diaper.

If your son will be circumcised at home in the traditional ceremony that signals the beginning of a boy's Jewish life, make sure that the *bris milah* is performed by an experienced *mohel*. *Mohalim* are often medical doctors; if yours is not, make sure he comes highly recommended and is experienced.

Newborn Care 101: Diapering

Some parents-to-be crack up when they get to the part in their birth-preparation class where they diaper a baby doll. Diapering is not quite so hilarious when you're grappling with a crying, wet newborn and you can't remember which end of the diaper is up. The first rule of thumb is to have a safe, flat space for changing and a diaper pail nearby (so you can toss the old diaper without leaving the baby). Position the baby on his back, with one of your hands on his belly. Then follow these steps.

1. Undo the diaper.
2. If the baby has had a bowel movement, clean off as much of the feces as possible with the front of the dirty diaper. Discard the diaper.
3. Remove the rest of the poop with a wet cloth or cotton ball, using a clean area for each wipe. A little baby oil will help remove stubborn or sticky feces (like meconium).
4. Use another wet cloth to remove urine and to clean the genitals and surrounding skin. Don't forget to clean the creases in the thighs.
5. Lift up your baby's legs by the ankles to wipe his bottom. Dry him with a clean cloth.

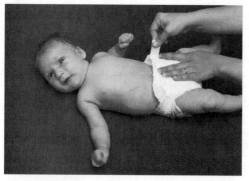

Even a very young baby can wiggle off a changing table. Always keep a hand on your little one while diapering

6. Open the diaper flat and slide it under your baby. Make sure the tabs are accessible on either side (if it's a disposable) or that there's enough cloth diaper showing for pinning.
7. Bring the diaper through baby's legs and up to his waist.
8. Open the adhesive tabs and pull each side over the front to fasten. For a cloth diaper, pull each side over and pin securely.
9. Check the fit. The diaper should fit snugly around your baby's legs and waist but not pinch or bind.

For a girl

- Always wipe from front to back.
- It isn't necessary to clean inside the lips of the vulva.

For a boy

- Be prepared for a stream of pee the instant you remove the diaper; plop a cloth diaper or towel on top of his penis to catch the spray.
- If he's not circumcised, don't pull back the foreskin.
- Position the penis so it's aiming down into the clean diaper (instead of up, where urine is more likely to come out of the top of the diaper).

If you're afraid of pins

- Try diaper covers with Velcro fasteners. A cloth diaper fits inside the cover and it's easy to get on and off, just like a disposable.

GOING HOME

The day that you've been waiting for is here. You may be incredibly eager to head home with your baby, or you may suddenly be wishing that you had just one more day in the protective environment of the hospital or birthing center. Checking out can feel just as momentous as checking in: you came in as two and after

Some hospitals like to roll Mom and Baby out the door in a wheelchair; others insist that the new arrival be carried out in his car seat.

I Don't Feel Like a Mom Yet? "Feeling like a mom" means a lot of different things to different people. Some women "feel" like a mom because they're high on the "I am woman, hear me roar" rush of having just delivered a baby. Others are suddenly scared of the new responsibility (and who isn't?). And still others are reeling from the birth experience and are too emotionally and physically tired to feel much of anything.

If you're feeling less than maternal, relax, give yourself a break, revise your expectations, and take care of yourself. Nothing happens instantly or easily, not even mother love. When you're less wiped out and your hormones are in better shape, you and your baby will bond just fine. In the meantime, don't let all the feeding, bathing, and burping get in the way of the fun stuff: the cuddles and kisses.

One day the "feeling like a mom" thing will catch up with you and take you by surprise: When you carry your baby through your front door. When she only has eyes for you. When your own mother first visits. When you haven't showered or slept for three days but still love your baby—that's when you know you're a real mom.

If you're feeling very blue . . . or have strong negative feelings about motherhood, you may be more than just weary. Tell your doctor (see "The Emotional Roller Coaster," page 154).

Q & A

"Why do my nurses keep asking me if I've had a bowel movement yet?"

Your nurses are asking because your bowels, your bladder, and your abdominal muscles have all taken a beating during labor and delivery and that can affect your ability to have a BM. So can fears about getting or aggravating hemorrhoids, or about tearing open your stitches (don't worry: you won't). Your bowels may also be sluggish as a result of having had an epidural.

If you are constipated, the best Rx is to eat well (lots of roughage and liquids), get a little exercise if you're up to it (walk around your room), and relax. (Good advice for when you get home, too.) If you do feel the urge to have a BM, put your feet up on a footstool when you're on the toilet and try not to strain. If you're very uncomfortable, try some breathing exercises. And if you're still constipated after a week or so of being at home, ask your doctor about a stool softener.

Don't . . . take mineral oil for constipation; this traditional remedy actually robs your body of needed nutrients.

a short roller-coaster ride you're leaving as three. No wonder you're a little bit dizzy. No wonder you're worrying whether you're really cut out for this. Don't worry, you are—and the hospital will make sure you and your baby are ready to go. Happy trails! And don't forget the car seat.

Before Mom Can Go Home

Now that women who deliver vaginally are allowed to stay in the hospital 48 hours, new parents are going home a little more rested, but the transition is still a biggie. Before the hospital staff lets you out the door, you have to convince them that you're well enough to take care of your baby on your own, and that you're armed with the necessary babycare basics. You should:

- Be feeling stronger, less light-headed, and at least a little rested.
- Be able to get to the bathroom by yourself and be urinating regularly.
- Have been given instructions for caring for your sore bottom, including how to give yourself a sitz bath, use an inflatable donut, and apply topical creams. If you've had a cesarean, you should know how to care for your incision (see "CHECK-LIST: C-Section Do's and Don'ts," page 44).
- Be able to administer your own pain medicine.
- Be aware of the signs of infection: fever, chills, change in your discharge, and so on.
- Know breastfeeding and bottle-feeding basics, and have numbers to call for breastfeeding assistance.
- Know how to change your baby; bathe, burp, and feed him; clean a circumcised penis; clean the umbilical stump.

GOOD ADVICE

Surviving the First 24 Hours at Home

"I put up a sign on my door that said 'Mother and baby are sleeping, please come back later.' Everyone did, even my father! This gave me time to just look at my child, breastfeed without interruption, and rest when I wanted to."

—*Anna Martin, Nashville, NC*

"Relax, take it easy, and let things go. The mistake I made was resuming my daily routine—picking up around the house, making breakfast, and so on. Although I had a vaginal birth, I didn't realize the time and rest needed for my body to get back to normal. I got really wiped out toward the end of the night and my body ached all over. So stay in bed or on the couch as much as possible. And let Dad help!"

—*Angel Au, Chino Hills, CA*

C-Section Do's and Don'ts

If you've had a cesarean, you'll probably be sent home four to five days after the surgery. Although you've had a few extra days in the hospital, major surgery can take its toll on your energy level and your strength. Take it easy.

Do

✔ Get extra help around the house. You may be able to sit with more ease than women who've had vaginal births, but your body needs more time to recover.
✔ Take pain medication if your incision still hurts. A mild pain reliever, recommended by your doctor, shouldn't interfere with breastfeeding.
✔ Expect to be reminded of your incision for several days. Itchiness or numbness around the scar is normal. Discharge or severe pain is not: call your doctor.
✔ Talk to someone if you're feeling depressed about not delivering vaginally. This is a not uncommon reaction to an unexpected C-section (see "The Emotional Roller Coaster," page 154).
✔ Be prepared for lochia. C-section moms are sometimes surprised that they, too, experience this vaginal discharge, which lasts several weeks. If it's foul-smelling or recurs after having stopped, call your doctor.

Don't

✔ Strain your abdomen. You can hurt your incision if you try to pick up your baby on your own. (Have someone hand her to you.)
✔ Start to exercise until you get a doctor's OK.
✔ Have sexual intercourse before checking in with your doctor. Your bottom may be ready but your incision may not be.

• Understand the dangers of jaundice and dehydration.
• Know the symptoms of postpartum depression.

Before Your Baby Can Go Home

In addition to the examination given by the pediatrician, your baby will be examined again by the hospital staff before leaving. She'll be measured and weighed again and her vital signs will be checked. The staff wants to be sure your newborn has a normal temperature, can suck and swallow, and has urinated and pooped during the last 24 hours. She may also receive a hepatitis B vaccine before she gets her walking papers.

Speaking of papers, you'll need to file for your baby's birth certificate be-

Newborn Skin Conditions

Condition	*Peeling*
Onset	*Birth to 1 week*
Symptoms	After weeks of being waterlogged, a baby sheds some of her old skin in preparation for growing a new layer. She may peel all over, or just on her hands and feet.
Treatment	None
Condition	*Milia*
Onset	*Birth to 3 weeks*
Symptoms	These little bumps, which resemble whiteheads, are often found on a baby's nose, forehead, and cheeks.
Treatment	Caused by a buildup of sebum, a skin lubricant secreted by sebaceous glands, the bumps will go away on their own once your baby's oil glands and pores are more mature. In the meantime, hands off: don't squeeze the bumps or wash them with harsh soap.
Condition	*Toxic erythema*
Onset	*Birth to 3 months*
Symptoms	This harmless rash with the scary name can make your baby's face look like it was lunch for a cloud of mosquitoes. Each red, irritated area has a white center.
Treatment	The rash disappears on its own after a few weeks and needs no special treatment.

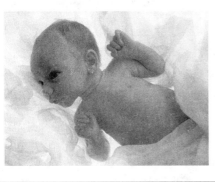

The natural lubricant that helped protect your baby's skin in the womb may now clog his immature pores and cause whiteheads called milia. This too shall pass.

fore you leave. The hospital will provide you with the forms. You'll save yourself trouble and expense if you carefully double-check all of the information you've filled in, including your baby's name. Changing his name or correcting any mistakes later is a hassle and can cost you. The hospital will register the birth certificate and the original gets sent off to a state government office. You can sign your child up for a Social Security number, usually on the same form. For a fee, you can ask the state to send you a copy of the birth certificate and your baby's Social Security card, which you'll receive in the mail in a few weeks.

How Baby Looks

You may be surprised that your baby's skin still looks bumpy and blotchy. Several weeks may pass before her skin begins to stabilize. In the meantime, many babies suffer from one or more skin irritations.

What You Need to Know About . . . Car Seats

Remember the traditional photo of a mom heading home with her baby? The proud mom was in a wheelchair holding Baby, about to climb into the front seat of the old Chevy. Today's photos show a scenario that's no less sweet, but a whole lot safer. I have pictures of my daughter being gently strapped into her bucket-style car seat in the hospital room, of me sitting next to her in the backseat of the car, and of her being carried in the front door still tucked into that car seat.

Car seats have become a necessary part of life with babies—and for good reason: you can reduce your child's risk of injury or death in a car crash by 70 percent if she's in a properly installed safety seat. In fact, your newborn can't leave the hospital any other way than *in* a car seat. Be prepared to bring the car seat up to the hospital room before you go. Bone up on these other car-seat basics:

- Your car seat must meet federal safety standards. Each year the American Academy of Pediatrics (AAP) releases a list of approved infant and child safety seats. Send a SASE to AAP, Department C—Car Seats, P.O. Box 927, Elk Grove Village, IL 60009-0927.
- For a list of car seats that have been recalled since 1981, call 800-424-9393, the Auto Safety Hotline for the National Highway Traffic Safety Administration (NHTSA). The recall list is especially important if you have a used car seat. Tell them the manufacturer of the seat, the model name and number,

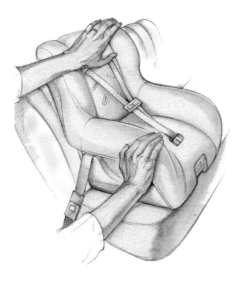

Check to make sure the seat is secure and resists side-to-side motion

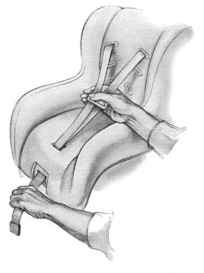

Lift up the harness adjustment lever to loosen and tighten straps.

and the date of manufacture—all information that can be found on the seat's label.

• Your baby should ride in a rear-facing car seat until she's 1 year old and weighs at least 20 pounds. Because it's the safest position and is recommended by the AAP, many parents wisely keep the seat facing backward well past the first year.

• The middle of the backseat is the safest spot for a baby. Side seats are more likely to get crushed in a crash. Front seats are definitely a no-no if your car has an airbag (more than 30 children have been killed by front-seat airbags), and they aren't a very safe spot even if you don't have an airbag (you've heard of the death seat). Even though airbags have been improved and can be deactivated, the backseat is still safest for *any* child. (In fact, the National Traffic Safety Board urges parents to *insist* that children under 13 ride belted in the backseat.) This *is* a matter of life or death.

- If you're worried about not being able to see your baby if she's in a rear-facing car seat in the backseat, buy one of the mirrors on the market that let you safely peek at her while driving.
- Read the car-seat installation directions carefully and then read them again. The NHTSA estimates that as many as 50 percent of car seats are installed or used incorrectly. Installation is not as easy as it looks, so read the directions and then have someone check that you've done it correctly.
- Use a locking clip that comes with the seat if you're using a shoulder harness, if the seat seems loose, or if the directions suggest one.
- If your baby seems lost in the seat, give her some neck support with a rolled-up towel or blanket, or buy one of the special car-seat cushions on the market. Soft pads that cover the car-seat straps can also be purchased.
- Check the security of the seat each time you put your baby in. Wiggle it to make sure it's fastened tightly. It shouldn't give more than an inch from side to side.

Newborn Care 101: Baby's Layette

Most hospitals and birthing centers provide diapers, T-shirts, and receiving blankets, so you needn't pack every outfit you received at your shower. In fact, most babies spend the majority of their time in a T-shirt and diaper, swaddled in a blanket. You might want to bring to the hospital:

- Little socks to keep your baby's feet warm
- A comfortable going-home outfit
- Baby's own blanket and a new stuffed animal
- Depending on the weather, a cool-weather cap with flaps or a sun hat, a light sweater or jacket, or a heavy-duty snowsuit

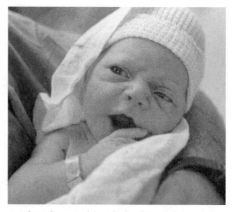

A white hospital hat helps keep Baby warm during his first hours out of the womb.

Remember . . . that your baby will be making the trip home from the hospital in a car seat; bunting or sack-style outfits don't work well with car seats that have a strap that buckles between Baby's legs. And don't forget to take home the

CHECKLIST

Baby Layette Buyer's Guide

Do

✔ Buy clothes with flat seams inside and out. Smooth inside seams don't rub against and irritate baby's sensitive skin.

✔ Choose easy-on and easy-off garments with wide neck openings or either snaps or zippers at the shoulders. Outfits should open in the front (not the back, which requires you to flip baby over to dress her—not an easy skill for beginners), and every crotch should have snaps or a zipper.

✔ Keep a soft cotton cap on your baby if she seems to like it. Her head will stay warm (as much as 40 percent of body heat escapes from the head) and she may feel more secure.

✔ Dress your baby in layers so that when there's a temperature change, you can simply add or shed a garment.

Don't

✔ Buy a turtleneck until your baby is 6 months old; make sure it's a snap-neck version when you do buy.

✔ Invest in fancy shoes or booties. It's a waste of money. Cotton socks with stretchy elastic tops are easier to get on and may even stay on; babies don't need shoes until they're standing.

✔ Buy anything with drawstrings. Strings that pull a garment closed at the neck are bad news for children of any age. Although your baby won't be crawling around for a while, it's best to avoid this choking hazard from day one. (Infant sacks, which have drawstrings at the bottom, are OK.)

✔ Forget baby's comfort. Even if fancy clothes and headbands are your style, it's more important in the first months that your baby is cozy and comfortable and that you're able to dress and change her as easily as possible. She has plenty of time for party outfits in the years to come.

✔ Keep baby bundled all the time. Parents are often tempted to keep their baby too warm. Use your own temperature as a guide and then add one light layer for your little one.

funny little warming cap that's often put on a baby's head right after she's born. It makes a nice keepsake. When your child is 3, she won't believe her head was ever that small (and you won't, either!).

Once you get home, the basic baby layette rule of thumb is this: You need enough clothing and related articles so that you don't have to do the wash every day. The list that follows is pretty basic; if you're using cloth diapers or if you have a big spitter-upper, you may need *more*:

- ☐ 3–5 receiving blankets
- ☐ 5 spit-up towels (cloth diapers work fine)
- ☐ 2–3 hooded towels
- ☐ 6 pairs of socks
- ☐ minimum of 30 newborn-size diapers (if using disposables); more if you're using cloth
- ☐ 5 bibs (to protect your baby's clothing from spit-up)
- ☐ 5 sleep sacks or sleepers
- ☐ 5 one-piece (snap crotch) T-shirts or T-shirts that have side ties (both are easier to get off and on than the over-the-head varieties)
- ☐ 5 one-piece outfits
- ☐ 5 outfits made up of separates: tops and bottoms
- ☐ 1–2 light sweaters or larger shirts for layering
- ☐ a few soft hats
- ☐ outdoor wear appropriate for the season

OTHER BIG DEALS

You wouldn't be human if you didn't ask yourself "What if something goes wrong?" at least once during your pregnancy and labor and delivery. Sometimes things don't go just as planned: a baby is early, a mom has complications, a baby is sick. Sometimes new parents are faced with a special challenge: multiples, a child with special needs, a baby who can't go home when you do. Worrying probably won't help much in any of these cases, but being armed with a positive attitude and knowledge can.

When Baby Is Too Little

Each year, about 300,000 babies fall into the premature or low birthweight category. A baby is considered premature if she was born any time before 37 weeks. The term *premature* is sometimes used interchangeably with low birthweight because preemies are often, understandably, underweight. (But a low birthweight baby—weighing less than 5 pounds, 8 ounces—isn't always a preemie.) In any case, these babies often need special care in the hospital and when they get home. Parents of these babies—who may be feeling sad, angry, or completely overwhelmed—also need some special TLC.

Because preemies often have a number of health problems, they're usually

A MOTHER'S VIEW

"Life with My Preemie"

Suzan Corcione went into labor during her 22nd week of pregnancy. She had emergency surgery to have her cervix stitched closed, then went on complete bedrest. But only four weeks later, Suzan gave birth to a baby girl. Delina Corcione weighed a mere 1 pound, 15 ounces.

When Suzan was sent home two days later, she'd held her baby just once. "Going home without Delina was very upsetting," recalls Suzan, who lives in Smithville, Missouri. "It was like leaving a part of myself behind."

She went right back to work so she could have time off when Delina was ready to come home. Suzan pumped at work and then rushed to the neonatal intensive care unit to feed the baby. "It was very demanding," she says. "And I felt cheated because Delina wasn't where Mother Nature intended her to be."

Before each visit, Suzan was required to put on a hospital gown and scrub her arms and hands for three minutes. At first, she "held" Delina by reaching into the isolette to cradle the baby's head and bottom, being careful not to tangle or disconnect the thicket of probes and tubes that surrounded her. As the baby grew and her nervous system developed, Suzan was able to take her out of the isolette for up to 30 minutes at a time.

After 10 weeks in the hospital, Delina was released. She weighed just 4 pounds, 12 ounces. "I was comfortable with her size," says Suzan, "but my husband was scared to give her a bath at first because she was so tiny."

Seven months later, the Corciones' "miracle," as they call her, is happy and healthy. Suzan's tips for adjusting to a premature delivery:

- **Let yourself cry, she says.** Your fears and worries are normal and healthy.
- **Take one day at a time.** It's easy to feel overwhelmed by all the medical caveats and cautions about a premature baby's prognosis, says Suzan. "You can't absorb it all."
- **Find a support group.** The best comfort comes from other parents of premature babies, says Suzan. "Only someone who has had a preemie can really understand what it's like," she says.
- **Take care of yourself, too.** You have to conserve energy for when the baby comes home.
- **Keep a daily journal of your feelings and your baby's condition.** It helps you stay connected and gives you a record to look back on.

ANATOMY OF
A Neonatal Intensive Care Unit

While in the NICU, your baby will be closely monitored by the trained staff and will be hooked up to machines that supply nourishment and measure her temperature, heart rate, breathing, and oxygen consumption. All the wires and tubes can look downright scary, but every piece of high-tech equipment has a role in helping your baby survive.

› **Isolette.** Many preemies spend their first days and weeks in the controlled environment of an isolette. The clear-plastic enclosed bassinet has openings where staff and parents can reach in and perform medical functions or just stroke the baby. Depending upon the baby's size and condition, she may rest in an isolette on a heated mattress, a water-filled mattress (to simulate amniotic fluid), or in a tiny hammock. She is usually naked so the staff can easily check her skin tone and breathing.

› **Oxygen and suction devices.** Since many preemies have undeveloped lungs, NICUs have equipment that delivers oxygen to the baby (via hood, ventilator, mask, or tubes in her nose) and devices that suction out the respiratory secretions that the baby can't eliminate herself. Preemies are often given doses of surfactant, a liquid substance that helps their lungs become more elastic.

› **Phototherapy lights.** This light treatment is used for babies with jaundice, a condition that often accompanies prematurity, thanks to their immature livers. Baby's eyes will be the only part of his body covered while he's getting the treatment.

› **Alarms.** A preemie's vital signs are being monitored constantly; alarms sound to let staff know if something goes amiss.

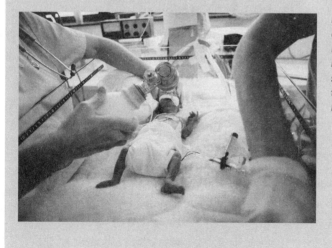

Preemies often have undeveloped lungs and need oxygen. A machine is sometimes used to suction out secretions that the tiny infant can't remove himself.

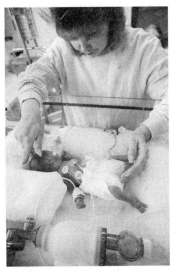

Most premature infants spend their first days in a warmed isolette in a neonatal intensive care unit. Parents are encouraged to visit.

kept in a hospital neonatal intensive care unit (see "ANATOMY OF: A Neonatal Intensive Care Unit," page 52) until they stabilize. Some preemies stay only a few days, others for months. Designed specifically for the care of newborns who are sick or tiny, these units are staffed by trained specialists.

If your hospital doesn't have a special-care unit for babies or if your preemie is very small or very early, request that he be moved to the nearest medical facility with an NICU. Studies have shown that high-risk babies (under 5 pounds) fare better in larger medical centers where the NICU staff may have more experience.

How Preemies Look and Act. Physically, preemies often look "unfinished." Their eyes are sometimes sealed shut, their genitals may be immature (in a girl, the labia, or lips of the vagina, may be undeveloped; in a boy, the testicles may be undescended), and their bodies may look especially scrawny, with no layer of fat to keep them warm. Preemies' reflexes are often very weak compared to full-term babies. And because of their undeveloped lungs, they can experience a variety of breathing problems, from grunty, raspy breaths to episodes of apnea, where they stop breathing altogether for a short time. For most preemies, these are temporary conditions.

The majority of babies born after 32 weeks will survive and develop normally. In fact, by the time they reach their 40-week "due date," their weight and physical development usually match those of their full-term peers. Until then, life with a preemie in the NICU can be quite an adventure.

Q & A

"How will I bond with my preemie?"

Luckily for parents of preemies, bonding comes in many forms and it doesn't have to be instant. Although you may not be able to achieve your "picture book" vision of bonding right off the bat, don't underestimate the value of just being there for your baby. As soon as you're up to it, visit your baby in the neonatal unit; the whole notion of having a baby or becoming a mother can seem unreal when your little one was whisked away before you got to hold and cuddle him. Send your partner if you're still bedridden or if the baby has been moved to another hospital; at least you'll be reassured by the secondhand reports that your baby is getting good care. And if your partner was around a lot during your pregnancy, chances are your baby will recognize his voice from the womb.

Once you're up to it, spend as much time as possible watching your newborn, talking to him, and stroking him through the holes in the isolette if it's allowed. Providing pumped breast milk is another wonderful way to connect with him.

As your baby becomes stronger, the opportunities for skin-to-skin contact will increase and soon you'll be able to actually hold him, feed him, and bathe him yourself. Ask the neonatal unit's nurses and doctors for other ways you can be a part of your baby's life.

For more help in caring for preemies, call Parent Care, Inc., 317-872-9913.

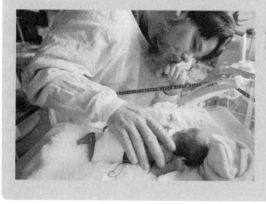

It may take parents a while to come to grips with how fragile and tiny their premature baby is. Skin-to-skin contact encourages the bonding process.

When Baby Has Complications

The great majority of full-term babies are born healthy and with no complications, but if the labor and delivery staff identified any problems in your baby's first examination, she may be taken to the NICU for further testing and treatment. What are some of the typical newborn medical problems?

• *Meconium aspiration.* Meconium is the tarry black stool passed by a baby within the first day or two after birth. However, in about 10 percent of all births, owing to stress or if the baby is late, the bowel movement may occur before the baby is born and meconium may get into the amniotic fluid and be "inhaled" in utero or right after birth. When a baby takes in her first breath after birth, stool particles may clog her airways and lungs.

If your water breaks and is dark or filled with particles, your doctor will be aware that this has happened and will take special care to suction out your baby's mouth, nose, and throat at birth. (In some cases, a C-section may be recommended.) If suctioning doesn't help ease your baby's breathing, she may have to be on a ventilator until her own body can clear out the stool debris.

• *Group B Streptococcus.* This nasty bacteria can do a number on your infant if he picks it up when he passes through your birth canal. Luckily, only one-third of all women have Strep B in their reproductive tracts and only a few babies born to those women become infected. Today, it's common for pregnant or laboring women to be screened and treated with antibiotics for this condition before they deliver. If an infection is suspected soon after birth, a newborn is given a variety of tests, sometimes including a spinal tap. Antibiotics may be administered for several days until the results of the tests are conclusive. Symptoms include breathing difficulties, kidney and heart problems, and fluctuating blood pressure. This is a very serious condition that can be fatal in 20 percent of the babies who get it. If a baby doesn't show signs of infection until later—a week after birth—meningitis may be a concern. This, too, is serious, but is more easily cured than the infection that sets in right after birth.

• *Anemia.* If your newborn shows a low red blood cell count during her tests, she may have anemia. This may occur if there were problems with the placenta, if your baby has an infection, or if she has a different blood group from yours. A variety of tests will be done to determine the cause of the problem, and iron supplementation or a blood transfusion may be recommended.

When Mom Has Complications

Some mothers suffer such severe exhaustion that they need a few extra days of rest before they're able to care for their babies. This may be particularly true if a woman has labored hard and then had a cesarean. The double whammy of labor and major surgery can wipe her out. If that happens, your hospital stay may be extended a few days and your baby will stay with you.

Hospital staff also watch new moms for serious bleeding. Hemorrhaging occurs in less than 5 percent of births, but if you do lose a lot of blood you need immediate help. Symptoms of excessive blood loss include chills, dizziness, heart palpitations, and nausea or vomiting.

In the great majority of cases of hemorrhaging after birth, the causes are uterine atony or a torn or retained placenta. In uterine atony, the uterine muscle fails to contract. Your doctor may try to help it along with medication and by massage. If that doesn't work, surgery may be necessary to stop the bleeding.

If your placenta isn't intact when it's delivered or just won't come out on its own, you'll be given an anesthetic to dull the pain so that the organ can be manually removed or the retained placental tissue can be scraped or suctioned out. Once it's entirely removed, the excessive bleeding should stop.

When You Have Multiples

Today, most twins are delivered at term. But multiple births are more likely to be premature than single fetuses and may suffer from prematurity or low birthweight.

By far, the logistics of caring for more than one baby at a time is the biggest challenge parents of multiples face. You may find that you need to write everything down to keep track of who had a bath, was fed, got burped. If you're able to do some tasks at the same time (feeding, burping one over each shoulder), you'll definitely save

After spending nine months together in the womb, twins are used to sharing the same space.

time. But that's not always possible; if you're bottle-feeding, you definitely need a second set of hands. In fact, the best thing you can do for yourself and your babies is to get extra help.

Q & A

"Will I have enough milk for my twins?"

The answer is simple: yes, your milk supply increases according to demand. The mother of twins, or triplets or more, simply has a much higher demand. Your breasts will respond with the appropriate amount of milk. If your babies are each soaking six diapers and having three to four bowel movements each day, they're getting enough. Tell that to the naysayers who think that breastfeeding multiples can't work.

Breastfeeding twins takes a little more work, but it can be done.

You may choose to nurse your twins simultaneously or sequentially. Either way, they'll be getting the nutrients they need and valuable bonding time with their mama. If your babies aren't wetting enough diapers or having the typical number of bowel movements, have them weighed and examined by the doctor to make sure they're getting enough.

For More Help: Multiples

- Center for the Study of
  Multiple Births
  312-266-9093

- International Twins Association
  612-571-3022

- National Organization of
  Mothers of Twins Clubs, Inc.
  505-275-0955

- Triplet Connection
  209-474-0885

When Baby Has a Congenital Condition

About 3 percent of babies born in the United States have some type of birth defect. These days, many congenital defects can be detected before birth, and they can begin to be treated right after birth. The conditions range from minor to severe.

- **Cleft lip and cleft palate.** These birth defects may or may not occur together; both can be repaired surgically during a baby's first year. A cleft lip can look like just a minor split in a baby's upper lip or extend all the way up to the baby's nose. A cleft palate, which occurs when the roof of a baby's mouth didn't fuse in utero, can cause problems with speech development.
- **Congenital hip dislocation.** When your baby's hips are examined, the doctor is checking that the upper leg bone fits properly into the hip socket. If it seems too loose, the joint will be repositioned and your baby may have to wear a brace for a few months. Even simpler, some doctors recommend rolling up several diapers and placing them between the baby's legs, then putting on a regular diaper. After her legs are kept in this spread position for several months, the dislocation should correct itself and disappear. If the problem recurs, it may be necessary to put a cast on your child or consider pediatric surgery. This problem afflicts more girls, firstborns, and breech babies.
- **Down syndrome.** Babies with this condition have three number 21 chromosomes. These infants may display common physical characteristics such as short fingers, large heads, small features, slanting eyes with folds in the corners, and decreased muscle tone. They may be mildly or severely mentally handicapped.
- **Spina bifida.** In this condition, the lower portion of the neural tube failed to close (the neural tube develops into a baby's brain and spinal cord during the first weeks after conception). The result can be a mild separation of spinal bones with no cord defect (spinal bifida occulta), or a more severe form in which nerve tissues bulge out of an opening in the baby's lower spine. Surgery is needed to close the opening. The baby may suffer severe physical and sometimes mental impairment.

WHAT IF...

Baby Can't Go Home with You? If your baby was premature or is sick, there's a good chance he won't be able to go home when you do. This, naturally, makes parents feel sad and guilty. When *can* your baby come home?

- When he's nursing well and starting to show a weight gain.
- When his temperature has stabilized.
- When constant medical care is no longer necessary.

In the meantime, spend as much time with your newborn as you can, call to check on him when you can't be there, and fill the rest of your time with positive thoughts of the happy homecoming.

A MOTHER'S VIEW

"Our Special Baby"

Linda Bullard Stoich of Larkspur, California, thinks of herself as a lucky woman. From the moment of her second son's birth, she got the help she needed to manage a situation that many pregnant women fear: Sam was born with a cleft lip and palate and with eyes that were fused shut.

"That first week, there were a lot of tears," says Linda. "Everyone expects a perfect baby, but he wasn't a perfect baby. Now, though, he is perfect. He's Sam."

Linda's first hurdle was figuring out how to feed Sam. Because of the hole in the roof of his mouth, he had to learn how to swallow without sending liquid up into and out of his nose. The nurses found a special squeeze bottle designed for babies with cleft palates and although no one was quite sure how it worked, "Sam figured it out," recalls Linda.

A plastic surgeon visited and explained what surgery could accomplish. A woman from Matrix, an organization that helps families with babies with special needs, visited Linda and Sam.

Sam went home three days after his birth. He had his first lip surgery when he was 3 months old. His second surgery to start the repair of his palate took place when he was 13 months old. He's scheduled for a third surgery at 21 months. But that doesn't seem to bother Sam. He's a typically exuberant, vocal 18-month-old boy. Linda's tips for parents of babies born with birth defects:

- **Give yourself time to deal with emotional adjustments.** "It took us a full month to get over the shock, the tears, the panic attacks about Sam's health," says Linda.
- **Take advantage of all the great resources.** The on-line community has been a lifeline for Linda. She found Cleft-Talk, an Internet conversation group where she got answers to both medical questions and questions about Sam's daily care.
- **Don't feel guilty if you can't be the "perfect" mom.** Linda gave up breastfeeding after the continuous pumping began to take all of her time.
- **Coach others on how to react to your child.** "Before Sam had his lip repaired, he looked weird," Linda says. When strangers would start swooping down to see a beautiful, new baby in the stroller, Linda would warn them: "He has a birth defect. It's a cleft lip, but he's going to be fine. It's amazing how kind people would be after that," she says.

- **Hydrocephalus.** Also called water on the brain, hydrocephalus is usually the result of too much fluid in the skull, which causes the head and fontanels (soft spots) to swell. In most cases, a shunt, or tube, is inserted to drain off the fluid. Mental development may or may not be affected.
- **Congenital heart disease.** Some babies are born with a heart that is not completely or correctly formed. For example, in one form of congenital heart disease there is a hole in the wall that divides the right and left ventricles of the heart (called the ventricular septum). The hole sometimes closes by itself; if not, surgery may be necessary.
- **Imperforate anus.** This is a rare abnormality in which the baby's anus has no opening. Surgery to create an opening usually corrects the problem.
- **Epispadias/hypospadias.** On rare occasions a baby boy's urethral opening will be in the wrong position on the penis. If the opening is on the top of the head of the penis, it's called epispadias. Hypospadias is when the opening is on the underside of the head of the penis. In either case, surgery is usually recommended when the child is 3 or 4. With surgery, the prognosis for normal urine flow and sexual function is good.
- **Clubfoot.** About half the time, this foot deformity can be treated right after birth by stretching and manipulating the foot, putting it in a splint or a cast, and having the child wear corrective footwear. In more severe cases, surgery is necessary. Clubfoot can affect one or both feet. In some cases, the sole of the foot faces down and inward; in others, the sole turns up and points outward.
- **Cerebral palsy.** The cause of this condition, which is an abnormality in the part of the brain that controls motor function, isn't always known. Sometimes cerebral palsy is caused by oxygen deprivation or bleeding in the brain that occurred during birth, or by an injury in early infancy. Other times, the problem can develop before birth for no known reason. Physical symptoms range from weak, floppy muscles to rigid, spastic behavior. The condition is sometimes associated with mental retardation and convulsions. Physical therapy and special education can help compensate for the lack of motor skills and learning disabilities. There is no cure.

For More Help: Babies with Special Needs

Alexander Graham Bell Association
 for the Deaf
202-337-5220

American Association for
 Home-Based Early Intervention
800-396-6144

American Cranial Facial Association
412-681-9620

American Foundation of the Blind
800-AFBLIND

American Speech-Language-
 Hearing Association
800-638-8255

Association for Children with
 Down Syndrome
516-221-4700

ARC
817-261-6003

Cleft-Talk
1-800-242-5338

Cystic Fibrosis Foundation
800-FIGHTCF

ERIC Clearinghouse on Disabilities
 and Gifted Education
800-328-0272

Federation for Children with
 Special Needs
617-482-2915

March of Dimes Birth Defects
 Resource Center
888-663-4637

National Autism Hotline
304-525-8014

National Down Syndrome
 Society
800-221-4602

National Easter Seal Society
800-221-6827

National Information Center for
 Children and Youth with
 Disabilities
800-695-0285

Sickle Cell Disease Association of
 America
800-421-8453

Spina Bifida Association of
 America
800-621-3141

United Cerebral Palsy
 Association
800-872-5827

It's amazing how this sweet bundle of joy changes your life. Within days you'll wonder how you spent your time before Baby.

CHAPTER **2**

THE FIRST THREE MONTHS

In the next several months your baby will grow from a helpless couch potato into a smiling, squealing boss of the household, struggling to let you know what he needs and when. Your life will be turned upside down, and at the end of the three months you'll probably have a new appreciation for the quotation "It was the best of times, it was the worst of times."

But take comfort from the knowledge that most of the "worst" is behind you. Your baby will still spend the majority of his time in a reclining position, and you'll still be running on too few hours of sleep, but with a few months under your belts, you'll both be smarter, more comfortable with each other, and more in love than ever. And you'll have shared some of Year One's incredible firsts, including: your first sleepless night at home together, your baby's first cry with real tears, and the first time he really smiled *at* you (not because of a digestive upset).

In the first three months your baby will probably . . .*

- Grow 2 to 4 inches and gain at least a pound a month
- Lose most of his fancy newborn reflexes
- Lift his head 90 degrees from a prone position
- Turn to your breast in anticipation (because he remembers that's where the milk comes from) instead of just instinctually
- Have had six vaccinations
- Have gone from sleeping eight hours during the day to five
- Begin to use his eyes together and focus on objects, even trying to follow a moving object
- Pause between cries to check if you're listening
- Attempt to swat at objects

*Every baby is different and has his or her own developmental timetable.

By the end of the first three months, **you** *will probably . . .*

- Be able to diaper, feed, and complete numerous other tasks while half asleep
- Still be swooning every time your baby smiles, whether it's from gas or not
- Have at least a vague idea of what your baby wants when he cries
- Be more tired than you ever thought possible
- Have become an expert at stain removal
- Be able to partake in sex again if you're so inclined (and if you can find the requisite time, energy, and privacy)
- Marvel at how boring your life must have been before Baby

YOUR BABY'S WORLD

The five senses are your newborn's gateway to her new world. Using her senses of smell, taste, sight, hearing, and touch, she gathers information about what's going on around her, and she figures out what it all means and how she fits into the grand scheme of things. To know best how to help her find her way, you need to put yourself in her booties for a while.

What Your Baby Hears

Even before your baby was born, she was developing an acute sense of hearing. In fact, your newborn may recognize a variety of sounds that she heard regularly during her time in the womb. She'll turn toward a familiar sound and may become very quiet or very animated when she recognizes it. Studies have also shown that a baby is more attentive to the sound of her mother's native language, even when that language is spoken by someone she doesn't know.

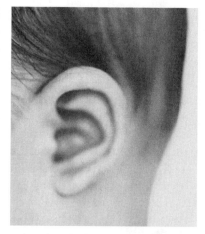

Babies love high voices. Some experts think a baby's preference for the female voice is a leftover survival tactic from cave-dwelling days when recognizing a friendly high voice was a matter of life and death. Whether they're conscious of their infant's preferences or not, many new moms and dads tend to pitch their voices higher when talking baby talk. And that's just dandy with Baby.

Babies love high voices, which may be why parents instinctively pitch their voices higher when they talk baby talk.

YOUR AMAZING BABY

Hair. Some babies have it, some babies don't. Others have it and then lose it. All babies get it, eventually.

Eyes. A baby is born with 20/200 vision. By 2 months, she'll begin to track objects and make real eye contact with you. By a year old, her vision will be 20/20.

Taste. Your baby can tell your breastmilk from somebody else's.

Mouth. A baby's mouth is an incredible touch center with very sensitive nerve endings that tell her a lot about what she puts in there.

Soft spots. It's okay to brush baby's hair or rub her head; her fontanels are covered with a tough membrane.

Ears. Your newborn may recognize sounds that she heard while in the womb.

Tummy. During the first weeks of life your baby's tiny stomach can hold only 1 to 3 ounces of milk. By a month old, she can manage up to 5 ounces.

Belly button. The umbilical cord stump usually falls off within two weeks.

What Your Baby Sees

From birth, an infant can focus on objects that are 7 to 10 inches away—roughly the distance to your face during a feeding. Some experts think that newborns just see what they need to see, thereby protecting them from being exposed to scary stuff they can't do anything about anyway (possibly the remnants of another survival tactic). Their 20/200 vision will improve dramatically in the first three to four months.

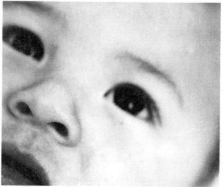

Your newborn can see about 10 inches—far enough to focus on your face during a feeding. He already recognizes your smell.

Newborns stare longer at new things—objects they haven't seen before—than at familiar ones. Given the choice between looking at a familiar design and a new design, studies have shown that an infant will look at the new one. Nonetheless their favorite thing to look at is your face.

They do see in color, but at this age they prefer the sharp contrast of black and white. They're also attracted to shapes that are curved and objects that move or are lit up.

By 2 months, a baby's eyes begin to work together better and to focus. He'll begin to track objects and make real eye contact with you. Up until then, he may look to the right or left of you but not right at you.

What Your Baby Tastes

Babies love sweet tastes, which is fine because breast milk is naturally sweet. Even when the milk is laced with strong flavors from something spicy or garlicky that mom ate, it's often OK with baby. Experts theorize that a baby's early exposure to such strong flavors may predispose him to favor the cuisine of his culture, or make him more likely to try different foods later in life.

What Your Baby Smells

Your baby recognizes your smell right at birth. Offered the choice between a breast that smells like soap and a breast that smells like milk, your savvy baby will go for the milky smell. She'll also choose a breast pad soaked with your milk over a pad with another mother's milk.

LIFE WITH ESTEBAN

Follow along with new mother Grege Lastra's month-by-month diary of her first year of motherhood.

Meet baby Esteban and his parents. In each chapter his mom shares a few entries from her new-mother diary.

IN THE BEGINNING

Esteban weighed in at 7 pounds, 2 ounces, and was 19 inches long at birth. His first moments weren't exactly ideal. He emerged with his umbilical cord wrapped around his neck.

This kid is a party boy. He's up all night and sleeps all day. From day one, he was breastfeeding every hour, maybe every two hours. But he's really a good baby, with a great temperament. When he's awake, he's all motion—little quivers, big yawns, and impressive hiccups. He kicks and stretches. When he does get to sleep, he really zonks out.

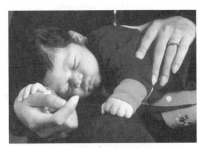

One of baby Esteban's favorite sleep positions is tummy down on Mom's lap, head hanging down.

MONTH 2

Steve is still floating—yesterday he came home with a New York Knicks outfit for Esteban, complete with little high-top sneakers.

No one can prepare you for how demanding life with a new baby will be. It's funny how I just have to run to him when he cries. At his first well-baby checkup, Esteban cried when he got his shots. I wanted to take him and run.

MONTH 3

Esteban is all movement. He holds his head up, inches up in his crib, coos, laughs—and can he kick hard! He's happy in his swing and loves his mobile. In the morning, he starts in with little rhythmic grunts to let me know he's awake. He gives me about three minutes to pull myself together for the day. For a while, as friendly as Esteban is, I wasn't sure he liked his dad very much—until I went out one day and left Steve alone with Esteban, no Grandma, no relatives or friends around. I suspect they played the whole time—and now their relationship is totally different. Esteban coos to his father the minute he comes into the room.

What Your Baby Feels

By around 3 months, your baby will begin to very briefly hold objects in his hands. He may try to aim them at his mouth. A baby's mouth is an incredible touch center with very sensitive nerve endings that tell him a lot about what he puts in there. Studies have shown that newborns can feel the difference between pacifiers with different textures.

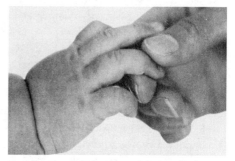

Since babies love to be touched, massage can be a mutually satisfying way to get to know each other in the first three months. Touch is so powerful, in fact, that research shows that premature babies who've been massaged grow faster than those who haven't.

Touch is incredibly powerful: Research shows that preemies who are massaged grow faster than those who are not.

CARE AND FEEDING

The word *responsibility* takes on a whole new meaning the day you take your baby home. Suddenly you're in charge of keeping her warm, dry, clean, fed, and happy. All this, and making sure you don't drop her, too!

The Art of Holding Your Baby

Babies love to be held almost as much as new moms and dads love to hold them. Some are wiggly and cross, though, until you find a hold that suits

Cradle hold. Baby's head and neck rest snugly in the crook of your arm. Your other hand supports his bottom and back. This hold lets you look at each other and provides lots of body-to-body contact.

Abdomen hold. Place your baby face down on one arm, with her neck supported in the crook of your arm, and her chest and abdomen on your forearm. Depending on her size, her legs may dangle off your hand. Use your other arm to provide additional support for the infant's lower body. Bring it up between her legs and under your other arm. Babies love this "airplane hold," especially if they need a little pressure on a gassy tummy.

Burping hold. Use one hand to hold your infant's head against your shoulder; support his neck with the same hand. Your other hand cups his bottom. If you're burping your baby, hold him a little higher with his head peeking over the shoulder while you gently rub his back; if he seems to need lots of comforting, hold him lower with more body-to-body contact.

them. These three holding techniques provide plenty of variety. Remember: always lean as close as possible to your baby when picking her up, and support her wobbly head, as shown in the photos on these pages.

Keeping Baby Fresh and Clean

To bathe or not to bathe . . . that is the question for many new parents. Yes, it's important to keep your newborn as clean as possible, but many parents go overboard worrying about cleanliness and diaper-rash prevention.

Until your infant's umbilical cord stump falls off, tub baths are not recommended. If you're cleaning his diaper area well at each changing, your baby doesn't even need to be bathed each day: a sponge bath every few days will be just fine.

Sponge-Bath Basics

Before you start a sponge bath, gather together a few supplies: a clean washcloth and towel, baby shampoo, a diaper, and mild soap. Any towel and washcloth will do, but baby washcloths are often softer, and a hooded baby towel is as cozy as it is cute. To clean the umbilical cord stump, you'll need rubbing alcohol and cotton swabs.

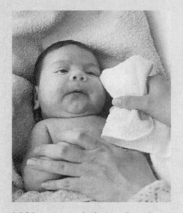

1. Wrap your baby in the clean towel and lay him on a comfortable padded surface. With a wet washcloth (always use lukewarm water), clean Baby's eyes, starting from each inside corner and working out. Wash his face and then pat dry.

2. You can wipe your baby's head with a damp washcloth, or hold him carefully over the sink, to get his hair clean. The sink method is often demonstrated to parents at the hospital by a baby nurse who makes it look easy—it isn't. If you're at all uncomfortable or anxious, skip it; it does take a steady hand and you must control the flow and temperature of the water. Instead, wash your baby's head with a damp washcloth and dry.

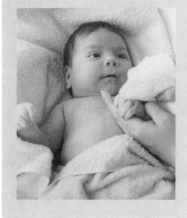

3. Bundle your baby up and move him back to the padded surface (if you used the sink). Do the top-to-toes routine, moving from his neck and upper body to his legs. Just unbundle the part of the body you're washing and rinsing at the time. Pat dry as you go along.

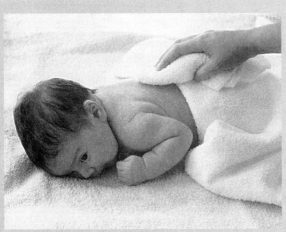

4. Turn your baby over gently to wash, rinse, and dry his neck and back.

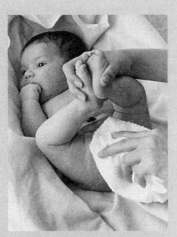

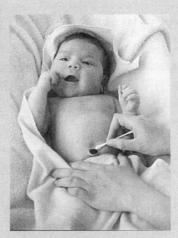

5. Turn him over again and remove his diaper. Wash his belly (but not his belly button) and then the genital area. His bottom should always be washed last, cleaning from the front to back. Lift up his legs to dry his bottom. (If your baby has been circumcised, keep soap and water off his penis until he's healed.)

6. Put on a fresh diaper. Make sure the diaper is folded down so that it doesn't irritate the umbilical cord stump. Dip a cotton swab in rubbing alcohol and wipe around the base of the cord as well as the stump. Let the area air dry, then dress your sweet-smelling package.

Time for a Tub Bath Once his umbilical cord stump has healed, your infant can move into a baby tub or take a bath with you. Even then, it isn't necessary to give your baby a bath every day. Take your cues from your infant: Some newborns love water; others hate it (usually because they don't like to be undressed). If bathing is an enjoyable ritual for both of you, go for it. If it's not, save the tub baths for days when he's really dirty or has had a diaper blowout.

For the reluctant baby, you can ease into the bathing experience by lying in the big tub with him on your chest, covered by a towel. Slowly and gently pour water over him as he's resting on you. Babies are incredibly slippery, however, so it's wise to have someone else at home to help you get in and out of the tub with your little one. If you're using a baby tub, make it more comfortable with a sponge insert that cushions his head and body (available at discount and baby-supply stores).

What You Need to Know About . . . Diaper Rash

The first thing you need to know is that most babies get diaper rash at one time or another. Given the combination of urine, loose stools, and baby's delicate skin, it's no wonder that your infant's bottom, inner thighs, genitals, or stomach can become red and irritated. To avoid a rash, or prevent a recurrence:

- Change the diaper as soon as it's wet or dirty.
- Make sure baby's bottom is clean and dry after each diaper change.
- Promote dryness by letting his bottom air dry, if possible. Powder has fallen out of favor because it can be hazardous when inhaled. Don't use any powder that contains talc, and always apply very sparingly.
- Coat the affected area with a soothing ointment that has a base of petrolatum or zinc oxide.
- Buy diapers that wick wetness away from baby's bottom.
- Use laundry soap (not detergent) if using cloth diapers; don't use fabric softener or antistatic sheets.

If the rash doesn't clear up in three to five days, talk to your child's doctor. You'll want to rule out a yeast infection or other problem (see "DEFINITION: Thrush," page 111).

Baby Wipes Can Irritate My Baby's Bottom?

Some babies' sensitive skin reacts to the ingredients or fragrances in packaged wipes—or in soap, for that matter. That's why most pediatricians recommend that you use a soft washcloth, water, and mild soap to clean baby's bottom during diaper changes.

Most of the backlash against baby wipes really stems from how much they cost, not how they smell. If you're like me, you may opt for convenience over cost. In that case, choose an unscented wipe with as few additives as possible. If your baby has a reaction, change to a different wipe or try the washcloth method. And don't use a baby wipe if your infant has diaper rash; if the wipe contains alcohol, it may sting your baby's already irritated bottom.

HOW TO
Trim Baby's Nails

Do . . .
- Use good-quality nail scissors with rounded tips. These are preferable to clippers as they're easier to maneuver around little paper-thin nails.
- Wait until your baby is sleeping deeply to trim.
- Follow the curve of the finger; straight-across cuts can leave sharp edges.
- Trim in one motion, if possible (instead of three little cuts), gently turning the scissors as you clip.
- Check your baby's fast-growing fingernails two or three times a week; slower-growing toenails will probably only need twice-a-month trimming.

Don't
- Trim too close. It's best to leave a little edge of white showing.
- Bite off your baby's nail, even if it's torn or jagged. Biting the nail is more likely to tear it down to the quick (where the nail meets the skin).

Use good-quality nail scissors with rounded tips (not clippers) to trim Baby's paper-thin nails. Never bite her nails.

Follow the curve of the finger when you're gently filing Baby's nails. And rule number one: Wait until she's asleep!

Baby Skin Conditions

Condition	*Cradle cap*
Onset	*From 1 week to 3 months*
Symptoms	This form of seborrheic dermatitis affects nearly half of all newborns during their first months. The symptoms: scaly, greasy patches found most often on a baby's scalp, but sometimes also seen around the nose, ears, eyelids, and hairline. The condition isn't at all painful and usually doesn't even itch. It's thought to be caused by a buildup of oil from the baby's active sebaceous glands.
Treatment	To remove the most crusty parts, smooth a few drops of olive oil into the baby's scalp to soften and then gently rub or brush off the scales with a washcloth or soft brush (some parents use a toothbrush). Follow with a good shampoo.
Condition	*Baby acne*
Onset	*From 2 weeks to 4 weeks*
Symptoms	As Mom's hormones work their way out of Baby's system, they can cause baby acne. Like most newborn skin troubles, pimples normally heal within two to four weeks and usually without any special care.
Treatment	Just wash with water and gently dry. Don't squeeze or pick the pimples or use lotion.

The Skinny on Skin

The same people who told you that all newborns are beautiful will tell you that nobody notices baby pimples or imperfections in your baby's skin. But it's not true. Each of my daughters had such bad cases of zits at 3 weeks old that even their adoring grandmother suggested they stay in for a couple of weeks. By the time your baby reaches the 2-month mark, though, her skin will probably be smooth.

Feeding Patterns

AGE	NEWBORN	1 MONTH	2 MONTHS	3 MONTHS
How often?	8–12 times/day	6–12 times/day	6–10 times/day	6–8 times/day (more often if breastfed)
How much?	A few mouthfuls to 3 ounces	3–6 ounces	3–8 ounces	4–8 ounces
When?	Erratic, whenever she wants	Every 2–4 hours	Nighttime feeding may taper off	May eat only every 4 or 5 hours at night; may have 1 or 2 very heavy feedings (more often if breastfed)

What Goes In . . . and What Comes Out

New parents are, understandably, interested in how much their newborn is eating, and how much—and what—she is producing in her diaper. Over the course of the first three months input and output may change dramatically, and, of course, every infant is different. Bottle-fed babies sometimes drink a lot more per feeding than breastfeeding babies and feed less often, but by the end of 3 months (and definitely by 6 months), many babies begin doing more of their eating during daylight hours.

Until then, an irregularly spaced feeding pattern is perfectly normal. In fact, some infants (especially if they're breastfed) feed every hour and a half for 30 minutes, which means you don't have much time in between feedings. Other babies eat every hour for just 10 minutes. Until your baby is at least 3 months old, just follow her signals and feed her when she's hungry.

Sometimes you'll notice that your baby has an unusually hearty appetite. That may correspond to spurts in her growth. It's thought that many infants have such a spurt at about 2 weeks, 6 weeks, 3 months, and again at 6 months. If you're nursing, you may suddenly feel as if you don't have enough milk—until all that extra nursing stimulates your body to produce more milk. Your body increases its production of milk to keep up with your baby's needs.

The Spit-up Story You don't really need to worry about overfeeding a baby—when he's had enough he'll let you know. If he's spitting up what looks like his whole feeding when you burp him, give him a little less at the next feeding (and rest assured that what looks like a lot of spit-up milk is probably only a teaspoonful or two). Try a gentler motion when you burp him (see "Burping Hold," page 69), and keep her in an upright position for 30 minutes. If you're bottle-feeding, check the size of the hole in the baby bottle nipple (see "Bottle-Feeding 101," page 86); a too-large hole may cause Baby to gulp down milk too quickly, which can result in gas or regurgitation.

An infant who spits up frequently and prodigiously may be suffering from gastroesophageal reflux (in which stomach acids back up into the esophagus), a milk or formula allergy, or a more serious problem. Let your doctor know if the excessive spitting up continues, if the spit-up is colored (typically it's whitish and may smell like curdled milk), if the episodes of spitting up occur after each feeding or are projectile, or if your baby is not gaining weight.

The Scoop on Poop Once you've lived through your baby's tarry meconium stools, you may think that nothing you find in her diaper can surprise you. Breastfed babies' poop can be especially colorful, however, as a result of what you've eaten. Their stools may be mustardy, runny, or grainy. Formula-fed babies typically produce firmer stools that are more tan than yellow.

How often should your baby have a bowel movement? There are some rules of thumb, but the range of normal varies widely. An infant on formula will probably have one or more bowel movements a day. Up until they're 6 weeks old, breastfed babies usually produce three or more stools per day; after 6 weeks, they may have only one a day or skip a day. Some breastfed babies move their bowels right after each feeding. Others, regardless of what they're drinking, go several days without having a bowel movement and make up for it later with impressive blowouts. After your breastfed baby is 6 weeks old, erratic

HOW TO

Remove Spit-up and Other Stains

You are now sporting the badge of new parenthood (along with bags under your eyes): a variety of gunk on the shoulders of everything you own. Blowouts and burp-ups have probably made your baby's togs less than pristine, too. Here's an "out damned spot" primer.

Stain Removal Tips

For This Stain . . .	Try This . . .
Spit-up	‣ Soak item in cold water
	‣ Wash in warm or hot water
	‣ Use chlorine bleach* in addition to detergent
Feces & urine	‣ Pretreat with a stain remover
	‣ Wash in warm or hot water
	‣ Use bleach* with detergent
Vitamins & medicine	‣ Pretreat with stain remover
	‣ Wash in hot water
	‣ Use bleach* with an enzyme detergent

*For nonwhites, use nonchlorine bleach.

Tips

- Don't let a stain sit around. Presoak or pretreat immediately for best results.
- Check all labels first. Some garments can't handle stain remover or strong enzyme detergent.
- Only colorfast clothing and whites can handle chlorine bleach; never pour chlorine bleach directly onto laundry.
- You can make a stain-removing paste for pretreating by mixing enzyme detergent with a little water.
- Always check to see if the stain has disappeared *before* you dry the item; if it's still there, try a second round of stain remover or detergent paste. Once you dry an item, stain-removal chances plummet.

bowel rhythms (and the occasional noisy passage of gas) shouldn't worry you—as long as your baby is wetting six to eight diapers per day (which shows he's getting enough fluids). Before that, however, do keep track of his bowel movements. Too few could mean he's not getting enough to eat. If his stools are infrequent or greenish, call the pediatrician.

Likewise, if your formula-fed baby has recurrent diarrhea, has gone more than a week without a bowel movement, or has blood in his stool, let your doctor know.

Breastfeeding: The First Days

Like most new moms, I was a little apprehensive about breastfeeding. I knew it was best for my baby, I wanted to do it, but I couldn't quite imagine that I could produce enough of anything to keep her happy and healthy.

Then my milk came in. With breasts filled to bursting, I had no more doubts about quantity. Instead I was stunned by how my breasts looked and felt. I actually had my mother take a Polaroid of my engorged breasts because I simply couldn't get over what I saw in the mirror.

The second shock was how the milk came out. Each nipple was like a mini–shower head! Milk didn't simply squirt out a hole in the tip like a sports water bottle; it spurted out of tiny holes *all over* the nipple. If I wasn't careful, it sprayed so hard that it shot innocent bystanders in the eye or poured down my daughter's throat so quickly that she choked.

In spite of all that, once you and your baby get the hang of breastfeeding, it can be an incredibly empowering experience. Many mothers marvel at how their newborns flourish just on breast milk and savor the intimate time spent feeding their baby. But it can take several days—weeks even—for breastfeeding to feel natural, and the path to successful breastfeeding is strewn with hurdles.

Engorgement You may be shocked, as I was, by how your breasts take on a life of their own. A postpartum drop in hormone levels combined with your infant's suckling are all your breasts need to kick into action. Your breasts already have

⌒ A MOTHER'S VIEW ⌒

"My Breasts Were Engorged"

Austin Madrzyk was born with a high fever and fluid in his lungs. He had to be fed intravenously and stay in the hospital for a few days after his mother, Kelly, was discharged.

The baby was going to be OK, but Kelly wasn't sure she'd survive. Although Austin couldn't nurse, Kelly's breasts filled up with milk even before she left the hospital. She pumped religiously, but her breasts were swollen, rock hard, hot, and painful.

"Those first few days were brutal," recalls Kelly, who wondered at the time why no one had ever told her how painful having your milk come in could be.

Even after Austin came home and was nursing regularly, Kelly had a hard time regulating her milk production. "I had no life," she says. "I had to take Austin with me wherever I went."

When Austin was 2 months old, Kelly attempted to go to a bridal shower. After stuffing napkins in her bra to staunch her milk flow, covering her damp blouse with her blazer, and then leaking through it, she gave up and went home. "I was afraid I'd scare the poor bride, so that she'd never want to have children!"

In spite of her ongoing problems with too-full breasts and leaking, Kelly believes breastfeeding is critical. "I nursed my son for 10 months and it was all worth it in the end," she says. Her tips about dealing with engorgement:

- **Use ice packs to reduce the hot sensation and to lessen the leaking.**
- **Try a pain reliever, such as acetaminophen.** When Kelly took a few Tylenols for a bad headache one day, she realized they also reduced the heat and pain of engorgement.
- **Keep your sense of humor and accept the situation.** Some women just get more engorged than others. There could be worse problems. And this, too, will pass, says Kelly, although not as soon as you'd wish.

plenty of colostrum for your baby, and within two to four days after your baby is born, they'll start to fill with mature milk. As they enlarge, your breasts may become swollen and sore. Some women fill up so suddenly and so much that their breasts become as hard as rocks. This can be very painful and can make it tough for your baby to latch on.

Engorgement is really just a simple (and fleeting) supply-and-demand problem. Once you're nursing regularly, your breasts will regulate themselves and become soft again. The best way to prevent engorgement is not to let too much time elapse between feedings.

To help ease the discomfort of engorgement, take a warm shower (this is sometimes necessary just to get the milk flowing) or apply warm compresses to the breasts before each feeding. The heat feels good and encourages letdown. Cold packs after each nursing session help reduce swelling.

Q & A

"How do I interest my baby in both breasts? My right breast is shrinking from disuse."

Although some women don't mind being lopsided and manage to nurse from just one breast, two breasts *are* better than one. Unless both your breasts are regularly stimulated and emptied, your baby may not be getting enough milk, and the ignored breast may be at a higher risk of a clogged duct or infection.
Some hints for turning baby into an equal-opportunity feeder:

- Start with the nonfavored breast at each feeding. A hungry baby is less likely to be choosy.
- Trick your baby into thinking she's getting the favored breast. If she prefers your left breast, when changing to the right breast simply slide her over to the other breast without changing the hold or switching arms. This may be uncomfortable at first, but is well worth it if it works. To avoid back or neck strain, place comfortable pillows under your most-used arm and sit in a supportive chair.
- Have a lactation consultant check how you're holding your baby and how he's latching on. There may be some subtle difference from breast to breast that's causing your baby to prefer one over the other. (In many cases, Mom is so much more comfortable holding the baby one way—in her left arm if she's right-handed, for instance—that the infant is just following her unspoken cue.)

In very rare instances, a baby rejects one breast because of an infection or tumor. If the less-used breast is sore or has a lump, call your doctor.

Trouble Latching On Engorgement can cause or aggravate latching-on problems. Nipples stretched out or flattened by too-full breasts are even harder for an infant to grasp. Before nursing, empty each breast a bit by expressing milk by hand or by pump. This should help soften the breast and pull the nipple out. If your baby can't connect because too much milk is coming out of your nipple or it's coming too fast, express some or let the milk flow into a diaper or cloth until it's not spraying out so forcefully.

Leaking Another supply-and-demand problem, leaking breasts can be embarrassing and make you very uncomfortable. Once your milk flow regulates, leaking should diminish, although some women continue to leak at night when they go longer between feedings. Invest in some absorbent cotton breast pads or make your own out of torn-up pieces of old cotton. Wash the pads often and try to keep your breasts as dry as possible to avoid infection. Breast milk washes out of most fabrics. To reduce leaking from one breast while you're nursing with the other, press down on the nipple.

Sore Nipples Members of the La Leche League (a breastfeeding support group) and lactation consultants like to tell you that breastfeeding, when done properly, shouldn't hurt at all. That sort of statement is meant to be encouraging, but it's not very comforting to the breastfeeding mom who is struggling to get her infant latched on correctly and who has sore or cracked nipples in spite of all of her efforts.

Of course, some mild discomfort may occur during the first weeks of nursing: Your nipples may need time to get used to the constant sucking, and your little one may need some time to learn how to latch on properly. But normal discomfort, the experts say, doesn't include severe soreness or nipples that are cracked or bleeding. These painful conditions are almost always the result of improper latching on. The experts stress that teaching your baby how to latch on correctly, so that her mouth is covering your entire nipple including the areola, is the key to breastfeeding success. (Besides causing nipple soreness, a baby who isn't latching on correctly may not be getting enough milk; see "What You Need to Know About . . . Dehydration," page 90.)

Yet in my case, in spite of having all sorts of knowledgeable folks repeatedly show me how to breastfeed properly, I occasionally had sore and cracked nipples both times I breastfed. I nursed my first daughter for six months and my second for nine months, and there were days when feeding was a breeze and others where just putting the baby to my breast was excruciating. I still enjoyed breastfeeding immensely and would recommend it wholeheartedly, but I was a little discouraged that nursing wasn't as "pain-free" as the experts said. What was I doing wrong?

Nothing, according to the lactation consultants who checked out my nursing style. I finally found a consultant who gave me great comfort by admitting that sometimes breastfeeding hurts more for some women than others, even when you're doing it right. If you're fair-skinned, fair-haired, or have light eyes or very pale nipples, you may have more discomfort than other women. (Some experts say this is an old wives' tale, but others are not so quick to write it off.) If your infant is large or is a particularly voracious, vigorous sucker, your nipples may take a tougher beating—even when the baby is latched on correctly. As your baby goes through growth spurts, there may be periods where he nurses harder and your nipples become more sensitive. And there may even be a physical reason that breastfeeding hurts. When my second daughter was 9 months old, her pediatrician discovered that she was tongue-tied—the tissue (called the frenulum) that connects the tongue to the bottom of her mouth was too tight. She couldn't move her tongue freely enough to latch on comfortably and so was always, literally, rubbing me the wrong way. A too-tight frenulum doesn't always interfere with feeding or require any treatment. In a worst-case scenario, the condition could result in your baby not getting enough to eat and even becoming dehydrated (see "CHECKLIST: Dehydration Warning Signs," page 90). In my case, it just meant that breastfeeding was a little more difficult, but no less worthwhile.

If you've gotten professional instruction in latching on and still experience sore nipples, what can you do?

- Pat a little breast milk (which is purported to have healing qualities) on your sore nipple and let it air-dry.
- Use lanolin cream on your nipples. You'll get all sorts of conflicting advice on this, but lanolin that's free of pesticides is safe for a baby to ingest. It's sometimes available from lactation consultants and centers, or from your hospital pharmacy. I found lanolin to be a true lifesaver; it helped my nipples heal more quickly and made nursing bearable during the tough times.
- Try wearing plastic breast shells with airholes in your bra. These provide a buffer between sore nipples and nursing pads. (They also help draw out flat nipples, so that your baby can latch on better.)
- Wear nursing bras (no underwires) and use breast pads that are 100 percent cotton. Moisture breeds infection, so buy enough pads to allow you to change immediately if they're wet. Pat your nipples dry after each feeding or let down your nursing-bra flaps and let your nipples air-dry.
- Nurse first with the less painful breast. Your infant may be satiated enough

HOW TO
Use a Breast Pump

Breast pumps come in many sizes and shapes and cost from $20 for a manual pump to about $200 for a high-quality electric model. It's also possible to rent a pump for $1 to $3 a day.

Although inexpensive, a manual pump requires quite a bit of work, time, and dexterity. It's fine if you're just expressing a little milk to relieve engorgement or to help Baby latch on. But go with an electric model if you plan to pump a lot of milk.

Electric pumps range from portable hand-held models to hospital-grade machines that have double-pumping capability. The cheaper electrics require that you push a button or cover a hole repeatedly to generate the pumping action. More expensive models generate the suction automatically and allow you to completely empty both breasts in less than 15 minutes.

A few pumping tips:

- All suction is not created equal. Some women complain that the suction generated by the smaller pumps can become painful. And pumps with weaker suction require that you pump longer. Ask for a pump recommendation from friends or a lactation consultant. Don't buy or use a pump that hurts! Try another model.
- Always make sure the pump's breast shield is snug to your breast and positioned so that your nipple is in the center. Incorrect positioning can cause nipple soreness.
- Practice good hygiene. Wash your hands before and after pumping, and clean the shield after each use.

Hospital-grade electric breast pumps generate suction automatically and let you empty both breasts in less than 15 minutes.

Manual breast pumps are fine for occasional pumping, but require quite a bit of dexterity and patience.

Electric breast pumps range widely in price and options. The more expensive models let you control the suction and pump both breasts at once.

GOOD ADVICE

Breastfeeding

"Before you go into labor, visit the hospital's lactation consultant to say 'Hi.' During labor, delivering, ask several nurses (one may forget) to send a message to the breastfeeding specialist saying that you're in labor and would like her to come to your room as soon as possible after you have the baby. When I tried to feed my baby for the first time, the lactation specialist was right at my side. This way you won't be trying to read those books on how to nurse while your baby cries to be fed."

—*Wendy Holmes, St. Louis, MO*

"When my daughter wasn't getting enough milk, I turned to my local La Leche League for help. Within 48 hours, I was producing more than ample milk. La Leche leaders are mothers who have breastfed their own children, and they receive additional training on special issues related to breastfeeding. You also can get support and tips from other mothers in the group and make friends for you and your child."

—*Reeves Rhodes, Brooklyn, NY*

"Breastfeeding doesn't have to be all or nothing. I was very committed to breastfeeding, but before my breast milk came in, I fed my 8-pound, 9-ounce baby supplemental formula. It made Jack much more content during those first days. While this technique doesn't work for all babies, in Jack's case it caused no nipple confusion or preference for formula over breast milk. He switches easily from breast to bottle, which gives me a break, and lets Dad and big sister help feed him. The lesson: Do what you're comfortable with."

—*Marianne Schermerhorn, Chicago, IL*

that he'll suck more gently by the time you move on to the sore breast.

- If nursing is too painful, use a high-quality pump to empty your breasts until your nipples heal. Sometimes the pressure from a pump is less painful or aggravating than a baby's mouth. Give the expressed breast milk to your baby by cup or syringe.
- Don't avoid nursing because you're in pain. Your baby may just suck harder the next time you feed, causing more damage to the nipple.
- Don't give up! Try another consultant or join a mothers' group so that you're getting the support you need.

Clogged Milk Ducts and Breast Infections You'll know it when you have a clogged milk duct; you'll feel a tender spot with a hard middle. The fastest way to unclog the duct is to apply warm compresses before and during nursing, and massage the hard knot during feeding. Start each feeding with the clogged side, in an effort to work out the hard knot. If the skin is red over the tender spot, you may have a breast infection. Call your doctor.

To avoid future clogs, don't miss a feeding, wear loose-fitting clothes (no tight bras or bras with underwires), and massage your breasts before a feeding (to make sure they're soft).

Left untreated, a clogged duct can develop into a breast infection called *mastitis*. The symptoms include a red area of skin over the clogged duct, fever, flu symptoms, and breast pain. You'll need a course of antibiotics, plenty of rest, and lots of fluids. You'll also have to continue nursing or pumping through the pain in order to keep your breasts emptied and your milk production up.

If you're experiencing a burning or stinging sensation spreading from your nipple into your breast, you may have a yeast (or monilial) infection (See "DEFINITION: Thrush," page 111). This occurs when your nipples become infected with yeast, usually passed from your infant's mouth to your breast, or if you've been on antibiotics. (You're more likely to pick up the infection if your nipples are cracked.) Signs of yeast in your baby include white patches on your baby's tongue or inside her mouth. If you suspect you have a yeast infection, you and your baby will both need medication.

Cracked nipples can also lead to a bacterial infection. Symptoms include nipple soreness and redness or a yellowish substance in the cracks. Oral antibiotics are the typical cure.

Food Reactions and Allergies If your baby begins to reject your breast or cries during or after a feeding, it may be due to something you ate. Coffee, chocolate, and spicy foods can alter the taste of breast milk, offending your baby's delicate palate or upsetting her tummy. If she's also congested, has a runny nose, red cheeks, diarrhea, or a rash, your baby may be allergic to something you're eating—but this is quite rare. If the condition continues, talk to your doctor and the baby's pediatrician. She may recommend an elimination diet—having you remove from your diet those foods such as cow's milk and other dairy products, eggs, citrus fruits and juices, wheat, or fish, that sometimes trigger an allergic reaction. Again, this is rare, and you shouldn't embark on an elimination diet without consulting a doctor.

Pumping Breast Milk

"I don't recommend trying to pump with your husband, baby, and mother-in-law looking on! It's a time to escape to a quiet, peaceful retreat. Just as I learned to relax every square inch of my body during a contraction, I tried to relax my tense muscles before I began to pump. I'd think about how Sam smelled and felt in my arms. That really sped things up. I could empty both sides in about five minutes."

—Sarah Normand Kerner, Plano, TX

"As soon as I would start to pump, my daughter would decide it was time to nurse. It sounds strange, but I figured out how to nurse my daughter on one side and pump on the other. It worked wonderfully, and I didn't have all the let-down on the unnursed side going to waste. The next nursing session I would switch sides. I froze the pumped milk and always had a ready stash when we would go out."

—Erin Martin, Inver Grove Heights, MN

"Start pumping a few weeks before you have to go to work. And get a good pump. With my first child, I tried using a single handheld electric pump, but that didn't work for me. I rented a Medella breast pump from a hospital supply store and got much better results. With my second child, I bought a Medella unit that is a lot nicer to carry around and that I use in my office."

—Cindy Gottfredsen, Green Bay, WI

Bottle-Feeding 101

Bottle-fed babies should be fed on demand just as breastfed babies are. Like their breastfed counterparts, bottle-fed babies don't need anything other than formula for the first six months of life. Feeding should be an intimate time for cuddling and bonding. A bottle can, of course, be propped and left with your baby (unlike a breast), but *no one* would recommend this practice. This increases the risks of ear infections and tooth decay, and you miss the chance to connect with your infant.

What Kind of Bottle Should I Use? Baby bottles come in 4- and 8-ounce sizes in myriad shapes and styles. Most people these days use plastic bottles. Some prefer the type that holds a sterilized plastic liner. If the huge selection

A Mother's View

"Why I Bottle-Feed"

"I had my heart set on experiencing the bonding that comes with nursing," says Carolyn Keys, a Phoenix, Arizona, mother of three. "But I kept having these horrible breastfeeding experiences."

Each time Carolyn tried to nurse, she would suffer from sore, bleeding nipples. Worse, her babies didn't seem to thrive on breast milk. Her second daughter lost more than 2 pounds in her first 10 days of nursing, and her third child, TJ, vomited or had diarrhea after each feeding. Five days after TJ was born, Carolyn gave up nursing once and for all. She's since found that her son has just as hard a time digesting formula.

Although she was greatly disappointed about not being able to nurse, Carolyn found that bottle-feeding definitely has its advantages. Her tips:

- **Use bottle-feeding as a way to get the whole family involved with the baby.** "My girls love feeding their little brother," Carolyn says. And bottle-feeding gives TJ's dad, who is away from home several nights a week for work, the chance to bond with his little boy (and give Carolyn a rest).
- **Fix several bottles at once so you're ready to roll.** Carolyn has found that bottle-feeding fits right into her hectic schedule of shuttling her two older children from activity to activity.
- **Don't let yourself feel guilty.** "I did feel disappointment and guilt," Carolyn admits. "It was as if my body could deliver a child, but not feed it." In the end, Carolyn was just happy that TJ was thriving: "At 10 months old, he's my biggest, healthiest child."

Bottle Basics		
IF YOU PLAN TO PREPARE . . .	YOU WILL NEED . . .	
A bottle at a time	2–3 bottles	4–6 nipples
A day's worth of bottles	8–10 bottles	12–16 nipples
Bottles with disposable liners	6–8 bottles	12–16 nipples

boggles your mind, ask friends for a recommendation.

The 4-ounce size is good for the first few months because it's unlikely that your baby will guzzle down more than that in one sitting.

How Many Bottles Do I Need? How much formula you plan to make at a time will determine how many bottles and nipples you need. (It's wise to have extra nipples handy, since—like socks and pacifiers—they seem to disappear just when you need them. You may also want to have a variety of shapes and hole sizes available until you determine which type and style your baby prefers.)

What Kind of Nipples Should I Buy? The right nipple is really important for a good start in bottle-feeding. Look at the shape of the nipple, which should resemble a human nipple as much as possible, and the hole size. A too-large nipple hole will let formula flow too quickly and can choke your baby; an opening that's too small won't let enough milk through and will frustrate her (and may cause gas). Luckily, many manufacturers have begun to label nipples with terms such as "slow flow" or "fast flow," which is very helpful. I've found that a small, clear nipple with a slow-flow hole is just right for a newborn, but by the time the baby is 2 to 3 months old, he may prefer a faster-flowing nipple with a larger hole. Keep experimenting until you find what's right for your child.

What Kind of Formula Is Best? There are two questions to ask when choosing formula: How much time do you want to spend preparing it? and What are the best ingredients?

You can answer the first question yourself. Do you want to walk to the kitchen and simply pour formula into a sterile bottle or are you willing to measure out powder or liquid and mix it with water? Formula comes ready-made in cans, in powder form, and in liquid that needs to be mixed with water. The

CHECKLIST

Safe Bottle-Feeding

✔ Wash your hands before you start to prepare or serve formula.

✔ Check the expiration date on the formula each time you make it.

✔ Keep all equipment clean: can opener, measuring spoons or cups, bowls.

✔ Boil water or use filtered water. Wash bottles and utensils in the dishwasher on high heat to sterilize.

✔ Test the heat of the formula on your inner wrist before feeding Baby.

✔ It's not recommended that you use your microwave oven to heat the formula. Even if the first squirt of formula feels only warm, in the middle of the bottle it could be burning hot. Shake up the bottle well and check the temperature in the middle, if you are warming bottles in the microwave.

✔ Don't top off bottles; the old formula may contaminate the new. Dump out unfinished formula if it's been out longer than an hour. (You can refrigerate an unfinished bottle one time if it has been out for 30 minutes or less.)

powder form, which is more convenient than the big liquid cans for travel, takes quite a bit of shaking to get the lumps out.

What kind of formula is best for your baby is a trickier question. To answer that, talk to your baby's pediatrician. Formula comes in cow's milk and soy varieties and with or without iron. There are also formulas on the market for babies who have trouble breaking down protein.

If your infant seems to be having a negative reaction to his formula, keep track of his symptoms—vomiting, diarrhea, rash, irritability—and call the doctor. Don't switch to another formula until your doctor has ruled out a tummy virus or infection. If your baby does have a formula intolerance or an allergy to a particular formula, switching brands before talking to the doctor will just hinder his ability to pinpoint the problem.

How Long Will the Formula Keep? Prepared formula in clean bottles can keep for 48 hours in the refrigerator. Once your baby drinks from a bottle, it's OK to have her finish it off later if you've returned it to the fridge within 30 minutes. Don't top it off with new formula. If the bottle has sat out for longer than 30 minutes, toss it; bacteria introduced into the bottle via your baby's mouth can multiply quickly.

A can of powdered formula that's been opened, if well covered, can be kept until its expiration date. It doesn't require refrigeration until it's mixed with water in a bottle. Opened cans of concentrated formula that you mix with water or that are premixed can be refrigerated for 48 hours. Prepared bottles are also good for 48 hours if they're kept refrigerated.

What You Need to Know About . . . Dehydration

Severe dehydration, which can be very dangerous in newborns, even fatal, is quite rare. But a few highly publicized cases raised awareness of the condition. Here, answers to common questions.

What exactly is dehydration and why does it occur? A baby can become dehydrated if she isn't taking in enough fluids or if she's losing too many fluids. Her brain and other organs need liquids to function properly. If dehydration isn't detected, it can cause serious problems in a newborn, including stroke and brain damage. In some cases, dehydrated babies have developed cerebral palsy; others have died.

Few breastfed babies become dehydrated, but since it's so hard to determine how much an infant is getting, you need to pay attention to your baby's condi-

---

CHECKLIST
Dehydration Warning Signs

Call your doctor if you notice any of the following, which could lead to or indicate dehydration:

✔ Your breasts show no sign of engorgement a few days after delivery or they don't seem to be emptying after a feeding.

✔ You have intense nipple soreness (a sign of improper latching on, which can interfere with milk production).

✔ Your baby is feeding less than eight times a day or going more than three hours between feedings without a fuss.

✔ He doesn't seem to be swallowing while feeding; you should be able to see or hear him gulping the milk.

✔ Your baby doesn't seem satisfied after a nursing session; a baby who's had enough to eat will be contented, not crabby; he won't be sucking the air or his fingers.

✔ He isn't wetting six to eight diapers a day and soaking one of them. (Because disposables absorb so well, it may be difficult to determine whether your baby is really soaking a diaper. You can insert a paper napkin or diaper liner in the diaper to get a better read on the degree of wetness.)

✔ Your infant's urine is dark colored or very strong smelling.

✔ Your baby seems to be losing weight.

✔ Your baby is inconsolable or difficult to rouse.

A MOTHER'S VIEW

"My Baby Was Dehydrated"

When Teri Winsor left the hospital in Mount Pleasant, Iowa, with her 2-day-old daughter, Anna, she felt happy and confident. Anna seemed to be catching on to nursing, and Teri felt recovered enough from her C-section to go home a day early.

Twenty-four hours later, it was a different story: the tops of Teri's nipples began forming scabs and were very sore. Anna cried endlessly. Teri assumed a little nipple soreness was normal but knew Anna's behavior wasn't when, two days later, the newborn fell asleep for hours and couldn't be roused for a feeding.

Anna was rushed to the pediatrician, where she was diagnosed as suffering from dehydration. She had lost a pound and a half in the five days since she was born. Although Teri thought Anna had been nursing just fine, the infant wasn't getting any milk because she was latching on to the end of the nipple, instead of putting the whole nipple, including some of the areola, into her mouth.

A lactation consultant showed Teri how to draw her nipples out with a pump to give Anna more to latch onto. Teri pumped to keep up her milk supply and began using a supplemental feeding system, which involves feeding a baby pumped breast milk through a tube. With this system, an infant who's having trouble nursing can be fed without the risk of becoming so used to a bottle that she rejects the breast.

"You're supposed to tape the tube onto your nipple," Teri says, "but Anna screamed out of frustration whenever I put my breast anywhere near her. We had to tape the tube to my finger." Finally, when Anna was 5½ weeks old, she began breastfeeding successfully. Teri's tips for surviving (or avoiding) a dehydration episode:

- **Give yourself a chance to learn how to breastfeed successfully.** "Limit visitors during the first 24 hours at home," Teri says, so that you can quietly nurse and get acquainted with your newborn.
- **Know the warning signs of improper latching on** (sore nipples, an unsatisfied baby) and don't be embarrassed to ask for help.
- **Look to the professionals.** A lactation consultant, the La Leche League, or another organization dedicated to promoting breastfeeding can provide the most knowledgeable advice.
- **Surround yourself with supportive people.** "Avoid people who tell you to just give your child formula," says Teri.

tion. Until your milk comes in, your baby should be fine with just colostrum (the nutrient-rich premilk fluid your breasts produce). Just make sure that she's feeding at least eight times in each 24-hour period, that you hear swallowing, and that by day 3 of life she's wetting at least six diapers in 24 hours. Once she's actually drinking your milk, it's critical that she continues to feed often and seems satisfied. A breastfed baby shouldn't need water (too much can actually harm her) or formula as long as she's feeding well every couple of hours. For more on babies and water, see "What You Need to Know About . . . Water," page 182.

How do I know that my baby is getting enough milk? Your newborn has an incredibly tiny tummy, with a capacity of only about 4 teaspoons of milk. Unless you're pumping your breasts and measuring your baby's intake by ounces per bottle, it's nearly impossible to figure out whether your breastfed infant is getting even that much. Try these less scientific (but very effective) ways to make sure that he isn't getting dehydrated:

- Breastfeed on demand. If your baby cries, feed him. If your breasts are full, feed him. Don't worry about overfeeding; within the first four weeks, a newborn should feed at least eight times within each 24-hour period.
- Focus on baby's output instead of input. If you're changing a wet diaper six to eight times a day, the chances of your baby being dehydrated are slim. By day 3, your baby should be having three or more stools per day.

When a Baby Isn't Growing

Sometimes a baby isn't dehydrated but still isn't growing as expected. The medical label for the condition is "failure to thrive." It may be that a baby is below the third percentile in weight and height, hasn't regained her birthweight by her two-week doctor appointment, or has a sudden slowdown or stop in growth in the first three months of life. The question the pediatrician must answer (with parents' help) is *why*.

The doctor looks first at how often a baby is feeding and tries to determine if the infant seems satisfied after each meal. If a nutritional deficiency (the most common cause of failure to thrive) is suspected, the baby needs more calories. To hike his calorie intake, he may be put on a strict feeding schedule to make sure he is getting fed regularly. A lactation consultant can help the breastfeeding mom figure out if sufficient breast milk is being produced at each feeding and whether or not the baby is latched on and sucking properly. If the problem is a low supply of mother's milk, she can pump in between breastfeeding sessions to increase milk production. The expressed milk or other supplement can be given to the baby until the mother's milk supply has increased.

If those tactics don't do the trick, a nutritional supplement may be prescribed, or, in rare cases, the baby spends a few days in the hospital being fed and observed.

If the baby seems to be eating enough but still isn't growing, the doctor will want to rule out the possibility that the infant is suffering from a minor digestive problem, has a urine infection, or is allergic to breast milk or to her formula. Sometimes a more serious diagnosis is made: diabetes, cystic fibrosis, or emotional deprivation can all cause a lag in growth. Typically, though, after a few weeks of scheduled feedings, a baby gets back on her growth track, no worse for the wear.

What You Need to Know About . . . Crying

Without a doubt, your baby will cry. And believe me, you wouldn't want it any other way: a baby's cry is the most natural thing in the world—and it's her only way of letting you know how she's feeling. Yet many parents are shocked to discover that their baby cries more than they thought was humanly possible—in some cases more than two or three hours each day.

Crying usually peaks at 4 to 6 weeks and eases off even more in the second three months. Until then, many new parents struggle to figure out just what all that noise is about.

Although a lot of crying can be hard on parents, too little isn't good, either. If your baby isn't crying much and is listless or limp, she may be dehydrated or have some other problem, in which case you should call your pediatrician.

What Your Baby Wants Simply put, a crying baby wants your attention. Crying, whimpering, sobbing, weeping—it doesn't matter what you call it—is your newborn's only way of communicating what she needs. At this point in her development, her cries aren't emotional calls for help. She's not saying I'm sad or lonely. The cries indicate physical needs: she's in pain, too hot or too cold, hungry, tired, wet, gassy, or just plain uncomfortable.

Once you attend to your baby's physical problem—you feed her or burp her or change her diaper—she'll probably stop crying. It may take weeks of trial and error, though, before you figure out which of her cries means what.

Of course, some babies cry more than others and are less responsive to your attempts to soothe them. You may have a baby who is extremely fussy and seems to cry all the time. This isn't colic, where your baby goes on a sudden extended crying jag every day about the same time (usually beginning in the late afternoon or early evening) and is inconsolable (see "The Curse of Colic," page

121). Excessive criers don't cry at a set time and usually can be comforted—eventually. They just seem to be cranky and let you know about it by fussing more than three hours a day, several days a week, for several weeks.

Excessive crying and colic are two of those particularly trying situations for which even the experts aren't sure of the causes. Some babies are more attuned to internal and external stimuli, causing them to cry when another baby might not. Whatever the reasons babies cry, the effect on a new parent is pretty clear: the inability to stop the crying can drive you nuts and make you feel like a failure as a parent. You should remind yourself that you're not to blame—excessive criers and colicky babies are born, not made—and that this, too, shall pass. Colic typically subsides as mysteriously as it began when Baby is 3 or 4 months old, and as your heavy crier becomes more mobile, she'll find ways to soothe herself.

How to Console a Crying Baby If your baby's physical needs are met and he's still making a racket, try some of these consoling tactics:

- **Nonnutritive sucking.** Some babies just need to suck a lot, whether they're hungry or not. Give him your clean pinkie (nail side down) to suckle, or try interesting him in his own little fingers, thumb, or fist. If breastfeeding is well established (usually after a month), try offering him a pacifier (you may have to hold it in for him if he's under 2 months old).

- **A little noise.** If your singing, humming, and shushing aren't working, try something different: run some water, turn on the vacuum cleaner, set the radio to static, or play an audiotape of nature sounds or white noise.
- **Get moving.** Step outside for a minute, go for a car or stroller ride, dance around the living room with your baby in a front carrier, sit in a rocker, crank up the baby swing.
- **Provide eye candy.** Have your baby gaze at the fish tank, at a moving fan, or out a window. Turn on your lava lamp if you have one.
- **Stay in touch.** Give your baby a relaxing baby massage (see "Leg and Foot Massage," page 144) or a soothing tub bath.

Crying is your baby's way of communicating her needs: she's wet, hungry, tired, uncomfortable, or overstimulated. Soon you'll know what each cry means.

Why Soothing Matters Whether your baby cries a little or a lot, make an effort to respond each and every time. Ignoring her cries in these early months is like telling her that communication doesn't matter. (Babies who're truly suffering from neglect, for instance, cry *less* than normal healthy babies. They've gotten the "don't bother to cry message" so clearly that they stop trying to communicate at all.) At this stage, your baby isn't willfully trying to break your eardrums or get her way.

Even if your fussy baby doesn't seem to be responding to your soothing, do it anyway. Leaving her alone to cry probably won't make either of you feel any better

DEFINITION

Shaken-Baby Syndrome

Crying and ignorance are two key elements in the vast majority of shaken-baby syndrome (SBS) incidents: A baby is crying relentlessly and an exhausted parent or caregiver—unaware of the extent of the danger—gives the baby a hard shake or two to teach him a lesson or to make him stop.

The baby, of course, doesn't stop and may be irreparably harmed—even from just one shake. He may suffer brain damage, including mental retardation, seizures, learning disabilities, speech disorders, and paralysis. Bleeding around the brain may also result, which can cause blindness. One out of four shaken babies dies from his injuries.

Because his brain is still forming (and because he does a lot of crying), a baby under 4 months old is especially vulnerable to SBS, although shaking can harm children as old as 5.

It's normal for a baby to cry and it's normal for caregivers to find that crying frustrating, even annoying. But if you have an impulse to shake or harm your baby, get help from an abuse hotline. And when you're interviewing prospective caregivers, ask about their tolerance to a baby's cries. Make it very clear to anyone who cares for your baby that:

- He is not to be roughly handled in any way.
- You don't believe a baby can be "spoiled."
- He should be comforted and picked up immediately if he is crying.
- Shaking can hurt—even kill—your baby.

Resources

National Child Abuse Hotline
800-422-4453

Shaken Baby Syndrome (SBS) Prevention Plus
800-858-5222

(unless you're at your wits' end, in which case getting away from the crying is a good idea). And your consoling efforts may be helping her even if she doesn't quite know how to pipe down. Make sure to give your baby lots of cuddles when she's not crying, too.

How Baby's Crying Pushes All Our Buttons The response to a baby's cry springs from more than just a desire to be a good parent or to turn down the volume. There's a real measurable physical reaction to a baby's crying that's a lot like the adrenaline rush you get when you're scared or called upon to react in a crisis. Symptoms of this fight-or-flight reaction include sweaty palms and an elevated pulse.

Perhaps our wired reaction to a baby's cry is nature's way of getting Mama over to her baby in a hurry in times of need. But too much crying and too much adrenaline can also bring out the worst in us. Add a big dose of sleep deprivation, and it's likely that you'll be nearly as cranky as your baby. If your crying baby is grating on your nerves or getting you down, take a breather by asking for help from family or friends. This is especially important for parents of heavy criers.

If all that crying is making you really anxious, depressed, or so mad at your baby that you feel you might hurt her, don't hesitate to immediately call your doctor, a mother's support group, or a counseling hotline (under "Emergency" in the white pages of most phone books). Parents need to remind themselves that a baby is crying for a reason; disciplining her or shaking her will not make her stop, and may cause serious damage.

SLEEPING

Two facts: (1) new mothers often claim they'd give anything to get some sleep; (2) newborns sleep an average of 16½ hours a day.

So what's the big deal? The problem, of course, isn't how much newborns sleep, but *when* and for *how long*. While their little internal clocks are still developing, most babies' circadian rhythms are out of synch. As any mother-to-be kicked awake by an acrobatic fetus at 3 A.M. knows, it's not much fun when one person's night is another's day. And so it goes for life with a newborn.

Baby's Changing Sleep Needs

Newborns sleep in short bits and pieces for lots of reasons. Besides their immature internal clocks, they're woken up by hunger. Their little tummies can hold only so much and when that's gone, they wake up for their next

How Much Babies Sleep (Hours)*

AGE	DAY SLEEP	NIGHT SLEEP	TOTAL SLEEP
1 week	8	8½	16½
1 month	7	8½	15½
3 months	5	10	15
6 months	3¼	11	14¼
9 months	3	11	14
12 months	2¼	11½	13¾

This is not uninterrupted sleep!

snack whether it's night or day. At first, your job is to wake when they do, feed them, burp them, and lull them back to sleep. And sleep when they do, if you can.

Soon enough—even in your baby's first 3 months—she'll gradually begin to adjust her sleep patterns to match yours. She'll still sleep more during the day than you'd like, but by the end of 3 months her daytime sleep will shrink to one-third of her total sleep time while her nighttime sleep grows to two-thirds. She'll go from four daytime naps when she was born to three during these early months. By the time she's a year old, naps will be down to two snoozes of a little over an hour each.

Nighttime sleep is another story. Even though your baby is sleeping more at night by the end of 3 months, it still wouldn't be accurate to say she's sleeping *through* the night. Consider yourself lucky if your child sleeps four or five hours in a row. Many parents are in seventh heaven if, by 6 months, their baby sleeps from midnight to dawn. Breastfed babies seem to take longer to sleep through the night than formula-fed babies. But all babies will soon catch on, with a little help from you. The chart above takes a look at typical sleep patterns during Baby's first year. Of course, some babies sleep more than the average; some sleep less.

Getting Baby to Sleep

At first, it's fine to let Baby doze off while you're nursing her or rocking her, but by the time she's 6 weeks old, you can start to help her fall asleep on her own. After all, good sleepers are made, not born. And it's up to you to teach your little one the slumberland rules.

GOOD ADVICE
Sleep Strategies

"Once, in a moment of desperation, I turned on the vacuum cleaner at two in the morning so the noise would lull my baby to sleep. It was noisy, but it worked!"

—Sharon Hoffman, Vail, IA

"Like most babies, mine had her nights and days mixed up. During the day I would wake her up every three to four hours. I'd undress her, change her, and massage her. Then I'd use a cold cloth to wipe her eyes, hands, and feet and let her fuss a little bit. I'd feed her when she was wide awake and aware of her surroundings. As she got a little older, each time she would stay up and awake longer. I would save her bath for the evening; it would relax and comfort her. After her bath and then a feeding, she'd be ready to sleep."

—Suzan Corcione, Smithville, MO

"At four weeks old, my daughter never slept. She cried constantly, and it tore my heart out. I finally read a book that suggested taking the baby to bed with you. The change was instantaneous. She was relaxed, she could nurse when she wanted to, and we all got a lot more sleep."

—Andi McWilliams, Spring, TX

That means you can begin to put her in her bassinet or crib when her tummy is full and she's drowsy, but still awake. In this contented state, she may be happy to look at her musical mobile, suck on her fingers (if she's found them and can navigate them into her mouth), or snuggle with a favorite blankie or a spit-up cloth that smells like Mom.

On the other hand, she may scream bloody murder. If that's the case, don't let her cry. She's too young to understand why you're not responding to her. Instead, resign yourself to sleeping when she does, and rest assured that over time, and with your continued patience, she'll learn to soothe herself to sleep. She'll also begin to pick up on your subtle cues (quiet, quick feedings) that nighttime is for sleeping. To encourage her to sleep when you do, wake her up before you go to bed and give her a big feeding then.

You may find that it's easier if you just keep the baby in bed with you between midnight and dawn, so that you can roll over and nurse her without either of you completely waking up. Some families find that keeping the baby nearby in a bassinet helps everyone sleep better.

ꙅ A MOTHER'S VIEW ꙅ

"In Defense of the Family Bed"

When Kim Holsapple was pregnant, she'd made up her mind not to let her baby sleep in bed with her. "My mom said that the baby belongs in the crib; she even bought us one," the Juppa, Maryland, mother recalls. "And a friend told me about her 3-year-old who still sleeps in bed with Mommy. Those stories influenced me!"

But when it came time to put little April Lynne in her new crib, Kim and her husband couldn't do it. "She was so tiny and it was easier to breastfeed with her next to me in bed," she says.

She and her husband, who is half Japanese, did some research on the family bed. "It's not uncommon in Japan to have kids in bed with you until they're eight years old," Kim says. "My husband thinks that April Lynne can stay with us until she's three or four."

The benefits of co-sleeping, according to Kim: "April Lynne doesn't wake up crying at night, she just snuggles with me." She also naps for long periods without her parents in bed with her. "I think she sleeps well during the day because she has such a positive experience at night."

Kim's tips for family-bed success:

- **Get a big bed.** "We think having a king-size bed really helps us all stay comfortable," Kim says.
- **Know the downside.** There are negatives to the family bed, she admits, but they're not insurmountable. One of them is adjusting your sleep schedule so that you go to bed when the baby does. That can mean hitting the hay as early as 8 P.M.
- **Don't give up on sex.** "We're hoping to resume our love life," says Kim, "and we'll probably have to go into another room. I know the baby won't understand what's going on, but I'd feel more comfortable."
- **Be prepared for criticism.** "Almost everyone tells me: 'Get her out of your bed. She needs to sleep by herself.' I listen to what they say, but gently remind them that this is what we want to do. The family bed has made us a much closer family, and we love waking up to her smiles every morning."

For more help on getting a baby to sleep, see "In Search of Sleep" (page 202).

Safe Snoozing

It's common for new parents to eagerly wait for their baby to fall asleep, and then to worry about her until she wakes up. Part of the anxiety stems from the sheer amazement that you have a baby and that such a small, fragile creature is in your care. That, combined with legitimate concerns about the safety of the baby's crib and sleepwear and worries about sudden infant death syndrome (SIDS), keeps many a parent up at night when they should be catching up on their own zzzs.

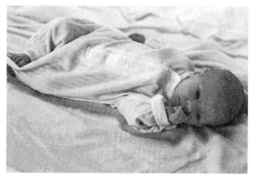

To put your own mind at rest, you need to make sure your baby can rest safely. *The number-one thing you can do to promote safe sleep is to put your baby to sleep on her back.* This has been proved to lower the risk of SIDS (see "What You Need to Know About . . . SIDS," page 101). If your baby prefers her tummy, you'll need to train her to sleep on her back. Some parents put their baby down on her tummy and roll her over after a few minutes of sleep. The second-safest position is to have your baby sleep on her side. This is preferable to tummy sleeping, but isn't nearly as safe as back sleeping.

To reduce the risk of SIDS, always put your baby to sleep on her back.

Some other sleep-safety basics:

- Examine cribs, bassinets, and cradles to make sure they've been assembled correctly and that everything is secure. Check for sharp edges and cracks. If your baby's bed is an antique or secondhand, make sure that there's no peeling paint and that the paint is lead-free. Crib slats must be less than 2⅜ inches apart, and head- and footboards shouldn't have fancy cutouts or posts.
- Make sure that there are at least 9 inches between the mattress and the top of the crib, bassinet, or cradle.
- Buy a mattress that is firm and that fits snugly into the bed. There shouldn't be room between the mattress and bedside or a big space in the corners (where Baby could get stuck).
- Check that crib bumpers are the exact size of the bed, leaving no space for Baby to scoot in between them and the bedside. Don't try to put crib

bumpers into a playpen or bassinet, for instance. Bumpers should be secured to at least six spots on the bed. Choose Velcro attachments or make sure that any strings are less than 6 inches long. Put bumpers in storage once Baby can stand.

- Remove pillows and animals from your baby's sleeping area. You may think they're cute and that they're all the way on the other end of the crib, but they're still a smothering hazard.
- Make sure that anywhere you put your baby to sleep is away from blinds, or from art, lamps, or draperies that a baby could pull down.
- Hang mobiles high enough so that a baby can't get tangled in its strings. And don't use strings to tie toys to the side of the crib (use Velcro).
- Have a working baby monitor in Baby's room.
- Dress Baby in comfortable clothes without strings. Short strings at the bottom of sleep sacks are OK. Many parents feel more comfortable when their baby sleeps in clothing that's flame retardant. Look for clothing that's labeled as sleepwear.

How Baby Sleeps

Your baby may make all sorts of noises in his sleep, from snorting to whimpering. He may smile. He may jerk. That's because 50 percent of the time newborns are in active sleep, called REM sleep (for rapid eye movement). You have REM sleep, too, but not nearly as much. And your nervous system is better equipped to tone down the fluttering eyes and twitching that go along with it. Your baby's noisy, active sleep is no cause for alarm, unless the jerking motions are constant or prolonged. In that case, you'll want to make sure he's not having some sort of seizure.

Babies also sometimes sleep quietly for a while and then make a couple of big snorting sounds. If your child does this repeatedly, watch carefully to make sure he is breathing during the silent periods. Some babies, suffering from apnea, actually stop breathing for a while and then snort themselves awake. Apnea is not uncommon among low-birthweight or premature babies. Babies usually outgrow the condition as their lungs mature, but it's best to report any apnea episodes to your doctor. Even healthy full-term babies sometimes stop 15 to 20 seconds between breaths.

What You Need to Know About . . . SIDS

At the rate of 1.2 deaths for every 1,000 live births, sudden infant death syndrome (SIDS) is the biggest cause of death in babies in the United States between the ages of 1 month and 1 year. In fact, 6,000 babies in the United States die of the syndrome each year.

⌒ A MOTHER'S VIEW ⌒

"My Baby Stopped Breathing"

One day, soon after she'd returned to work, Jayna Sattler of Bartlesville, Oklahoma, got an emergency call from her baby-sitter. Her son Travis was having "blue spells." The 3-month-old would suddenly stop breathing for 30 seconds or more.

After a week of consultations with doctors, Travis was diagnosed with sleep apnea, a condition that is not uncommon among premature or low-birthweight babies. Travis, born a month early, had weighed only 5 pounds, 12 ounces.

During the day, the Sattlers or their baby-sitter would keep a constant eye on Travis. Usually a gentle shake or a tap on his foot was all it took to encourage the baby to resume his breathing.

But nighttime was a special challenge. Travis's pediatrician prescribed an apnea monitor to alert the Sattlers whenever the baby stopped breathing. Two electrodes connected to the monitor would trigger a loud alarm any time the baby's chest movement stilled. "We would have seven to eight alarms a night," says Jayna, "and I never got used to it."

The sound of the alarm usually startled Travis enough to start him breathing again. One night when the alarm sounded, though, the Sattlers found Travis lying completely still in his crib. When Jayna couldn't gently rouse him, she picked him up. "He was totally limp and his lips and fingertips were blue," she says. Jayna was getting ready to start CPR when the baby began to scream.

It was then that Jayna decided to quit her job to stay with Travis. "I felt like I needed to be with him," she says. He never left her sight during the day.

"It was a rough introduction to parenthood," Jayna admits. But by Travis's eighth month the alarms had dwindled to the point where the Sattlers felt comfortable returning the rented monitor. Travis is now a healthy 16-month-old. Jayna's tips for dealing with sleep apnea:

- **Ask your pediatrician about a sleep monitor.** Since Travis slept in a crib in his own room, the monitor gave his parents the confidence they needed to catch a few winks of their own.
- **Learn infant and child CPR.** It will help you feel more confident if an emergency arises.
- **Don't smoke in the house.** Secondhand smoke contributes to the incidence of sleep apnea and SIDS.

But researchers have made great strides in identifying factors that put a baby at risk for SIDS. And SIDS awareness campaigns telling parents how to avoid the risk factors are having a significant impact: the number of SIDS deaths is dropping. Here are answers to parents' most common questions:

What Causes SIDS? Even with all the new research, experts still aren't sure why some babies stop breathing in their sleep. Studies continue, however, especially of the respiratory system, and researchers believe they're getting closer to understanding why some babies are more likely than others to fall victim to SIDS.

- One possibility is that babies who've died of SIDS have defective carbon dioxide sensors in their brains. When carbon dioxide builds up, most babies receive a brain signal that tells them to rouse themselves or to take a deep breath. A baby who doesn't get the signal may simply stop breathing and die.
- Another study has shown that the heart rate of SIDS babies may not fluctuate as much as that of healthy babies during changes in sleep or respiratory patterns.
- Babies who are at risk for SIDS may move the muscles of their upper airways in a different way than normal babies do. By using a computer to analyze the sounds of babies' cries, researchers are hoping to be able to identify which babies have this problem.
- An infant's ability to breathe may be affected by high levels of certain chemicals found in the spinal fluid.

How Can I Prevent SIDS? Given that sudden infant death syndrome is still so mysterious, there's no guarantee that anything can prevent SIDS. The best any parent can do is to eliminate as many risk factors as possible.

- **Put your baby to sleep on her back.** If your baby insists on sleeping on her tummy, wait until she's asleep and then roll her over. Over time you can train her to sleep in the safer position. You might invest in one of the sleeping blocks on the market that are designed to keep tummy sleepers on their backs. Don't wedge a rolled-up blanket next to your baby to keep her in a back position; the blanket could come unrolled and cover her face. And insist that all caregivers—from grandparents to baby-sitters and child-care providers—put your baby to sleep on her back. *Why:* Babies who sleep on their backs are at a much lower risk of SIDS, studies show.
- **Keep up with your baby's health basics.** Have her immunized regularly and breastfeed if you can for as long as possible. Call your doctor if your baby shows signs of a chest cold or seems to have trouble breathing. *Why:* Studies done by the National Institute of Child Health and Human Development (NICHD) indicate that babies in poor health or who are not breastfed are at a higher risk of SIDS.

> **For More Help: SIDS Awareness**
>
> *Organizations*
> • **American SIDS Institute**
>   800-232-SIDS
>
> • **SIDS Alliance**
>   800-221-7437
>
> *Books and Other Resources*
> • *SIDS: A Parent's Guide to Understanding and Preventing Sudden Infant Death Syndrome*
>   by Dr. William Sears (Little, Brown and Company)

• **Use a firm mattress, a fitted sheet, light covers.** Your baby shouldn't sleep on or under anything that's fluffy, puffy, fuzzy, or furry. Banish pillows and stuffed animals. Use light covers only. No heavy comforters, quilts, sheepskins, or blankets. *Why:* Thirty percent of SIDS victims were found with their noses and mouths covered by soft bedding, according to the U.S. Consumer Product Safety Commission. Studies also show that significant levels of carbon dioxide from exhaled breaths can collect in the pockets of fluffy bedding; your baby may end up rebreathing exhaled air that's full of carbon dioxide.
• **Don't overheat your baby.** A baby's bedroom should be kept comfortably cool and he should be dressed in a thin, comfortable sleeper. Don't swaddle him at naptime and bedtime or allow his clothes or blankie to cover his face. *Why:* An overheated baby may sleep more deeply and be unable to wake himself up if he experiences breathing problems.
• **Ban cigarette and cigar smoke.** And don't take your baby to smoky places. *Why:* Babies whose parents smoked while they were in utero are at a much higher risk of SIDS. If you or your partner smoke now, in any part of the house, your baby is two to three times more likely to die of SIDS. No matter where you are, exposure to secondhand smoke increases the risk.

HEALTH AND SAFETY

With good preventive health care, and by taking sensible safety precautions, you can ensure that your baby gets a healthy and safe start in life. That's why your baby will visit the pediatrician at least six times in his first year, and why

My Baby Shouldn't Go Out Until She's 3 Weeks Old? It is true that babies don't have the same immunities against disease that adults have. But parents these days are often out and about with their newborns (properly attired and snug in their car seat) by the end of week one. Use your own common sense about whether you should stay in or go out.

In either case, it's always wise to have eager-beaver helpers wash their hands before they hold your baby (and that means you, too; wash your hands every time you walk in the door and after every diaper change), and keep your baby away from cigarette smoke and people with colds.

parents soon become experts about such things as DPT, RSV, and CPR.

Baby's Three-Week Checkup

Unless your baby has jaundice or some other problem, his first trip to the pediatrician's office will be when he's 3 to 4 days old to 2 weeks old. For many parents, this first doctor visit is a milestone in itself. They've survived the first weeks of parenthood, and now they get to see how much their baby has grown.

After you check in (which often requires that you show an insurance card and fill out lots of new-patient paperwork), you'll be sent to the

CHECKLIST

Well-Baby Visits

Make appointments and mark your calendar for the following well-baby appointments:

✔ 3–4 days to 2 weeks
✔ 2 months
✔ 4 months
✔ 6 months
✔ 9 months
✔ 12 months
✔ 15 months
✔ 18 months
✔ 24 months
✔ 30 months
✔ 36 months

Thereafter, well-child visits are usually scheduled once a year on or around her birthday, or a month or two before the school year starts.

waiting room or taken to an examination room. Many pediatricians' offices have a separate waiting area for well children; if yours doesn't, sit as far as possible from the sick kids.

Once you're in the exam room, a nurse will talk to you for a little while to find out how things are going, and then you'll undress your baby. Usually you go to a nurses' station where your baby will be measured and weighed.

Your pediatrician will look your baby over from head to toe, repeating many of the examinations that were done in the hospital, including checking baby's vital signs, organs, hearing, vision, and reflexes. The baby's legs will be examined for dislocation or hip-joint abnormalities.

Some doctors examine the baby while she's in your arms; most place her on a high padded examining table. You can stand nearby while she's being examined and have a blanket ready if she gets cold.

Here's what else most doctors cover on the first visit:

HOW TO
Create Baby's Health History

It isn't too soon to begin to keep track of your baby's health. Your pediatrician will have complete records, but it's important for you to be the record keeper and historian of your own family's health. Here's what to include for each child:

- Date of birth, where born, name of hospital, and attending doctors
- Weight, Apgar score, head size, length at birth
- Complications during pregnancy or delivery
- Any feeding difficulties or early food allergies; if baby was breastfed, for how long
- Each doctor visit
- Immunizations (what, when, any reactions)
- Congenital problems (such as heart murmurs)
- Chronic or recurring conditions (such as asthma, frequent ear infections)
- Long-term-use prescription drugs
- Major surgeries or other significant medical treatments
- A brief history of major diseases in the family
- Dates of childhood diseases (chicken pox, for example)

Resources

- Ask your physician for a free booklet developed by the American Academy of Family Physicians and the U.S. Health Department. It contains record-keeping advice, charts, and reminders.
- For two other booklets—"Personal Health Guide" and "Child Health Guide"—send $1 each to R. Woods Consumer Information Center, Pueblo, CO 81009.

• **Baby's growth.** Her measurements will be plotted on a graph, which helps the doctor identify any significant changes in growth.

• **Feeding and wetting.** You'll be asked how often and how much your baby is eating. If you're breastfeeding, the doctor will want to know how it's going and whether you have any particular problems. Because dehydration is a serious concern, the pediatrician will want to make sure that your baby is getting enough fluids; besides weight gain, another way to measure that is by checking how many diapers he's wetting and soiling each day. For a breastfed baby, three or more yellow, seedy stools each day is a sign that he's getting enough breast milk.

• **Development.** At each checkup, he'll ask you what the baby is doing and how she's acting. Is she alert? sucking her hands, and the like? Your reports on your baby's actions will help the doctor in his evaluation of her neurological, psychological, and physical growth. He'll tell you about the developmental milestones to expect, but he'll be relying on your powers of observation to keep him posted on your baby's progress.

• **General well-being.** Your doctor may ask how the whole family is coping with the new arrival, lack of sleep, and so on.

• **Immunizations.** You'll discuss the upcoming vaccinations and why they're important.

Pediatricians are incredibly busy, but these well-baby visits should be more relaxed than sick-baby visits. Do write down questions beforehand so that you have a list of things to cover with the doctor. It's easy to forget what you wanted to ask when your baby is crying and the doctor is rushing in and out of the room. It's important to speak up if you are concerned about your baby or about something the doctor has said. Although the doctor has the medical degree, you're the expert on your own baby—even with only a few weeks of parenthood under your belt. Develop a solid partnership from the beginning by keeping communication open. For starters, you might want to read *The Intelligent Patient's Guide to the Doctor-Patient Relationship* by Barbara Korsch, M.D., and Caroline Harding (Oxford University Press).

What You Need to Know About . . . Immunizations

For the first 18 months of your baby's life, it will seem as if he's getting an immunization during each well-baby visit. In fact, he'll have had 18 immunizations by the time he reaches his first birthday. (By the way, babies typically get their shots in the meaty part of their thighs, not in their upper arms; as your baby gets older and stronger, you may be called upon to restrain his arms while the nurse holds down his legs for the injection.)

CHECKLIST

Immunization Watch

After a vaccination, call the doctor if your baby:

✔ Has a temperature of 105°F or higher
✔ Has a stiff neck
✔ Seems excessively sleepy or cranky
✔ Has a high-pitched or unusual-sounding cry
✔ Seems unusually pale or still
✔ Becomes unconscious or is hard to rouse
✔ Has a seizure

Frankly, it's no fun to watch your baby scream and turn purple after having a shot. It breaks most parents' hearts. But immunizing your baby against infectious diseases is one of the most important things you can do for him. The fleeting pain of a vaccination is a lot easier to deal with than the complications of a disability caused by a preventable childhood disease.

Babies are born with a certain amount of immunity, passed on from their mothers. But the protection wears off during the first six months of life, during a time when your little one may be most vulnerable to disease. Vaccines help babies and children build their own defenses against infectious diseases by providing antibodies that guard against them.

Some of the shots have side effects, although serious complications are rare (see "CHECKLIST: Immunization Watch," above). In most cases, giving your baby acetaminophen before the immunization can help ease the pain. So can warm compresses on the injection site. Ask the doctor or nurse (most doctors delegate the fun of shot-giving to another staffer) about pain control *before* the vaccination is given.

Before your baby gets *any* immunization, get detailed information about what he's going to be given, and what the possible side effects are. If you have any questions, don't let your child get the shot until they're answered. It's usually necessary for you to sign a parental consent form before a vaccination. If your child has a fever, the pediatrician may suggest that you hold off on the shot until he's better. (Make sure to reschedule the immunization so his shot schedule doesn't get too out of whack.) Your doctor will keep scrupulous records in your child's file, but you should keep your own schedule, too. (See "How To: Create Baby's Health History," page 106).

Immunization Schedule

VACCINE	PROTECTS AGAINST	AGE GIVEN	POSSIBLE SIDE EFFECTS
Diphtheria-tetanus-pertussis (DTP or DTap)	Diphtheria, tetanus (lockjaw), pertussis (whooping cough)	*Five Shots:* 2 mos. 4 mos. 6 mos. 12–18 mos. 4–6 years old Every 10 years thereafter (no pertussis)	Injection site soreness, including redness and swelling; fever.
Haemophilus B (Hib)	Meningitis and pneumonia	*Four shots:* 2 mos. 4 mos. 6 mos. 12–15 mos.	Low-grade fever; sometimes sore, inflamed injection site
Hepatitis B	The virus that causes liver infection	*Four shots:* birth–2 mos. 2–4 mos. 6–18 mos. 11–16 years	Red, tender, or swollen injection site
Measles-mumps-rubella (MMR)	Measles, mumps, and rubella (German measles)	*Two Shots:* 12–18 mos. 4–6 years	Low-grade fever, rash, swelling around the joints, jaw, or neck. Drowsiness. Symptoms appear 5–12 days after the immunization
Polio	Polio	*Four shots:* 2 mos. 4 mos. 6–18 months 4–6 years	Sore injection site, low-grade fever. Paralysis occurs in fewer than one in a million vaccinations with the oral dose
Varicella zoster	Chicken pox	12–18 mos.	Sore injection site, plus fever, crankiness, fatigue, nausea

First-Year Immunization Schedule

	DTP	HIB	HEP B	MMR	POLIO	TB TEST	VARICELLA
Birth–2 months			•				
2 months	•	•	• (2–4		•		
4 months	•	•	months)		•		
6 months	•	•					
6–18 months		•	•		•		
12–15 months		•		•		•	•
12–18 months	•						

Infant Health Worries

Anytime a baby under 6 months gets sick, it's wise to let the pediatrician know. At this age, your baby can have misleading symptoms, and what seems like a simple cold may really be respiratory syncytial virus (RSV) or pneumonia (see "Lung Infections," page 111). If the doctor has ruled out a serious illness and your baby has the sniffles or a little cough, she's probably fallen victim to one of the more than 100 different cold viruses out there. (For more common childhood illnesses, see Chapter 3.)

The Common Cold Cold symptoms can be scary, especially if your baby also has a low-grade fever. But the temperature, coughing, and sneezing usually mean your baby is fighting off the cold. Here's how to make her more comfortable:

- Drain her nose with your trusty bulb syringe before she eats. If she can't breathe well, she can't eat well.
- If the crusty stuff in her nose is hard to get out and is keeping her awake at night, try saline nose drops. These nonprescription drops are really just salt water that helps soften the crusties so they can be secreted or sucked out of Baby's nose. A drop of breast milk may soften the nose secretions and may help fight the virus topically.
- Run a cool-mist humidifier in her room to keep the air moist. Clean the device every day to prevent bacteria or mold from growing in it. A dirty humidifier can contaminate the air, causing allergies and other breathing difficulties.

(Don't put Vicks Vapo-Rub in the vaporizer or on an infant's nose or chest; this is not recommended for a baby this age.)

Babies under 6 months are rarely given over-the-counter cough medicines, nasal sprays, or cold treatments. Many of these remedies cause side effects; some even make a baby more congested. Don't use them unless your doctor specifically recommends a particular remedy for a particular ailment.

If your baby's cold is accompanied by a raspy cough that sounds like a seal barking, she may have croup. If she's struggling to breathe, call your doctor immediately.

Lung Infections Sometimes the cause of a cold is respiratory syncytial virus (RSV), an infection that's highly contagious. An older child or adult may have RSV with only minor cold symptoms, but a baby often has worse symptoms. RSV is the most common cause of pneumonia and bronchiolitis, an infection of the lungs' small breathing passages.

One-third of children with their first RSV infection develop a serious respiratory-tract illness; every year, 100,000 children with RSV (half of them babies) end up in the hospital. The infection, which can be life-threatening, is usually treated with antiviral agents. Scientists have high hopes for a nasal spray in the future that delivers virus-fighting medicine directly to the lungs.

If your baby has the following symptoms, with or

DEFINITION

Thrush

This common infection has freaked out more than one parent, but it isn't very serious. It's characterized by white cottage-cheesy spots on Baby's gums, tongue, cheeks, or the roof of the mouth. When you gently wipe the white patches, the inside of Baby's mouth can become sore and red; it may even bleed a little. The infection isn't dangerous, but it can spread to a breastfeeding mom via her nipples (see "Clogged Milk Ducts and Breast Infections," page 85), and it can interfere with Baby's feeding. If you think you or your baby have thrush, tell your ob-gyn and the pediatrician. Breastfeeding mothers will need to treat their nipples at the same time as the baby's mouth is being treated.

Thrush is caused by an overgrowth of *Candida albicans*, a fungus that is usually found in harmless amounts in the mouth and vagina. Many women are familiar with Candida as the culprit in their own monilial (yeast) infections, usually triggered by hormonal changes or by antibiotic use. In fact, newborns often catch the fungus as they pass through the birth canal; older babies may have an outbreak after taking a round of antibiotics.

My Baby Gets Sick Late at Night? No one knows why, but it seems that many illnesses do get worse at night. It may just seem that way because medical reassurance isn't available to us in the middle of the night, and that makes us uncomfortable. But you can get help at night. If you think your baby is having any sort of medical emergency or is seriously ill, don't hesitate to call the pediatrician or an emergency number (see "CHECK-LIST: Health Basics," page 116), or take her to an emergency room.

Before an emergency ever arises, it's wise to decide on a hospital. Ask your doctor for a recommendation. If there's a children's hospital or a hospital emergency room especially equipped for children in your area, that's probably your best choice (see "What You Need to Know About . . . Emergency Rooms," page 214). Find out exactly where the hospital is so that you know how to get there in a hurry. Keep your insurance cards and medical records handy. And once you're there, keep your cool. Most hospitals are run on the triage system, which means that patients are sorted and seen based on the seriousness of their condition. You and your baby may not be seen in the order that you arrived—the most serious cases are treated first. The wait can be frustrating, but with a baby 3 months old or younger, you can be sure they'll get to you pretty quickly.

without the typical cold symptoms—fever, cough, runny nose, listlessness—call your doctor:

- Difficult or rapid breathing
- Nostrils that flare with each breath
- Wheezing
- Bad color; especially pale, ashen, or gray
- Not eating well

What You Need to Know About . . . Fever

By definition, a fever is a rectal temperature higher than 100.4. It's usually a sign that the immune system is doing its job; the rise in temperature indicates that the body is fighting off an illness.

That's all well and good, but it's still pretty scary for many new parents when their baby feels even the least bit hot. And when that baby is 3 months old or younger, let the pediatrician know about any fever. Young babies' immature

CHECKLIST

The Well-Stocked Medicine Cabinet

Your medicine cabinet is about to become more than just the place where you store your dental floss. With the right supplies, it can become a household first-aid station. You'll need the following:

✔ Thermometer—axillary (underarm) or rectal
✔ Infant acetaminophen or ibuprofen—to reduce fever and pain from injections
✔ Rubbing alcohol—for cleaning umbilical cord stump or cleaning thermometer before use (do not put on Baby)
✔ Cotton balls and swabs—for cleaning umbilical cord stump or sensitive or hard-to-reach areas
✔ Zinc oxide—for treating diaper rash
✔ Nasal aspirator—to suck gunk out your little one's stuffy nose
✔ Saline nose drops—these natural drops help loosen nasal congestion
✔ Petroleum jelly—for lubricating rectal thermometer
✔ Measuring spoons or syringes—for getting the right dose of baby medicine
✔ Topical teething gel—use only as recommended by your doctor
✔ A small flashlight—great for examining sore throats, removing splinters
✔ Anti-itch lotion—for bug bites and rashes; check with your doctor before using on a baby
✔ Syrup of ipecac—used to induce vomiting in children who have ingested a suspected poison. Always call the doctor or poison center before using
✔ Tweezers—for splinter removal
✔ Notebook and pen—to keep track of medicine
✔ Self-adhesive bandages—for pint-size injuries
✔ Sterile gauze pads and bandage tape—good for odd-sized boo-boos
✔ Small scissors—for cutting bandages or gauze

For suctioning out stuffy noses, the aspirator is an essential.

A syringe lets you gently squirt medicine into the side of your baby's mouth, where she's more likely to swallow it rather than spit it out.

Keep small blunt-ended scissors handy for cutting bandages or gauze.

HOW TO

Take Baby's Temperature

There are several methods of taking an infant's temperature: rectally, axillary (under his arm), or with an ear thermometer (called a tympanic thermometer). You should hold off on the oral method until a child is 5 years old; a younger child has difficulty keeping the thermometer under his tongue and could choke on it or bite off the end.

Regardless of the method you choose, a thermometer should be cleaned before each use: disinfect it with rubbing alcohol or soapy water, rinse well, and dry. (Follow manufacturer instructions for an ear thermometer.)

If you're using a mercury bulb thermometer, shake it down to below a reading of 96°F before you start; switch on the digital or ear models.

Wait until your baby is quiet and calm before taking his temperature and, if possible, enlist a helper. An extra pair of hands will come in handy if you're a beginner or if your baby is squirmy.

With a rectal thermometer

1. Apply a dab of petroleum jelly to the tip of the thermometer.
2. Lay your baby on his belly on a changing table or on your lap.
3. Hold him steady with one hand on his back.
4. Gently insert the thermometer tip a half inch into his rectum. Hold it in place between your second and third fingers.
5. After two minutes, carefully slide out the thermometer and read.

To take your baby's temperature using a rectal thermometer, gently hold your baby in a tummy-down position in your lap or on the changing table.

With an axillary thermometer

1. Make sure your baby's underarm is clean and dry.
2. Cradle your baby in the crook of your arm or in your lap.
3. Place the tip of the thermometer in her armpit.
4. Press her elbow to her side to keep the thermometer in position.
5. After four minutes, remove and read.

Add two degrees to the reading when you take your baby's temperature under her arm.

With an ear thermometer

1. Lay your baby on a safe, soft surface.
2. If you're right-handed, hold the thermometer in that hand and insert it into your baby's right ear; if you're left-handed, use your left hand and your baby's left ear.
3. Use your other hand to pull back on his ear so that the thermometer can point straight into the ear canal.
4. Activate the thermometer while continuing to hold the canal open.
5. Wait for a beep. If you're not sure you've done it right, repeat the process and use the highest number.

Since a baby's ear canal is very small, it's critical that you position the ear so that the thermometer has a clear "view" of the tympanic membrane. Gently pull your baby's ear until the thermometer can go straight in.

For an accurate reading, an ear thermometer should be in far enough so that the canal is completely sealed. (Even so, many doctors believe this method is unreliable for babies under a year old.)

CHECKLIST

Health Basics

When to call the doctor . . .
✔ If your baby has a temperature over 100.4°F.
✔ If he is sleeping more than usual or is unresponsive.
✔ If your baby won't eat.
✔ If he isn't wetting at least four diapers a day.
✔ If he's having trouble breathing.
✔ If your baby has a seizure.
✔ If his vomit or diarrhea contains blood or won't stop.
✔ If he has difficulty breathing.

What information to have ready when you call the doctor . . .
✔ Your name, your baby's name, your doctor's name, your insurance information.
✔ What the problem is: the symptoms and when they started (if your baby has a fever: what it is and with what method you took his temperature).
✔ Why you're particularly worried and whether your baby has any history of this problem or any other medical problem.
✔ What you've done to alleviate the symptoms or make your infant more comfortable and whether you've had any success.
✔ How your infant is eating, breathing, sleeping, responding, and acting, and whether or not he is wetting the usual number of diapers.
✔ Your pharmacy's phone number.

immune systems aren't always well equipped to fight off an infection, and your little one may not have any symptoms other than a fever, even if she's very sick. (Feeling your baby's forehead, by the way, is *not* as reliable as using a thermometer. See "HOW TO: Take Baby's Temperature," page 114.)

Fever: When to Worry Although fevers aren't dangerous, when combined with particular symptoms, an elevated temperature can indicate a serious problem such as meningitis, pneumonia, or appendicitis. During the first three months, call the doctor if your baby:

• Has a temperature higher than 100.4°F
• Seems particularly out of sorts: very irritable, doesn't want to be held, sleeps through a few feedings, doesn't react to loud noises
• Refuses to drink fluids or breastfeed

- Is breathing fast or with difficulty
- Becomes very pale, bluish, or has mottled skin
- Seems to be in great pain, or can't hold down any liquids

The pediatrician may want to see your baby to rule out any serious ailment. She may decide to treat the illness that's causing the fever—having your child take antibiotics for an ear infection or nose drops to relieve the symptoms of a cold, for instance—or she may admit your infant to the hospital if she thinks the ailment is more serious or if your child is dehydrated. Most likely, she'll recommend that you just let the fever run its course. Most fevers do go away on their own within a few days (if the fever lingers, call the doctor again).

How to Keep Your Baby Comfortable Because fever alone isn't dangerous, you don't need to treat it, but to make your feverish newborn more comfortable, try any or all of the following:

- **Increase fluid intake.** To avoid the possibility of dehydration, make sure your baby is drinking lots of breast milk or formula. Older babies can have water or juice, too.
- **Turn down the heat.** Don't bundle up a baby when she's sick; she'll be more comfortable if you keep her cool. Take off a layer of her clothes, remove heavy bedding, turn a fan on low (don't blow it right on her). A baby's room should be a pleasant temperature, but not cold.
- **Give medication.** Ask your doctor if it's OK to give your baby a fever-reducing medicine such as acetaminophen or ibuprofen. Follow package instructions carefully, making sure to wait the allotted time between doses. Don't *ever* give a baby aspirin (even children's aspirin), which has been linked with Reye's syndrome. Infants under 2 months old shouldn't be given fever-reducing medicine. (For a well-stocked medicine cabinet, see "CHECKLIST: The Well-Stocked Medicine Cabinet," page 113.)
- **Bathe her in tepid water.** Fill a baby tub with an inch or two of lukewarm water and wipe your baby's body with a washcloth. Let her air-dry and then repeat every five minutes. (Do *not* rub her down with alcohol; it's now known that alcohol can be absorbed through Baby's skin in dangerous levels.)

Safety from the Start

You look at your sweet, sleeping baby and wonder, *How could she possibly get into any trouble?* It's true that, in the first few weeks of your baby's life, it's more likely that *you'll* have an accident—stumbling around in the dark to get up to feed her, falling asleep while slicing the bread—than she will.

But safety precautions are just that—precautions. You don't learn how to handle medical emergencies *after* you've had one; you learn before, so that you're prepared. Likewise, baby-proofing shouldn't wait until your baby is mobile. It's an ongoing, continuing process.

Baby-Proofing Basics As your baby approaches the rolling-over stage, you don't want to wake up in the middle of the night with an anxiety attack of giant proportions: *This house is an accident waiting to happen. How can I keep my baby safe?!* Now is the time to get the baby-proofing basics down. Here's where to start:

- Double-check that all smoke detectors and carbon monoxide detectors are working. (A carbon monoxide detector is a must if you have a wood-burning stove or fireplace or a gas furnace.)
- Always have a working monitor turned on in the baby's room when you're in another part of the house.
- Check the size of all toys. Nothing should be smaller than a baby's fist (or it could be swallowed).
- Give playthings the test. Pull on all pieces to make sure that they can't fall off, including sewn-on buttons and fabric pieces on stuffed animals.
- Check the safety and stability of your changing table. The table should have a padded surface, a strap for buckling your baby in, and a tall side. Don't ever leave your baby on the changing table unattended.
- Make sure all mobiles and dangling things are out of grabbing distance. Babies older than two months should be able to swat at mobiles, but not pull them down.

For More Help: Keeping Baby Safe

Organization
- National Safe Kids Campaign
  202-662-0600
  Offers a $2 child-proofing
  primer called "Safe Kids
  Gear Up Guide"

Catalogs of Safety Products
- The Right Start
  800-LITTLE-1

- Perfectly Safe
  800-837-KIDS

- Remove all pillows or stuffed animals from the crib—they're smothering hazards. So are puffy quilts and sheepskins. Babies shouldn't be laid down on anything that's puffy or furry.
- Do a string check on your baby's wardrobe. Baby clothing shouldn't have any drawstrings (except on the bottom of sleep sacks). And no pacifiers on strings around your baby's neck.
- Don't put the baby's bouncy chair anywhere but on the floor. Although it may look as if they're not even moving, babies have been known to scooch their chair or car-seat carrier off the edge of countertops, kitchen tables, and beds.
- Buckle your baby in even when she's sleeping in her stroller or carriage. When my second daughter was 3 months old, I was reading the newspaper outside on the grass, a few feet away from where she was napping in her carriage. After about 20 minutes of reading, I went over to check on her. She wasn't there. Naturally, I freaked. Where was she? She was 8 feet away, on her back on the ground, gazing up at a magnolia tree. How did she get there? I'm not sure, but I think she squirmed out of the leg hole in her carriage (it was a dual carriage-stroller) and then rolled down a gentle slope to come to rest under the tree. Obviously, she wasn't hurt or fazed a bit—she hadn't let out a peep. But you can be sure I buckled her in from then on.
- Keep the cat out of the baby's crib and room.
- Do a crib safety check (see "Safe Snoozing," page 100).

Lifesaving 101 Even if you know adult cardiopulmonary resuscitation (CPR), it's important to take a refresher course once you become a parent. CPR and the Heimlich maneuver are different for infants than for adults; in fact, they're different for children over age 1 than they are for your baby. Call the Red Cross and sign up for a class today. In the meantime, review the basic infant CPR steps below.

CPR is performed when a baby has stopped breathing. If you discover that your baby can't breathe because an object is blocking his airway (food or some other small item), do the infant Heimlich maneuver.

1. **Call for help.** If you think your child isn't breathing, even after you've tried to rouse him, have someone immediately call 911 (or your local emergency service if you don't have 911) while you get started on CPR. If you're alone, go through the CPR routine once, then carry your child to the phone with you. Continue CPR while you're calling, if possible.
2. **Do a 5-second breathing check.** With your baby on his back, tilt his head back and lift his chin. This should open his airway and allow you to listen to

check whether air is passing in and out. Watch to see if his chest is rising and falling. If you don't detect any signs of breathing, go to Step 3.

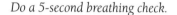

Do a 5-second breathing check.

3. **Start mouth-to-mouth resuscitation.** With your baby's head still tilted back, cover his lips and mouth with your lips. Create a seal. Give two slow breaths and let the air flow back into your mouth between breaths. You should be blowing hard enough so that his chest rises. If it doesn't, retilt his head and try the breaths again. If there's still no rise in the chest, assume that there's an obstruction in his airway and begin the Heimlich maneuver.

Start mouth-to-mouth resuscitation.

4. **Check for a pulse.** If your breaths have gone in, press two fingers against the inside of your baby's upper arm to feel for a pulse. *If a pulse is evident,* but the baby isn't breathing, continue giving a slow breath every three seconds, stopping to check the pulse every minute or so. As long as there's a pulse, repeat the one slow breath every three seconds until the baby begins to breathe, or until help arrives. *If you can't feel a pulse* and the baby isn't breathing, place two fingers in the center of his chest about an inch below his nipples. Press five times firmly and quickly (within about three seconds). The baby's breastbone should go in about an inch each time you press. Follow the five compressions with one breath. Repeat the compression-breath cycle about 20 times during the next minute. Then check the pulse again. Continue until you feel a pulse or help arrives.

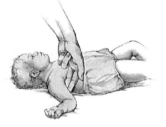

Check for pulse.

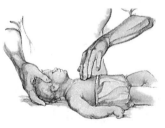

Begin CPR.

OTHER BIG DEALS

Crying that lasts all evening, nannies who scare you to death, siblings who pinch the baby—who knew that parenting included all this?

The Curse of Colic

One out of every five babies will experience some degree of colic during her first three months. Beyond mere crankiness, colic crying spells:
- Usually occur every evening around the same time.
- Last three to four hours.
- Typically begin when a baby is around 3 weeks old, peak at 6 weeks, and wane or stop completely around 3 to 4 months old.
- Sometimes include signs of physical discomfort, such as a distended tummy and gas; the baby often pulls her legs up to her tummy and screeches.
- Aren't easy to quell; a colicky baby may respond or settle down for a few moments, but often can't be soothed at all.

There are all sorts of theories about the cause of colic but no real answers. Is it just a natural developmental stage that's the result of a newborn's immature digestive system? Is it caused by the intolerance some babies have for cow's milk protein in their formula or, if their moms eat a lot of dairy, in their breast milk? And given that most colic strikes in the evening hours, does fatigue somehow trigger it? Experts continue to research all these theories and more. In the meantime, parents keep trying new ways to help their babies—and themselves—survive what can be three months of living hell.

Colic can be totally unpredictable: a soothing trick that didn't work yesterday (the breast, the bottle, a pacifier, a ride in his swing or around the block, a musical tape with a rhythmic beat) might work today; it pays to try and try again. Many parents also discover that motion and massage are powerful pacifiers. What works?

The Colic Carry Lay your baby facedown on your forearm with her belly resting on your hand. Her head will be in the crook of your arm and her legs will be dangling down. Use your other hand to hold her back in place. Apply gentle pressure with the hand under her tummy while you sway her back and forth. Try any variation of this hold that seems to work.

The Sling Carrying your baby next to your body in a carrier or sling has many advantages: he feels your closeness and warmth and is lulled by the motion as

On Living with Colic

"Adam, my first baby, had colic for almost three months to the day. The best solution I found was to lay him tummy-down on my tummy. We would sleep like that all night—or at least until the next feeding."

—Liza Murphy, Cornwall, Ontario, Canada

"We relieved our child's colic with the modified colic carry. I would put my arms under his stomach, and keep his legs dangling while we walked around. He outgrew the colic after about a month."

—Meta Neuschuler, San Diego, CA

"I would hold my baby in my arms on her side and pull her up real tight into a ball with her knees close to her chest in a sort of fetal position."

—Liz Marshall, Spring, TX

"I dealt with colic by walking outside with my baby. His colic would start at about six in the evening and continue until about ten at night. It was the combination of holding him tight and the fresh air, I think, that soothed him. It worked especially well when I used a pouch, because his stomach would be close to mine and his legs would be loose—not all cramped up. But the main problem for my son was my diet. As soon as I got completely off dairy, the colic stopped. He only had it for about three weeks in all."

—Fran Proce, Albuquerque, NM

"A specialist recommended that I keep a crying diary. I would write down when Alex started crying, as well as his feeding and naptimes. The idea was to see if the crying was related to lack of sleep or nourishment. I can't say we made any connection, but the diary gave me concrete proof of why I was going so crazy. I saw for the first time how much time he actually spent crying each day."

—Abby Gowans-Crawford, Corvallis, OR

you go about your business. This feeing of security combined with the motion of riding in a sling may help calm a colicky baby. A study in Botswana revealed that babies who were attached in this way to their mothers all day long cried much less than typical American babies.

⌒~ A MOTHER'S VIEW ~⌒

"Waiting Out Colic"

Colic was double trouble for Lynda Morris of Bedford Hills, New York. Her twin boys, Brendan and James, had colic that just wouldn't quit. "I'll never forget the day the colic started—January 15—and the day it ended—May 10," Morris says. "When the twins first started screaming, I called the doctor and he said, 'Oh, you just think they have colic because there are two of them.'

"But the crying went on and on. I tried everything: driving in the car, putting their bouncy chairs near the dryer. I even tried something called Gripe Water that my cousin told me to get at a local deli, and colic tablets that you buy at a health-food store. I ordered $200 devices that attached to the bottoms of their cribs that simulated the vibrations of a car going 50 miles per hour. Luckily there was a money-back guarantee and I returned them both."

After three months of trying music, and the vacuum cleaner, and even dipping the twins' feet in warm water (a suggestion from her sister), Morris learned that:

- **Sometimes nothing helps colic and it's nobody's fault.**
- **To save your sanity, it's OK to give yourself a time-out:** "Occasionally I just had to put the boys in their room and close the door for a short time."
- **The only true cure is time.** Morris remembers, "The day the colic stopped, I said to myself, 'God, they were good today.' The next day I said the same thing, and then I rejoiced. It ended that abruptly."

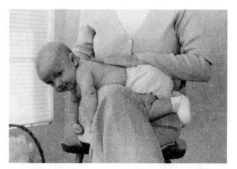

When colic strikes, try the colic carry: One hand massages Baby's belly while the other hand rubs his back.

Using the tummy trick, the colicky baby's tummy rests on your knee while you rub her back.

Some babies I know who ordinarily reject a pacifier will take one when curled up in a snuggly or sling. When you're ready to tear out your hair after three hours of crying, the pacifier-sling combo is definitely worth a try.

The Tummy Trick Another way to try to relax your colicky baby is to massage her tummy. Lay her across your knee. While you gently rub her back, your knees will gently rub her middle. A twist on the tummy trick: put a warm hot-water bottle or heating pad on your knees first (always check the temperature before putting Baby on it).

What You Need to Know About . . . Infant Childcare

Whether you're looking for a baby-sitter for just a few hours a week or for full-time childcare, you're probably nervous about leaving your baby. And who wouldn't be? You're about to entrust your child's well-being to somebody else. There's nothing more important than choosing the right person and place for that important job.

For some parents, that means finding an individual who'll care for their baby at home (usually a nanny or au pair); others are interested in child-care that's near or on their way to work (a family daycare in another person's home or a childcare center). Everyone is looking for someone who is loving and qualified.

What Your Baby Needs Infants have some very particular needs in the first three months of life, and your childcare situation—whatever it may be—should accommodate those critical needs:

- **Attention.** Beyond the basics—his diaper is changed when needed, he's fed when he's hungry—your baby needs to know that someone is going to pick him up when he cries. A one-on-one relationship is the best way to get that kind of attention, but family care or a daycare center with a low child-to-adult ratio can also provide it. In the birth-to-12-month-old age-group, the ratio recommended by the National Association for the Education of Young Children is one adult to three babies. Most parents are happy if they can find a one-to-four ratio in a center, with a maximum of eight babies in one room.

- **Affection.** In order for your infant to develop secure relationships, he needs caregivers who are loving. During interviews with caregivers and tours of centers, watch for lots of hugs and cuddles and coos. Choose a caregiver who understands the importance of giving affection and providing lots of eye contact, and who seems to genuinely love babies.

- **Playfulness.** Professionalism in the childcare business doesn't require a person to be serious and dour. In fact, physical contact and cheerful interaction is essential for babies this age as they learn how to socialize and play.

- **Consistency.** For healthy development, a baby needs to bond with her caregiver. That's pretty difficult if she has several different adults caring for her each day or if caregiver turnover is high. In fact, one study has shown that babies who had lots of different caregivers may have a harder time feeling comfortable in social situations later in life. If you're putting your child in a large daycare center, find one that has a low turnover and that assigns a primary caregiver to each baby. Even if that caregiver changes from day to day, at least your child will have consistency throughout the day.

- **Safety.** Anyone who cares for your child should be trained in infant CPR. You're best able to control the safety of his environment if he's being cared for in your own home. If he's in a family daycare or center setting, refer to the CHECKLIST: "Childcare Health and Safety," page 131.

- **Patience.** Babies sometimes cry a lot. They need constant attention. Your child's caregiver—especially if this person is at home alone with your child all day—needs to understand this about babies and needs to have a great deal of patience. A caregiver needs a certain amount of maturity to be able to handle the demands of an infant.

It's sometimes hard to tell how mature a person is in an interview. It's certainly difficult to figure out whether she has a hair-trigger temper or no patience. You can ask questions probing how that person feels about a baby who cries a lot or ask about what pushes her buttons. Find out how the caregiver would handle a baby who's been fussy for three hours, and so on. And make sure to get—and check—references.

❧ A MOTHER'S VIEW ❧

"Why We Chose Family Daycare"

Julie and Steve McGill, of Danville, California, chose family daycare for their 12-week-old son Jeffrey because they wanted him to have one consistent caregiver, not several, and they were looking for a very low caregiver-baby ratio. "We also felt that with fewer kids around, Jeffrey would have less exposure to germs," says Julie.

They decided to have their baby spend each day with Louise High, a certified caregiver who takes only four children at a time.

"Louise keeps photos of all the kids she's cared for in the past twenty years on her refrigerator," Julie says. "I feel very comfortable talking to her—I often call when I have questions about Jeffrey's health or eating habits. I consider her part of our family." Julie's tips for finding quality family daycare:

- **Get a referral from someone you trust.**
- **Interview the caregiver in her home.** Ask if she is certified and knows CPR.
- **Look for a parenting style that matches your own.** Julie liked the fact that her caregiver had a living room full of playthings and empty of furniture. "Jeffrey had plenty of room to move around in. She lets the babies explore as much as they can within boundaries."

What Parents Need Your baby isn't the only one who has special needs in these early months. Most parents have their own set of standards that need to be met in order for them to feel comfortable with a childcare situation:

- **Confidence in the person or place.** For many parents, knowing their baby is in a center or family daycare that's licensed is a confidence builder. Look for a daycare center that is accredited by the National Association for the Education of Young Children (NAEYC). Each state also has its own health and safety requirements for centers.

It's a different story for family daycare and in-home caregivers. Some states do require licenses for individuals who care for two unrelated children, whether that's in your home or at theirs. Other states require licenses only for health and safety. But a health and safety license isn't necessarily a reflection of the quality of the care, and many states don't have any licensing at all for nannies or family daycare.

Licensing aside, to know whether a prospective childcare situation is right for you, the wise thing is to ask the right questions (see "10 Questions to Ask the Childcare Provider," page 129) and to spend some time with the provider in your home or at the center. Sometimes it just boils down to a gut reaction about a situation. If you're at all nervous about how the caregiver's home or center is run or looks, find someplace else. If you sense your au pair candidate is more interested in checking out the night scene in America than in responding to your baby's needs, or doesn't have the maturity to handle eight hours a day of babycare, find someone else.

If you're uncomfortable with the whole notion of childcare, you're not alone. A large proportion of the 1.7 million new moms who march off to work each day worry about their childcare situation and wonder whether they're doing the right thing. Some reassuring news: a recent study conducted by the National Institute of Child Health and Development suggests that high-quality childcare doesn't threaten the mother-baby bond. It's critical, though, that you find the right care for your baby and that he's getting sensitive care from you, too, when you're together.

- **Experience.** If you're a first-time parent, you may be looking for someone who can help you understand and learn more about your new baby. Try to find an experienced caregiver who's a parent herself. She'll know what to ask you about your child (Does she cry differently when she's hungry versus when she's wet? How does she like to be held?), even if you're not yet sure what's important and what's not.
- **TLC.** Although taking care of your baby will be the childcare provider's first priority, you'll need a bit of tender loving care, too. Separating from an infant

Comparing Childcare Options

	CENTER	FAMILY DAYCARE	HOME PROVIDER
Pros	• Licensed • Interaction with other babies • Trained staff • Daily stimulation and learning games may be played • You know what's happening through out the day • Flexible hours • Backup is always available	• Homelike environment • Feels like family because of different-age kids • Usually a small group • Flexible hours possible	• One-on-one interaction • Baby gets to stay home (easier on parent, too) • Caregiver becomes part of family; may do housework • Flexible schedule • Less exposure to germs
Cons	• Lots of kids means lots of chaos • Limited one-on-one attention • Schedules may be for center's convenience, not baby's • Exposure to germs • May close during holidays or summer	• May not be licensed • Caregiver may not be trained • Limited one-on-one attention depending upon size of group • If caregiver is sick, you need to arrange for backup	• Limited interaction with other kids • You can't really be sure what caregiver is doing during day • If caregiver is sick or quits, you need backup • You'll need to pay employment taxes
Monthly Cost	• $400–$2,200	• $300–$800	• $900–$2,600

can be very painful; you'll want a caregiver who understands how you're feeling and who's experienced enough to realize that your anxiety doesn't reflect on her. Finding a person with whom you can have a good rapport is particularly important if the caregiver is going to be in your own home. I've known moms who were so intimidated by their nannies that they were too afraid to ask them basic questions about their baby's day. Anybody who takes care of babies should be warm and responsive—to you and to the infant. If you're the sort of person who likes to check in a lot or get lots of feedback on your baby, make sure you choose a provider who's parent-friendly. Some daycare centers, for instance, are run like institutions, while others feel more like a family.

• **Ability to drop in.** You must be able to drop in to visit your baby whenever you want, not just at times convenient to the center. If this is discouraged by a caregiver, find another one. Not only is this a safety issue, but a caregiver's willingness to have parents visit reflects her (or the center's) philosophy regarding parent-caregiver-baby relationships. This is your baby we're talking about, not an animal that's being boarded or a vacuum cleaner that's being serviced. At first, you may feel that casual drop-ins are an invasion of your caregiver's privacy, but you need to be intimate with how the place runs—and that means being able to check up on your baby whenever you want.

• **Flexibility.** A center or caregiver that best serves your needs is going to have to jibe with your schedule. Get all the details about hours of operation, late-pickup fees, holiday closings, and so on before you sign on the dotted line.

As with most things in life, choosing a childcare situation does require making sacrifices. Decide what's most important to you and your baby, and take it from there. (See "Comparing Childcare Options," page 128.)

10 Questions to Ask the Childcare Provider

1. What is the infant-to-caregiver ratio?
2. What are the credentials of the center or individual: Do they have a license? Certification? Training in CPR? If it's a center, how are caregivers screened before hiring? Are police checks run to rule out a criminal record? Fingerprints taken?
3. Can you have the names of other families who've used the center or caregiver so you can call and get the inside scoop? (A provider shouldn't hesitate to provide references and names of current clients.)
4. What is the center's staff turnover rate?
5. Will someone always be available to answer your calls? If an answering machine picks up calls, how soon before someone will call you back?

⤳ A MOTHER'S VIEW ⤶

"Why We Chose Center Care"

"**O**ur first priority was finding childcare close to either my office or my husband, Steve's," says Stacey Levy, of Livermore, California. "We also wanted our daughter, Jordyn, to be exposed to lots of other kids during the day, but to still have individual care and attention." After interviewing several centers in the area, the Levys chose one close to Steve's office that offers care for children from 6 weeks of age to kindergarten age. "We get the sense that the caregivers are there to give our daughter love and to make her feel secure," Stacey says. "They're always holding the babies, singing to them, and giving them kisses." Stacey's advice for finding good center care:

- **Make sure the center has separate rooms for little ones.** "There are only five other babies in Jordyn's room at the center, and at any given time, there are two or three caregivers attending to them," Stacey says.
- **Ask what kind of feedback the staff will give you about your infant.** "Each day the caregivers at Jordyn's center write down how much she eats, the number of diaper changes, and the length of her naps."
- **Check out the center's visitation policy.** You should be able to drop in at any time. "Our center is very receptive to my husband, who visits Jordyn every day at lunch."

CHECKLIST

Childcare Health and Safety

✔ All childcare providers (even if they're part-time) should know infant CPR and the Heimlich maneuver.

✔ Any family care or daycare center should be able to show that they've met local health and safety requirements. They should have approved fire exits, extinguishers, detectors, and so on.

✔ Infants should be kept in an area away from older babies (who can trample them) and their toys (which they can choke on).

✔ All cribs, playpens, and changing areas should be up to current standards.

✔ Basic baby-proofing should be evident: plug protectors, cupboard locks, cords protected or put away (even barely mobile babies can pull down a cord or chew on it and be electrocuted).

✔ There should be separate areas for changing diapers and preparing formula and food. And a sink should be handy so that caregivers can wash their hands after every diaper change.

✔ Babies should have their own pacifiers, blankets, and other personal items.

✔ The front door should be secure so that strangers can't come in and out; parents should be required to sign their baby in and out.

6. What kind of feedback will you get about your child—daily reports? monthly conferences? Are caregivers available to talk at the end of the day or only by appointment?

7. Are infants separated from older children? Do they have their own toys, play space, sleep area, changing area?

8. How many people will be caring for your child each day? Is a primary caregiver assigned to each baby?

9. Are babies fed on demand and allowed to sleep when they're tired? Or is a schedule forced on them? Is scheduling flexible?

10. What is their general philosophy about infant care? Are they loving and responsive? Are they OK with breastfeeding moms and feeding babies expressed breast milk? Do they like having parents around? (Make sure you ask any caregiver you hire about discipline; babies this age don't need any sort of discipline.)

The Sibling Situation

When your "baby" suddenly becomes the big kid, you can expect a few fireworks at home. After all, your firstborn was your little one when you headed off

⌒ A MOTHER'S VIEW ⌒

"Why We Chose Nanny Care"

Jeff and Helene Altmann, of Berkeley, California, wanted their son to have constant individual love and attention. "As much as I could provide myself," says Helene, who went back to work eight weeks after Julien was born. They decided to have the baby cared for in their home by a nanny. They hired Wessne Gebrmedhin. "There are a lot of qualified nannies, but we liked Wessne, who is from Ethiopia, because of her warmth, charm, and great attitude. And she is flexible with her hours, which helps when we have to work late." Helene's tips for hiring a nanny:

- **Register at an agency.** "I didn't feel comfortable picking someone from the newspaper, so we registered, at no cost, with five nanny agencies and interviewed fifteen people."
- **Consider sharing a nanny if cost is an issue.** "For only Julien, we paid eight dollars an hour," says Helene. "But we began sharing Wessne with another family who brings their nine-month-old to our house. For two children, Wessne charges ten dollars, cutting our cost significantly."
- **Realize that you're going to be very dependent upon one person.** If your nanny is unable to come one day, you'll have to cover for her.

For More Help: Childcare

- Au Pair in America, 800-727-2437, ext. 6188
- Child Care Aware, 800-424-2246
- Internal Revenue Service, 800-829-1040
- National Association for Family Child Care, 800-359-3817
- National Association for the Education of Young Children, 800-424-2460
- U.S. Information Agency, 202-401-9810

---

to the hospital, and now he's the big guy. Many moms have told me how their first child suddenly looked like a giant in comparison to the new baby. Your giant may be pretty peeved about this state of affairs and, depending upon his age, act out in lots of normal ways, such as:

- Clinging and crying to be held; pitching fits
- Showing signs of anger when the baby is fed or held
- Ignoring you or pretending the baby doesn't exist
- Regressing in his development (going back to diapers if recently potty trained, for example, or coming into your bed at night)

Adjusting to a new baby can be particularly hard on an older infant or toddler who doesn't understand what's happening. Even a well-prepared sibling who is preschool age or older may show signs of jealousy after the novelty has worn off ("When can we take him back to the hospital, Mom? You mean he's *staying*?! Waa-a-a!").

To nip sibling rivalry in the bud, experts suggest that parents make the new big brother (or sister) feel as important as possible:

- **Recognize his new status.** Acknowledge your older child's important new position in the family with the gift of an "I'm the big brother" T-shirt or pin.
- **Plan special activities.** If relatives are visiting, they may want to take the older sibling on a long-awaited outing or to a special restaurant.
- **Keep the routine.** Even with all the fuss over the new arrival, and with special treats for the sibling, your aim should be to show your older child that most things haven't changed. Life will go on much the same with naptimes, trips to the zoo, preschool, and so on. Now, more than ever, your child will need this consistency. If he used to crawl into your bed with you every morning, try to keep up that routine even if it means losing a little (more) sleep or putting the baby in the crib for a while.

ᕲᐧᐧ A MOTHER'S VIEW ᐧᐧᕳ

"This Isn't Sibling Rivalry—It's War"

When 20-month-old Monica Chin arrived at the Portland, Oregon, hospital to meet her baby brother, she wouldn't go near her mother. "It was devastating that she didn't want me," recalls Jennifer Weigel. "I knew she was really upset."

Monica's rejection of her mother was just the first sign of protest against baby Eric. Monica ignored him for seven days. "The first time she acknowledged him, she hit him over the head," says Jennifer.

Not an auspicious start—and six months later the situation had barely improved. "For the first eight months we were telling our friends that we had our kids way too close together," says Jennifer, "but by nine months things were improving."

Her tips for dealing with persistent sibling rivalry:

- **Acknowledge your older child's negative feelings.** Help her try to channel them in nonviolent ways—by drawing pictures about how she feels, for instance, or by working out frustrations in hard physical play.
- **Make an effort to have one-on-one time with the jealous sibling every day.** Find ways for the two of you to have special outings.
- **If your time and attention are stretched to the max with the new baby, look for ways you can pay attention to your children at the same time.** Monica would fetch book after book for Jennifer to read to her while Eric was nursing.
- **Use the baby's adoration to help the older child feel important.** It's hard to ignore a sibling when he thinks you're great.
- **Persevere.** After eight months of warfare, Monica now tolerates her brother. Try to think of it as a phase.

For More Help: On Parenting an Adopted Baby

The first days at home with an adopted baby are full of their own joys and challenges. Here's where to look for advice and support.

- Adoptive Families of America, 612-535-4829
- Families Adopting Children Everywhere (FACE), 410-488-2656
- National Council for Single Adoptive Parents, 202-966-6367

- **Provide extra hugs.** Whatever you do, don't shuttle your child off to visitors or your spouse all the time. To find his new place in the family, he really needs physical signs from you that he's still loved, still important to you. Cuddle, hug, snuggle as much as possible—even if it means handing the newborn off to someone else for a while.
- **Supply one-on-one attention.** Carve out time every day for you and your eldest to be alone together, reading a story, playing a game, whatever.
- **Build a family.** Depending upon your child's age, he may like to bring a small gift to the hospital for the new arrival. Or once everyone's home, he may be able to hold the baby or fetch items you need: a clean diaper, a blanket, a bottle. Praise him for being a great helper.

Spend some time talking about when he was a baby and how you nursed him, too, and how special he was—and still is. Talk about what you're going to be able to do as a family and how the baby will soon be able to respond to him. If the baby wants a finger to hold, see if she'll hang on to big brother's finger; he'll be thrilled and, possibly, smitten.

Sometimes siblings try to vent their anxieties on the baby, not knowing that an infant can be easily hurt. If your child is under 4 years old, and seems especially angry or out of control, keep an eye on him and the baby for the first months. In any case, all siblings should be taught some rules about safely handling the baby.

Before you know it, your two children will be fighting over blocks or the TV—then you'll know the real meaning of sibling rivalry!

YOUR GROWING BABY

What kind of world you create for your baby during her first three months— cozy or sterile, stimulating or boring, accommodating or unresponsive—helps shape her attitude about life and herself. And, not surprisingly, her world also affects her physical, mental, and emotional development. A baby who is given the chance to get down on the floor, for instance, will soon learn to roll over. An infant who is cuddled and cooed over while being diapered will feel more connected to her caregiver than the baby who isn't. The newborn who knows that a parent will come when he cries will learn to trust the world. The 3-month-old who is talked to and read to and exposed to a colorful world will eventually be more likely to think learning is fun.

What You Need to Know About . . . Stimulation

Not long ago, it was thought that when a baby was born, the structure of her brain was already set. Now the scientific community believes that early childhood experiences have a dramatic impact on how—and how well—the brain develops. In fact, a review of recent research, "Rethinking the Brain," reported that in the first months of life the number of synapses (connections between brain circuits) in a baby's brain can grow from 50 trillion to 1,000 trillion. The interesting news is that if a baby doesn't use or exercise the synapses—if she isn't mentally, emotionally, and physically stimulated—she may lose some of those connections. Brain scans of institutionalized Romanian orphans, for instance, showed that lack of stimulation during the early months stunted the growth of the parts of the brain that regulate emotions and the senses. Apparently the unused synapses withered away.

What does this mean for new parents? They should do what they planned to all along: give their baby as much love and attention as possible. Talk to your baby, hug him, play with him. Age-appropriate stimulation combined with lots of love is just what the synapses need.

This is not to say that you should run right out and buy some newborn flashcards, a language-instruction tape, or a baby balance beam for your newborn. A baby doesn't need fancy toys; she's got you. Playing gentle games of peekaboo, singing a lullaby, talking baby talk—this is the sort of stimulation that your developing baby will find pleasing. And remember, there *can* be too much of a good thing: If your newborn turns away or gets fussy, she's telling you she needs a break.

Physical Development

Height and Weight Although every infant is different, most gain 1 to 2 pounds each month during their first year. They are likely to double their birthweight by 5 months and triple it by their first birthday. The average newborn grows 7 to 10 inches in the first year.

Average Growth				
	0–3 MOS.	4–6 MOS.	7–9 MOS.	10–12 MOS.
Height	+2½ in.	+2½ in.	+2½ in.	+2½ in.
Weight	+3 lbs.	+4 lbs.	+4 lbs.	+3 lbs.

During the first critical month when feeding is being established, you and your pediatrician will want to watch your baby's growth especially carefully. A baby's weight can sometimes be the only indication of whether or not he's getting enough milk.

Once feeding is well established, your pediatrician will monitor your baby's weight and height and head size in a couple of ways. She'll measure his growth and compare it with other children's growth by calculating a percentile (see Q&A, below). She'll also plot how much your baby grew this month compared to last month and will create a personalized growth curve. A baby can be above or below national averages for his age and still be right on target for his personal rate of growth. What's important isn't necessarily how much your baby grows, but that he grows steadily and that he appears healthy and happy.

Q & A

"My 2-month-old is in the 75th percentile for weight. What does this mean?"

A percentile chart gives height, head circumference, and weight averages for children at different ages. In your baby's case, being in the 75th percentile for weight simply means that 75 out of 100 babies her age weigh less than she does; 25 weigh more. She's still within the normal weight range for a baby her age.

At each visit, the pediatrician will plot your baby's growth on the percentile chart. Over time, she may move up or down on the chart until she stabilizes at the percentile that's determined in large part by genetics.

Motor Skills Your baby was born with an impressive array of involuntary reflexes, from coughing up mucus to blinking when exposed to bright lights. It won't be long before he'll replace those automatic responses with voluntary large and small motor skills that will be just as impressive:

• **The stare.** As the first months pass, you'll notice that your baby has learned

DEFINITION

Motor Skills

Motor development—how a baby learns to move and use the different parts of his body—is divided into two parts: large and small. Large motor development includes kicking, holding his head up, crawling, walking, and so on. Small motor development includes abilities such as eye-hand coordination, grasping, and manipulating objects.

to follow an object as it moves across her path of vision. Eye muscles develop first in a baby (development seems to move from the head down, and from the trunk outward to the hands). She'll also develop that deep-thinker stare; she'll appear to intently study her hand or another object for several minutes.

Hurray for the baby push-up! Your baby is strong enough to hold her head—and her shoulders—off the ground.

• **The head lift.** A newborn's lack of head control often strikes fear in a new parent's heart. Luckily, your baby will soon gain more control of his floppy neck and his heavy head. At first he may only occasionally turn his head from side to side or raise it a bit for a brief time. But by the end of 3 months, he'll be able to lift his head to a 45-degree angle and may even move it back and forth in search of you or something else particularly interesting. Much to parents' delight, he'll also be able to keep his head steadier when he's held in an upright or sitting position.

• **The baby push-up.** After she can pick up her head a little, it won't be long before your junior gymnast wiggles her little shoulders off the ground, too. She won't be able to stay in the push-up position for long at first, but as the months pass, she'll get stronger and stronger.

• **The whirlwind.** Your baby may begin to "show off" when he's lying on his back, waving his arms and legs rhythmically as if he's cycling. Some babies even try to roll over partway by the third month. This new activity level increases the need for vigilance: now there's even more reason to use the straps on your changing table and to never leave him unattended.

• **The grasp.** Your newborn's tightly clenched little fists will begin to unfurl, and by the time she's 3 months old, her hands will be open enough to make attempts at grasping toys, rattles, your little finger, your hair. This is a voluntary action under her own control, not a reflex. Even at rest, your baby's hands will now be unclenched.

• **The reach.** He may still be uncoordinated, but by the third month, your little one will try to reach out and swat, grab, or bat something. He'll probably be able to navigate his hands and fingers into his mouth (although he may still poke himself in the eye occasionally) and may discover (if you're lucky) that sucking on his own fingers is very soothing. The 3-month mark is a great time to introduce a mobile above his crib or changing table.

Over time, your baby's control of her body will become more and more sophisticated. If you gently poke her hand during the first three months, she's likely to fuss and move her hand and her whole body. After six months or so, she'll have learned to move just her hand.

> ### *MILESTONE*
>
> **THE STARE**
> "Now that my daughter India is two months old, she's more alert and loves looking at her fists. She stares directly into our faces, making gurgling sounds. She wiggles and smiles a lot and sticks out her tongue."
>
> —Hillary van Kleeck

By the end of the third month, your baby will make a game of trying to reach out and swat, grab, or bat nearby objects.

Mental Development

Cognitive Behavior Your baby was born knowing how to cry and suck. These automatic actions require no thought and are called reflexive. Within days, however, your baby will learn to suck more efficiently, to turn toward the breast for a feeding, and to cry if the feeding isn't coming fast enough. These are your baby's first cognitive actions and are just the beginning of his intellectual development.

By the second month, he'll have sharpened his ability to anticipate, to the point where he'll begin to mewl if he even sees his bottle or smells your breast. And by the third month, some babies smack their lips or make sucking noises in preparation for a feeding.

Memory Memory plays a big role in your baby's mental development. To be able to learn, to retain and process information, memory is essential. And memory is important in the development of attachment and love, as well. A baby begins to remember that this nice person fed and played with him last night, and the night before, too. By 3 or 4 months, he'll recognize whether or not a familiar person is holding him. That doesn't mean he'll miss you if you're not there (that comes later); it just means he knows it's not you who is picking him up.

HOW TO
Make a Mobile

Satisfy your baby's developing swatting skills with a homemade mobile.

1. Screw a hook into the ceiling above the crib.
2. Tie fishing line, dental floss, or nylon thread to the hook.
3. Hang bright objects from the thread, such as a set of colorful plastic measuring spoons or your baby's favorite key rattle. Or attach a metal hanger to the thread (close the hook of the hanger into a circle so it won't slide off), and tie on a variety of items, from empty spools to squeeze toys. Just make sure they're securely attached and far enough away so that your baby can't get a grasp.

Using fishing line and a ring of baby spoons, make a mobile for your curious baby. Hang it low enough so that he can touch it but not yank it down.

Babies prefer black and white over color? Newborns seem to be more attracted to black-and-white images because they can focus on black and white so much better than on pale colors.

Mental Development Month by Month

BY THE END OF . . .	MONTH 1	MONTH 2	MONTH 3
Attention Span	Fleeting moments of attention	15 minutes	May pay attention to you for 30 minutes at a time
Vision	Sees light and dark patterns	Looks at one object at a time, likes faces and moving objects	Looks from one object to another, can focus on object whether it's near or far, prefers 3-D to 2-D
Coordination	May try to weakly grasp object if it's placed in hand	Tries to grasp object out of his reach (usually in vain)	Swipes at object with better aim, holds toy for a short time

You may think that it's your baby's memory that's at work when he begins to show an interest in a mobile. It looks as if he may be thinking: "If I hit the dangly thing, it will move." But this development isn't so much an understanding of cause and effect or the result of his miraculous memory as it is his newfound ability to make a connection between two things: he swats at something and it moves. This sort of associative learning can result in great fun with toys that move.

Social Development

Language During the entire first year, a baby expresses himself mainly by crying. And after just a couple of weeks, an attentive parent can usually begin to make sense of her baby's cries. Familiarity helps Mom decipher the sounds, but the baby is also doing his part to improve communication. During months 2 and 3, he'll usually cry less and add cooing, squealing, and squeaking to his repertoire. A cry may mean "I'm hungry"; a coo, "I'm glad to see you." He may even begin to pause between his vocalizations, waiting for you to answer.

Indulge him in this primitive form of conversation: Baby whimpers a bit and then stops; Mom or Dad says, "What's the matter, sweetie? Do you want a cuddle?" Baby cries again and pauses, Mom replies, "OK, little one, let's get your diaper changed and go sit in the rocking chair." Even if you don't have a clue what he's trying to say to you, your replies teach him (even at this tender age) that you're trying to respond to his needs and that communication is a two-way street.

By the end of month 3, your baby may also demonstrate:

> ## MILESTONE
>
> ### THE ATTENTION SPAN
>
> "Sarah, who's three months old, absolutely loves her baby quilt, which has black and white and red patterns on it. It makes me dizzy, but she focuses on it for a long time. I keep wondering what she sees."
>
> —*Becky Specker, Cincinnati, OH*

• **The vowel sounds.** His coos begin to sound like stretched-out vowel sounds—*ah-h-h, eh-h-h*, or *oh-h-h-h*—and he'll start to have more fun "talking" to you by varying the length of the sounds. He'll like it if you babble some vowels at him, too, especially if you stretch them out and make funny faces at the same time.

• **The shout.** He may shock you (and himself) by how loud he can screech—and then delight in your surprised response. When you tire of this noisy game (and you'll undoubtedly tire of it before he will), try a whisper and see if he lowers his pitch.

• **The laugh.** It's more than a gurgle or a giggle now. It's a bona fide laugh, and when parents first hear it coming out of their baby's mouth around the 3- to 4-month mark, they can't quite believe it. When my oldest daughter let out her first belly laugh, I immediately called my mother to report the good news and tried to get her to do it again. (Of course, Halley Rose had no intention of laughing, or doing anything else, on cue.) That didn't prevent me from spending the next several days trying to figure out what tickled her budding sense of humor—and delighting in every single chortle.

Most parents are understandably eager for their child to "talk." But as thrilling as communication is, it's best to keep your conversation simple these first months. Get down to your baby's level and look him in the eye; use simple words and sentences and exaggerate your facial expressions a bit; speak in a singsongy voice pitched an octave higher than usual; and always give him a rest if he looks away from you or begins to fuss.

Interaction with Others Between week 1 and week 12, your baby's social skills will have undergone a transformation. By the end of the third month, she'll be quiet when you hold her, look directly at people and follow them visually, and show signs of recognizing you. Your baby's smile has evolved from a newborn's random involuntary action to a prewired reaction to any human face to a real, full-blown "I know you" smile. At 3 months old, she may smile for lots of folks she knows well, but there may be a special smile for Mama.

Many babies this age are beginning to organize their schedules to fit into a more predictable pattern of family life. They have more time for socializing because they're sleeping less during the day and more at night.

Touch Your baby will use touch, like each of his other senses, to learn more about his surroundings: the slide of the water in his bath, the texture of his blankie, and the special feel of his parents' hands. He craves, and actually needs,

Social Development Month by Month

BY THE END OF . . .	MONTH 1	MONTH 2	MONTH 3
Smiling	Random smiles	Smiles at faces and smiles when you do	Smiles to say hello to special people
Eye contact	Looks around you rather than at you	Makes eye contact for 5–10 seconds, beginning to track	Follows you or object with eyes, stares
Body language	Molds body to yours while being held	Flaps arms and legs when excited	Extends arms for play

to be touched. A simple cuddle, stroke on the cheek, or pat on the back may be all it takes to quiet him at this age. Studies show that babies who're touched or massaged often are happier and healthier than babies who aren't. Not only has massage been proven to reduce crying and colic, and to improve circulation and body awareness, it has also helped premature or sick babies gain weight and go home from the hospital sooner.

But beyond the scientific, skin-to-skin contact is a relaxing nonverbal way for you and your baby to socialize. It may even boost your confidence as a parent by building your awareness of your baby's likes and dislikes. Try massaging him when you want to reconnect after a busy day or when he is particularly fussy. During the early months, start with your baby's feet and legs and move on to his tummy. Save a head or chest massage for when he's a little older. If he doesn't seem to like being massaged, stop and try again another day. The massages that follow were originally created for PARENTING'S BABYTALK magazine by masseuse Vimala Schneider McClure.

> ### *MILESTONE*
> ---
> **THE SMILE**
>
> "At seven weeks, Anne smiles for anyone who talks to her in a high-pitched voice, especially our three-and-a-half-year-old daughter, Erin, who mimics the way I talk and sing to the baby."
>
> —Leslie Mishu,
> Knoxville, TN

Leg and Foot Massage

1. Lay your baby on his back on a comfortable, safe surface. Start each massage by asking him if he wants one. Put olive oil on your hands and stretch them out as a sort of invitation. It may sound ridiculous, since he won't know what you're talking about at first, but eventually your baby will recognize the massage cue and will let you know if he's interested.
2. With one hand, raise his leg up by the foot and run your other hand from under his bottom along the inside of the leg to the foot. Masseuses sometimes call this firm but gentle motion "milking." Repeat the same motion on the same leg but with your other hand.
3. Next, hold his leg near the ankle with both hands (as if his leg were a bat or tennis racket). Move your hands from the ankle to the top of the thigh, very gently twisting and squeezing in opposite directions with each hand.
4. Then, move to the bottom of his foot. Massage the foot with your thumbs from the heel to the toe. Squeeze each toe from underneath.

5. Now, apply pressure to the top of the foot with your thumbs, moving from the base of the toes up to the ankle. Continue using your thumbs to make small circles all around the ankle.
6. Repeat with the other leg.

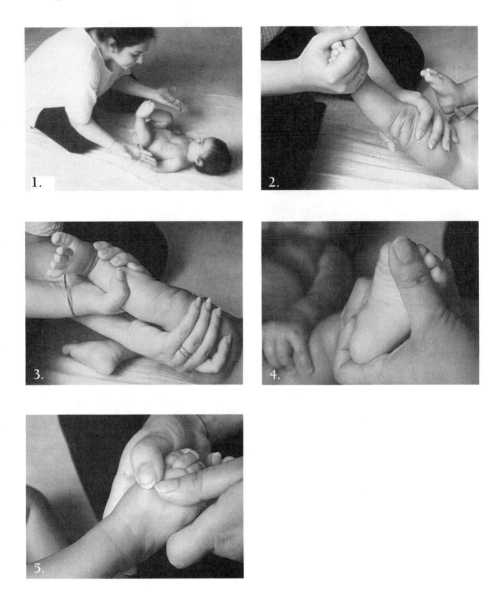

The Tummy Rub

1. Use the palms of your hands to make alternating paddle strokes on your baby's tummy. Start right below his rib cage and move down. Use your left hand to lift up your baby by the ankles while paddling down his tummy with your right hand.

2. Your baby's tummy should now be more relaxed and ready for a little deeper massage. Place a thumb on each side of his belly button and press gently to the side.

3. Make a smile (or a half moon) on his stomach with your right hand. Start with your palm on the left side below his navel and move it up to the right in a half circle. Rest your palm on his belly.

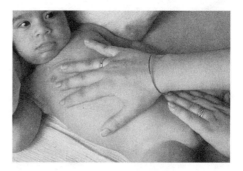

4. Leave your right hand resting on his belly while moving your left palm to the left and below his belly button. Move it up into a circle (or sun) shape.

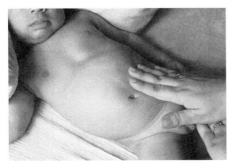

5. Move the palm of your right hand down his tummy to spell "I."

6. Use your left hand to move across his belly and down, to make an "L" for "Love."

7. Make the "U" for "You" by moving your right palm from the left side of his navel, up and over to the right side of his belly.

FOR INFORMATION ON . . .

Baby massage. Call the International Association of Infant Massage to find a certified instructor near you, 800-248-5432. To order Gentle Touch Infant Massage, an instructional video, call 888-333-3936.

What You Need To Know About . . . Baby Temperament

Some parents swear that their baby was born with his or her temperament intact. "Zach has been sunny from day one," his mother says. "Nothing ever seems to get Melanie excited," another mom says. Was Zach born jolly and Melanie born mellow?

Experts today believe there are genes linked to shyness, fear, and some mental illnesses; they've even isolated a gene they believe is connected to thrill-seeking behavior. But most scientists also think that genetics and environment work together to determine a baby's personality, a sort of nature and nurture duet.

Take sunny Zach, for example. He may have been born with a cheery disposition or he may have just learned that when he gurgles and coos, Mom smiles and coos right back at him—and because that's pleasant, he keeps it up. Melanie may be less outgoing than most babies, but if her mom would continue to be loving and cheerful with her, Melanie might learn to interact more readily. In this way researchers now believe that positive personality traits can be encouraged and negative ones can be redirected. Shyness or aggressiveness needn't be your baby's destiny. In fact, some scientists estimate that by the time a child grows up, experience takes the upper hand and only 10 percent of his adult personality will be inborn.

In any case, during the first three months it's pretty difficult to tell whether your baby is shy or just sleepy, crabby or overstimulated, innately happy or simply pleased because she just passed gas. What's essential during these early months is that you meet your baby's needs, regardless of her temperament and regardless of whether it matches your own. If you're finding it difficult to develop a nurturing relationship with your baby because of his temperament (or for any other reasons), it's important to discuss this with your pediatrician.

CHECKLIST
Developmental Warnings

Every baby has her own developmental timetable, so don't worry if your infant seems to be developing at a different pace from the baby down the street. There is a very wide range of normal. Instead of comparing your baby to another child, compare her to herself. Last month she didn't seem to be looking right at you; this month she's actually following you around the room with her eyes. If you're at all concerned about your baby's progress, talk to her pediatrician, especially if by the end of three months your child:

✔ Can't lift her head up
✔ Isn't able to push up on her arms 45 degrees
✔ Still has limp limbs or a flopsy-mopsy posture
✔ Holds her arms and legs very stiffly or close to her body
✔ Doesn't turn when you speak or respond to loud noises
✔ Isn't repeating sounds you make, such as coos
✔ Isn't following you around visually

DEFINITION

Attachment

Psychologists use the word *attachment* to describe the emotional tie that develops between a baby and his primary caregivers. It's thought that the quality of the attachment developed during Baby's first year profoundly affects how he will eventually feel about himself and the world. A baby is prewired to attach to Mom; he recognizes her voice, her smell. But a baby can form multiple attachments—to his father and to a daily caregiver, for example—in addition to his mother. This is probably nature's way of protecting him from the loss of his main caregiver.

Predictability is an important factor in attachment. Once your infant realizes that life is predictable—that if he's wet someone changes him, hungry someone feeds him—he's on the road to love and attachment. If you're satisfying your baby's needs, you're well on your way to building a strong, nurturing relationship.

A PARENT'S LIFE

Call them clichés, but a couple of old and overused sayings ring true when it comes to parenthood: "Life will never be the same again" and "You'll understand when you're a parent." In the process of getting your life back to normal during these first three months, you'll discover that so much has changed—your body, your relationship with your partner, your heart—that nothing will ever be "normal" again. You'll also find (after you get some sleep) that that's OK.

The First Tiring Weeks

Each time I was in the hospital after having a baby, I couldn't wait to be left alone. I was sick of the staff poking and prodding me all the time. By the end of the first week at home, I was tired of family and friends hogging the baby, telling me to take a nap, putting the dishes away in the wrong cupboard, and being overwhelmingly "helpful." *Why doesn't everyone just leave me alone,* I thought to myself.

A crisis came for me on day 9 of my daughter Gracie's life. My husband was going out of town for two days on business on the same day that my own parents had to head back home. The visitors and food deliveries had stopped coming. My 2-year-old suddenly came down with a fever and I couldn't, in good conscience, drop her off at daycare for even a three-hour respite. Sore, bone-tired, overwhelmed, suddenly I didn't feel so strongly about being left alone. I burst into tears the minute my mother walked out the door. My 2-year-old took

GOOD ADVICE

Surviving the First Weeks

"When he got home from work every day, my partner, Adam, took care of Robert. For two hours, I wasn't even allowed to touch the baby. It gave me a chance to spend some time alone, either reading or sleeping."

—*Carrie Courter, San Jose, CA*

"My husband and I made it a point to go out one night a week to see a movie or have dinner. It was hard to leave the baby—even for just a few hours—but it gave me a chance to relax."

—*Heather Goff, Memphis, TN*

"At first I acted like a martyr—I refused help. But eventually I had to pick up the phone and ask my mom to come over. Going to a new moms' group was a life-saver. All the mothers had the exact same concerns and strains as me. It was a great support."

—*Smita Patel, Marlboro, NJ*

"I took a couple of evenings and went to the school where I teach and did a little work. It made me feel like the 'other' me, my old self."

—*Jody Hepp, Bryan, OH*

"We set aside two nights a week for friends to come over and see the baby. Otherwise, people would have been stopping by all the time."

—*Carolyn Gruning-Jones, Blackwood, NJ*

one look at me and burst into tears, too. It wasn't long before Gracie joined us in our group cry.

Well, nobody said it was going to be easy. In fact, some instructors of birthing and new-parent classes go out of their way to tell parents-to-be just how hard the first months with Baby can be. But it's hard to believe, until you've lived through it, how tough life with a newborn can be. My own Lamaze teacher had the whole class laughing at her horror stories: imagine a sleep-deprived dad coming home to a messy house, nothing to eat, a bedraggled, teary-eyed mom still in her bathrobe. Hah-hah-hah, we all tittered. My teacher's point: chaos *is* normal at first. Lower your expectations. Let the house be a mess. Order takeout food. Do whatever's necessary to spare yourself the guilt and get through the first incredibly taxing weeks. You can't

Four Good Reasons to Cry

✔ You'll feel better afterward. In a Minnesota study, 85 percent of women and 73 percent of men said their mood improves right after a good cry.

✔ Tears wash away stress. Tears that are brought on by emotions (as opposed to pain, for instance) contain pain-relieving chemicals called endorphins, according to researcher William Frey of the HealthPartners' Tear Research Center in St. Paul, Minnesota. He believes those are by-products of stress streaming down your face.

✔ Crying is healthy. One study of crying patterns found that folks who were physically healthy cried almost twice as often as the patients who were ill.

✔ You'll get some sympathy. In the right situation (as in the months after childbirth, for instance), a little weeping can, literally, be your cry for help. It's an effective way to tell the people around you that you need some TLC.

do it all, so do what's important: take care of your baby and yourself. She was right.

The Fatigue Factor Sleep deprivation may be the number-one "I wish I'd known" in conversations with new moms. Few parents are prepared for waking up five times a night and getting no more than two hours of uninterrupted sleep at a time. We're talking about the kind of fatigue that makes your bones hurt, your good temper

Keeping Your Cool

"My son has been very independent and headstrong from the beginning. When I start to lose my cool, I've learned to remind myself (sometimes several times) that he was sent here to bring out the best and the worst in me. And I've realized that there are some things I need to work on (like not always having to be the one in control). This has helped me relax and focus on the good times, instead of the bad."

—*Shawn Trego, Simpsonville, SC*

sour, and your patience and confidence flee. It's like being permanently jet-lagged. Everything gets blown out of proportion when you're low on sleep: any feelings of inadequacy you may have become exaggerated, you may cry more often, the idea of making a sandwich may seem exhausting. So how can you prevent turning into a zombie?

• **Sleep when the baby sleeps.** Experts claim you get more energy from a catnap in the P.M. than the A.M. But, hey, take a nap whenever you find the time.

ᨈ A MOTHER'S VIEW ᨈ

"I Was Scared Stiff"

*T*he hardest thing Michele White ever did was bring her new baby, Madeline, home from the hospital. For Michele, motherhood meant instant worries: was Madeline dressed warmly enough for the cold winter in Lennon, Michigan? Was she getting enough to eat? Was she safe in her crib?

Most new moms have similar fears, but every night Michele's anxiety went over the top. "I would be fine during the day," recalls Michele, "but at bedtime I couldn't go to sleep. I would cry and cry." She was terrified that the baby she had tried for 10 months to conceive would die in the night. Michele's fear of SIDS was so great that she would wake up every hour of every night to check on the baby.

It was baby Madeline who finally helped ease Michele's fears. "At five weeks I remember looking at her and worrying about whether or not I was doing everything right, and she looked up at me and smiled," Michele says. "I felt like she was telling me, 'I'm fine, Mom. Relax.' So I did."

She also feels blessed that Madeline has been an ideal baby for a nervous first-time mother. "Even when I was weeping, it didn't faze her," says Michele. "She taught me to relax." Here's what else Michele learned:

- **Cut yourself some slack.** It's difficult to feel like a competent mom if you're trying to keep the house spotless and gourmet meals on the table. "Use your time to enjoy your baby and gain your confidence," she says.
- **Accept all offers of help, especially from Dad.** "After all, both of you had the baby," says Michele.
- **Sleep when the baby sleeps.** That's the only way that Michele could catch up on all those hours of sleep she missed when constantly checking up on Madeline.
- **Realize that fears are a normal part of parenthood.** "Even now, at six months, I still look in on Madeline all the time," admits Michele. "I just don't feel foolish about it anymore."

Because everyone will tell you to do it, because you have 10 million other things to do while the baby is napping, you may resist taking a nap. Don't. You may think that going to bed at 9 P.M. when the baby goes down is ridiculous. It isn't. "Sleep when the baby sleeps" is possibly the best advice ever given.

• **Eat well.** You need the right kind of fuel to get you through the night (and day). If you cut back on calories because you're too tired to eat or are dieting, you're cheating your body of the energy it needs. (Calorie-cutting can also sabotage your milk production if you're nursing; you need 500 more calories a day, just as you did when you were pregnant.) Eating plenty of vegetables and fruits will help keep you regular, and drinking lots of water keeps your milk flowing.

• **Get help.** Don't fall into that supermom trap right off the bat. If relatives, friends, or neighbors want to offer food, housecleaning, baby-sitting an older sibling, whatever—accept! If you can afford it, hire a baby nurse or a *doula* for a day or two. The nurse takes care of the baby; the *doula* (which is Greek for "maidservant") takes care of you by doing household chores and keeping visitors at bay.

• **Get out of the house.** A simple change of scenery may be just the thing to give you a little energy spurt.

• **Connect with other new mothers.** Being a new mom can be pretty isolating, especially if you're alone with the baby all day. To stay sane, many mothers find it helpful to get together formally or informally with other new moms to share their experiences. There's nothing so comforting as finding out you're not alone—in your moments of misery or joy.

Even if you do all of the above, it may still take months for you to erase the sleep debt

HOW TO
Find a Mother's Group

Word of mouth is a wonderful way to find out about other new moms and to locate a mothers' group near you. Or call the following to find out if they know of any local mothers' clubs:

- Your obstetrician or pediatrician
- Your Lamaze or prenatal class instructor
- The hospital or birthing center
- Children's toy or clothing stores
- Your neighborhood association
- Your place of worship
- La Leche League
- The human resources department at your office

Some new mothers have met and chatted on-line before they get together in person. Use your good judgment when you're getting together with someone you don't know for the first time.

accumulated in the first weeks of parenthood. It took you nine months to grow a baby; it may take a lot longer to get used to living with her.

The Emotional Roller Coaster Although becoming a mother may be the most incredibly happy time in your life, you may be feeling low. How low depends upon your fatigue level, how realistic you are about what a new mom can really handle, how much help you're getting at home, and your sensitivity to hormonal changes. If, for instance, you have a history of severe premenstrual symptoms, your body may be sensitive to hormonal activity and may have a stronger postpartum reaction to the precipitous drop in estrogen that occurs after birth.

Feeling a little depressed, a little tired, a little anxious and weepy is normal and quite common among new mothers. According to some studies, these "baby blues" typically strike 50 percent of postpartum moms a few days after the baby is born and disappear within a month. Medication is rarely prescribed or necessary. Getting more sleep, accepting more help, sharing your feelings of inadequacy with your partner and friends—plus the passage of time—should help you feel better. Breastfeeding, too, is thought to help minimize the effects of plummeting estrogen.

For some women, though, the effect of hormonal shifts on the neurotransmitters in the brain is more dramatic, and can result in a variety of forms of postpartum mood disorders. Altered brain chemistry, alone or combined with not enough support, severe fatigue, and the general stresses associated with childbirth and new motherhood, can trigger some very scary symptoms. Women who have a personal or family history of depression may also be harder hit than those who don't.

Because many of today's moms hesitate to admit any weakness or that they can't "do it all," they may be reluctant to talk about how they're feeling. But being open about depression is the first step toward getting better. If you have any of the symptoms of the following disorders, see your doctor immediately.

• **Postpartum depression (PPD)** is more than a minor case of the blues; it's a serious clinical condition that is most likely to strike one day to six weeks after the baby's birth. (It can show up later in breastfeeding moms, after they wean the baby.) Symptoms include an inability to sleep or eat, extreme anxiety, unfounded and inconsolable concerns about your baby, and, sometimes, thoughts of suicide. In severe forms, these feelings are constant and overwhelming. PPD affects up to 20 percent of new moms, and treatment typically includes psychotherapy and medication. Support groups can also be very helpful.

❦ A MOTHER'S VIEW ❦

"Why Moms Need Other Moms"

"My main reason for joining a mother's group was to find friends for Kathleen," says Amy Hatch of Corte Madera, California. But she soon realized that her 3-month-old daughter wasn't nearly as interested in socializing as she was—and that a mothers' group could inject some much-needed stimulation and support into her new life as a mom.

She found out about a local mothers' club one day while she was strolling through the mall with Kathleen. "Another mother introduced herself and asked me if I'd joined yet," Amy recalls. She was invited to a coffee get-together with veteran mothers of 2- and 3-year-olds. "It was nice to hear about their experiences as new mothers," she says.

Before long, the club's playgroup coordinator had put Amy in touch with another new mom, and the two started their own playgroup. When Kathleen hit 5 months old, the group had grown to four moms; by the time she was 6 months old, it was 10. "The group is like a party," says Amy. "At first it was mainly for the moms, but once the kids started sitting up, they started paying attention to each other."

Going though childbirth and raising a child is an incredible experience, says Amy, "and only another mother can really understand it." Her advice about mothers' groups:

- **Don't wait until your baby is born to join.** "In my group, moms who join before their babies are born get cooked meals delivered to their doors after the birth," Amy says.
- **Shop around to find a group size that suits you.** There are small groups that provide a more intimate relationship with other moms or larger groups that offer a whole slate of activities. Amy's group has both: in addition to small playgroups, her 150-member mothers' club offers special events and speakers each month. "It's interesting to listen to the speeches, but it's really great just to have an hour or two for myself," says Amy.
- **Search out mothers with the same parenting style.** "Once in a while, a mother will give her opinion on a parenting question and everybody else will agree and I don't," says Amy. "Then I'll feel like I don't fit in." As time goes on, like-minded moms sometimes break off into smaller groups of their own.

• **Postpartum anxiety or panic disorder** often occurs in conjunction with PPD. It can rear its ugly head any time between birth and six weeks, but also sometimes strikes after your baby has been weaned. Symptoms include strong feelings of doom and/or panic, shortness of breath, and dizziness. The condition affects 5 to 10 percent of postpartum mothers, and psychotherapy and medication is prescribed.

• **Postpartum obsessive-compulsive disorder** affects less than 5 percent of new mothers. Here, too, women suffer from deep bouts of anxiety in which they worry about being left alone with their baby, harming their baby, and protecting him. Typical treatment: a combination of medication and psychotherapy.

• **Postpartum psychosis** comes on suddenly after birth and is extremely frightening. Symptoms include severe confusion, hallucinations and delusions, inability to sleep or think clearly, and violent or bizarre behavior. In some cases, women have hurt themselves and their babies. This condition is relatively rare, affecting only 2 out of every 1000 childbearing women. It requires immediate emergency treatment, medication, and hospitalization.

For More Help: Postpartum Disorders

Organizations

- Depression After Delivery (D.A.D.)
  908-575-9121

- Postpartum Support International (PSI)
  805-967-7636

Books and Other Resources

- *This Isn't What I Expected: Recognizing and Recovering from Depression and Anxiety After Childbirth*
  by Karen R. Kleiman, MSW, and Valerie Raskin, MD; Bantam Books
  Provides detailed information on the subject along with exercises, action lists, and resources.

- *Fragile Beginnings: Postpartum Mood and Anxiety Disorders*
  InJoy Productions; 303-447-2082
  An informative and reassuring videotape on postpartum mental health. Also available on audiotape.

⌁ A MOTHER'S VIEW ⌁

"My Rocky Start"

When people would ask Jackie Garcia, "Don't you just love being a mom?" she would stare at them in horror. "I didn't share any of those warm feelings about motherhood," the Lafayette, California, mom recalls.

In fact, during those first months, she says, "I was never more miserable in my life. Ariel wasn't cuddly or cute. He didn't smile. He just cried all the time. You can't imagine before a baby is born that he will cry all the time, and that you will be doing anything and everything you can to get him to stop."

When Ariel would cry, so would Jackie. Soon she became so emotionally and physically exhausted, she was shouting at him in the middle of the night.

Was Jackie depressed or just severely sleep deprived? She wasn't sure; all she knew was that the combination of "baby blues" and a relentlessly fussy baby was taking its toll on the whole family.

By the time Ariel was 6 months old, life was on a more even keel. Ariel fussed less and slept more. And Jackie started feeling better after discussing her frustrations and fatigue with friends and a counselor. Her tips for coping with a less-than-perfect introduction to motherhood:

- **Get counseling.** Jackie regrets that she didn't talk to someone right away about how she felt. Once she met with a counselor, she was able to put her struggles with Ariel into perspective and better learn how to deal with his fussiness.
- **Take time off from your baby.** "It's not going to ruin his life if you leave him with a sitter for a few hours," says Jackie, who found that she could better cope with Ariel's crying when she'd had a breather. And he seemed happier when he spent a few hours a week with other babies.
- **Don't underestimate how not getting enough sleep can affect you.** Jackie learned that sleep deprivation is a powerful contributor to negative feelings about parenthood. Once Ariel began to sleep better, Jackie did, too. She soon realized that fatigue had played a big part in her depression.

Many women feel guilty and embarrassed that they have to take medication to control their depression and that they're not the jolly supermom they thought they would be. It's important to understand that all forms of postpartum depression are a type of mental illness caused by a number of biochemical and psychological factors out of your control. These disorders go beyond normal fatigue and the natural pressures of new parenthood. If you have a serious disorder, you'll do yourself and your baby a favor by getting treatment so that you can more cheerfully and competently care for him. And there's good news: some new antidepressant drugs can be used while continuing to breastfeed.

Taking Care of Yourself

Now that your top priorities are the baby, the baby, the baby, and getting some sleep, it's not surprising that eating right, exercising, and monitoring your own physical health may have fallen by the wayside. But all that you've heard people say about the importance of mothering the mother is true: if you're not healthy, your parenting skills will suffer.

In the first month after childbirth, it's especially important to watch for any warning signs of pregnancy-related infection.

Report any problems to your doctor at your six-week postpartum checkup, or sooner if you're feverish or in severe pain. Women who've had C-sections often have a three-week appointment to check their incision.

At many ob-gyn offices it's traditional to bring in the new baby with you for your checkup. The nurses, doctors, and staff who've seen you through your pregnancy gather around and ooh and aah over the baby and congratulate you on a job well done. It's a nice time to thank them for their support, too. (If all goes well, this will be the last time you see them until your next regularly scheduled Pap test or pregnancy test.)

You'll start out your appointment with a blood pressure check and weigh-in. A urine sample isn't usually collected unless you've been having problems or suspect a urinary tract infection. Your blood pressure should be back to normal (even if it was slightly elevated near the end of your pregnancy) and you'll probably have lost 17 to 20 pounds. The doctor will check:

- To see if your uterus is returning to its prepregnancy size
- The condition of your cervix, which may still be pink from engorgement
- To see if the muscle tone of your vagina is tightening
- How your episiotomy or tear(s), or C-section incision, are healing
- Your breasts for any signs of lumps or abnormalities

Postpartum Health Watch

PROBLEM	SYMPTOMS	PREVENTION/RX
Breast infection	Breasts that are painful, swollen, pink, hot; high fever, flu-like symptoms	Apply warm compresses, massage breasts while nursing, empty breasts completely, nurse regularly or increase nursing; a doctor visit and antibiotics if condition persists
Incision infection	Sharp pain, unusual tenderness, or pus-like oozing from C-section scar	Keep area clean, don't lift heavy objects; see your doctor
Episiotomy opening or infection	Pain, bleeding, or foul-smelling discharge.	Clean perineum with sitz bath and squirt bottle, wear clean cotton panties (not panty liners, which can encourage bacteria growth); call your doctor if you're worried
Uterine or vaginal infection	Fever, abdominal pain, foul-smelling discharge, soreness	Same as above
Urinary tract infection	Blood in urine, burning sensation, fever	Drink lots of fluids, especially cranberry juice; call your doctor if there's blood or burning urination
Urethral damage	Difficulty urinating or total inability to relieve yourself	Force fluids, take a sitz bath with warm water; call your doctor

- Hemorrhoids or varicose veins that may have developed during pregnancy or childbirth.

In addition, she may have a list of questions to go over with you:

- Have you resumed sexual relations with your partner? How do you feel about having sex again? Have you experienced any pain or unusual sensations? What sort of contraceptive are you using or planning to use (see "What You Need to Know About . . . Birth Control," page 172)? Are you experiencing vaginal dryness? Do you have plans to have another baby? When?
- How much sleep are you getting? Are you eating right? Do you have enough help to give you a break during the day?
- How are you feeling emotionally? Any mixed feelings about the baby or episodes of depression?
- Are you breastfeeding the baby and, if so, how is it going? How long do you hope to continue?
- Have you started to exercise? Do Kegels? (See "HOW TO: Kegels," page 172.)
- How are you feeling generally? Is there anything bothering you or that you'd like to talk about?

Have a list of your own questions to review with the doctor, and use the checkup to air any concerns that you have.

Eating Right Even though you'll be eating with just one hand for quite a while, steer the hand that's not holding the baby toward the high-energy nutrients you need:

- **Water.** It's not a food per se, but drinking lots of water can help you fight the fatigue that comes with dehydration. And if you're nursing, you need to drink at least eight tall glasses a day.
- **Iron.** Your doctor may have suggested that you continue with your prenatal vitamins while you're nursing. You can also help replace lost red blood cells with a daily serving of an iron-rich food such as spinach, dried fruit, or lean red meat. Many cereals are also iron-fortified.
- **Calcium.** A nursing mom's RDA of 1000 milligrams of calcium (that's five servings a day) can be fulfilled with more than just milk. Some orange juice and cereals are calcium fortified, and flavored yogurt delivers a calcium punch, as does nonfat ice cream. Calcium is also found in broccoli, salmon, sardines, tofu, and, of course, your favorite cheese.

- **Protein.** Fish and lean meat are great sources of protein, and so are low-fat dairy products such as cottage cheese and yogurt and tasty treats such as peanut butter. You need two to three servings of protein each day.
- **Fiber.** To prevent painful constipation, eat several daily servings of fruit, vegetables, and beans. If your breastfeeding baby tends to get gas, however, avoid veggies such as broccoli and cauliflower.

Knowing what you should be eating is a far cry from having the time and energy to prepare (and actually sit down and eat) healthful foods. Once the well-intentioned but fat-laden casseroles stop coming, it's time to simplify your life and treat yourself right with a few easy, tasty menus. Here's one day's worth of good food that provides more than just a nursing mom's dietary requirements—it packs a lot of variety and flavor into 24 hours. Recipes and menu plans were created by Kathy Gunst, mother of two and author of The PAR-ENTING *Cookbook*.

BREAKFAST: *Quick Scramble*

Preparation time: 5 minutes
Cooking time: about 5 to 6 minutes
Yield: 1 to 2 servings

Breakfast seems to be an easy meal to ignore when you're busy with a new baby, but with this quick egg dish you'll have no excuse. Add your favorite cheese and herbs and serve with toast, muffins, bagels, or warm tortillas.

> 2 eggs
> 1 tablespoon chopped fresh dill, basil, parsley, or favorite herb, or
> ½ teaspoon dried
> Salt and freshly ground black pepper
> 1 teaspoon olive or vegetable oil
> 1 scallion, thinly sliced
> 1½ tablespoons grated cheese
> 2 tablespoons finely chopped fresh tomato

In a small bowl, whisk the eggs, half the herbs, and salt and pepper to taste.
Heat the oil in a small skillet set over moderate heat. Add the scallion and cook about 2 minutes, stirring frequently. Raise the heat to moderately high and add the beaten egg. Using a fork, whisk in the cheese and tomato and cook 2 to 3 minutes, or until the egg is set and the cheese is melted. Serve immediately.

Calcium-Rich Foods

½ cup broccoli	36 mg
4 ounces cottage cheese	102 mg
½ cup tofu	130 mg
2 ounces sardines	217 mg
8 ounces low-fat milk	297 mg
8 ounces fortified orange juice	300 mg
8 ounces low-fat yogurt	415 mg

SNACK: *Spinach Spread*

Preparation time: 10 to 12 minutes
Cooking Time: 5 minutes
Yield: 1 cup

Full of iron and calcium, this spread or dip is incredibly versatile. Smear it on a bagel, crackers, or toast, dip raw vegetables into it, toss it with pasta, or spoon it on top of cooked chicken breasts or fish fillets.

For a quick snack, thinly slice French bread and toast on one side. Spread 1 heaping tablespoon of this spinach spread on top of the untoasted side, sprinkle with 1 teaspoon of grated Parmesan cheese, and toast until the cheese is bubbling.

10 ounces fresh spinach (one 10-ounce bag), stemmed and rinsed
½ cup regular or low-fat sour cream
Salt and freshly ground pepper
⅛ teaspoon grated nutmeg

Place the spinach with the water still clinging to the leaves in a large skillet set over high heat. Cook for 4 to 5 minutes, stirring frequently, until wilted and softened. Drain the spinach in a colander and rinse with cold water to stop the cooking; drain again.

Place the spinach, sour cream, salt, pepper, and nutmeg in a food processor or blender and blend until smooth. Taste for seasoning. The spread will keep, covered and refrigerated, for 24 hours.

LUNCH: *Mediterranean Salad*

Preparation Time: 10 minutes
Cooking Time: 5 minutes
Yield: 2 servings

If you steam the beans ahead of time, you can put this salad together in about 5 minutes. Serve with toast, French bread, or crackers

   1 cup green beans, trimmed
   1 teaspoon prepared mustard
   Salt and pepper
   2 tablespoons balsamic or wine vinegar
   4 tablespoons olive oil
   2 cups assorted greens
   ⅓ cup crumbled or cubed feta or other cheese
   1 small red bell pepper, cut into slices

Place about 1 inch of water into a steamer or medium saucepan and bring to a boil. Add the beans and steam about 5 minutes, or until just tender. Drain and rinse under cold running water; drain again.

In the bottom of a medium salad bowl, mix the mustard with salt and pepper to taste. Mix in the vinegar and then the oil. Add the greens, then scatter on the beans, cheese, and pepper slices. Toss before serving.

DINNER: *Brazilian Beans and Rice*

Preparation Time: 10 minutes
Cooking Time: 15 minutes
Yield: 2 servings

Beans are high in iron and twice as rich in protein as grains. This dish transforms canned beans into an exciting dish with exotic flavors.

   1 cup quick-cooking white rice
   1 tablespoon olive oil
   1 medium red or white onion, finely chopped
   1 garlic clove, finely chopped (optional)
   1 teaspoon dried thyme
   ¼ teaspoon ground cumin
   Salt and pepper

1 15-ounce can black beans or white cannellini beans, drained and rinsed
1 cup chicken or vegetable broth
1 orange, cut into wedges
1 to 2 scallions, very thinly sliced

Place the rice and 2 cups cold water with a pinch of salt in a medium saucepan and bring to a boil over high heat. Reduce the heat and let simmer, covered, for about 10 minutes, or until the water is absorbed and the rice is tender.

Meanwhile, heat the oil in a large skillet over medium heat. Add the onion, garlic, thyme, cumin, and salt and pepper to taste, and sauté about 5 minutes, or until the onion wilts. Stir frequently to keep the onion from browning. Add half the beans and the broth and, using a masher or the back of a spoon, mash the beans into the broth and onion. Let simmer about 5 minutes, or until thickened. Add the remaining beans and let simmer another 5 minutes, or until heated through. Taste for seasoning.

Serve the beans on top of the rice, surrounded by the orange wedges, and sprinkle with scallions.

Easing into Exercise You can begin eating well right after you have your baby, but exercise is something you need to ease into. One thing you can do soon after birth is resume (or begin if you skimped before) your daily dose of Kegels (see "HOW TO: Kegels," page 172). These will help strengthen your vaginal muscles.

Once you're feeling a little more rested, some daily stretches or a walk around the block with the stroller may actually invigorate you. Hold off on aerobic exercises, however, until you get your doctor's OK at your six-week postpartum checkup.

The gentle exercises that follow focus on stretching and on toning those classic postpregnancy trouble spots: the tummy and thighs.

WARM-UPS

Full-Body Stretch
For a full-body stretch, lie on your back with arms relaxed at your sides.

1. Stretch arms up over your head.
2. Point your toes.
3. Hold for a count of 5.
4. Relax and repeat.

Q & A

"My doctor says I have diastasis and should hold off on exercising. What is this and how can I make it go away?"

Diastasis is an abdominal condition that sometimes occurs after childbirth. There are two muscles in your abdominal wall called recti abdominis muscles. These side-by-side muscles, which stretch vertically, can separate during pregnancy; even nonstrenuous exercise can aggravate the condition. To strengthen and repair the separation, your doctor will probably suggest that you either give it some time to heal on its own or hurry it along with the following regime: lie on your back with your knees bent, hands over your stomach. Breathe in. Put gentle pressure on the two muscles and push them toward each other as you exhale. Simultaneously, lift your head slowly. Don't strain.

Gentle exercises to heal a diastasis. Lie on your back with your knees bent, hands over your stomach. Breathe in. Put gentle pressure on the two muscles and push them toward each other as you exhale. Simultaneously, lift your head slowly. Don't strain. (Always ask your doctor before trying any new exercise.)

Seated Full-Body Stretch

To focus your warm-up on your upper body, sit in a cross-legged yoga position. This two-part stretch will really get the boulders out of your shoulders and will unkink your neck. To start, your back should be straight but not rigid, your hands resting on your knees, your breathing and body relaxed.

1. Raise your shoulders up to your ears, count to 5, release. Repeat.

Seated full-body stretch, step 1.

Seated full-body stretch, step 2.   *Seated full-body stretch, step 3.*

2. Let your head fall forward for part two. Bring your chin as close to your chest as possible, without strain.
3. Slowly raise your head and bring your right ear to your right shoulder.
4. Return your head to the center and repeat the movement to the left.
5. Repeat five times, each time remembering to suck in your belly, but keep the rest of your body relaxed.

BELLY SHAPERS

Pelvic Tilt

Almost anyone who's had a baby in recent years has heard of the pelvic tilt. The trick to this abdominal exercise is to always breathe through it, and to keep the movements small and controlled. Lie on your back with your knees bent and arms relaxed at your sides. Your lower back should be touching the floor.

1. Breathe in through your nose.
2. Exhale through your mouth, while pushing your lower back to the floor.
3. Tighten your abdominal muscles.
4. Raise your pelvis 1 or 2 inches off the floor (no higher!).
5. Tighten your vaginal muscles (like doing a Kegel).
6. Hold for a count of 2.
7. Relax.
8. Repeat five times.

Pelvic tilt, step 2

Pelvic tilt, step 4.

Seated Pelvic Tilt

This is basically a sitting-up version of the pelvic tilt.

1. Sit yoga style with hands relaxed on your knees. Always inhale through your nose, and exhale through your mouth at the beginning of each repetition.
2. Roll your head and spine forward while tightening your stomach muscles.
3. Inhale and begin the roll back up.
4. Repeat the exercise, but this time Kegel your vaginal muscles.
5. Alternate the two moves, for a total of six repetitions.

Seated pelvic tilt, step 1.

Seated pelvic tilt, step 2.

LEG STRETCHES

1. Sit on the floor with your legs straight out in front of you. Your back should be straight but relaxed. This exercise will firm your thighs and give your whole leg a nice stretch.
2. Put your hands on your right knee and slide it up and toward you. Your foot should remain flat on the ground.
3. Lift your left foot 1 inch off the ground.
4. Point your toes and draw circles with your left foot, first 10 in one direction, then in the other.
5. Repeat with the other leg.

1.

2.

3.

How Dad Is Feeling

The new father probably feels a lot like Mom: he's tired, overwhelmed, incredibly proud, worried about the cost of college. But there's something else to add to his list: Dad may be feeling left out. In most families, Mom is the primary caregiver. The baby spends a lot more time with her, especially if she's breastfeeding. And if Dad works all day, he's probably coming home right about the time that Baby is most out of sorts and Mom is most exhausted. Not a great welcome.

Dads and babies need their own special time to get to know each other.

It may be harder for a new mom to let the new father "help" than it is to do everything herself—not because Dad is incompetent, but because Mom is

HOW TO
Get Dad Involved

Many new fathers are eager to play an equal role in caring for the new baby, but either they don't know exactly what to do or their wives—unwittingly—just won't give them a chance. Break the cycle with the following tactics.

- Have Dad join in when you play with, feed, or bathe the baby. Eventually he'll be confident enough to do these things on his own.
- If your breastfed baby fusses every time you give her to Dad, make sure she's been fed before the handoff. That way she won't be looking for breasts that aren't there.
- Suggest that your partner put on the baby carrier or sling and get close to your infant that way.
- Don't just pass off the baby to Dad when she's cranky and expect either of them to have a good time. Wait until they're both in a good mood to get them bonding.
- Encourage Dad to do the night feeding if your baby is on formula or to fetch the baby if you're breastfeeding.
- Don't criticize your partner. Let him find out the best way for him to hold the baby or to sing a good-night song. Besides, there are several "right" ways to do almost anything.
- Give him time alone with his child. If you pop in all the time, the baby will be distracted by your voice.

⤙⤍ A FATHER'S VIEW ⤏⤚

"My Life as a Dad"

Before he became a father, Tom Lombardo's household chores were a cinch. His wife, Hope Dlugozima, cooked dinner and he cleaned up afterward.

That all changed with the arrival of baby Lucy. "For the first three months, I did all the cooking, cleaning, diaper changing, and clothes washing," says the Portland, Oregon, dad, who had arranged to work from home during that time. He and Hope had agreed that her postpartum jobs would be limited to nursing the baby, eating, and sleeping. And Tom did all the rest.

The "rest" included getting Lucy back to sleep each night. "Whenever she woke, Hope would nurse her and then go back to sleep. I would deal with Lucy," Tom says.

After Lucy's 5 A.M. feeding, Tom would head to his computer to do a little work, with Lucy snuggled up next to him in her baby bundler—a piece of cloth 10 feet long and 2 feet wide. "Sitting there at the computer and looking down at her on my chest was really special," says Tom. Lulled by the heat of her daddy and the sound of his heart, Lucy would nap until her 8 A.M. feeding.

By the end of three months, Lucy's sleep habits had changed considerably and everyone began getting more rest. "Looking back at that time, I think: 'That was a lot of work,' " says Tom. "But I also felt joy, elation, and responsibility."

Tom's tips for surviving—and enjoying—the first chaotic months with baby:

- **Don't expect to accomplish too much.** If by the end of the day, all Tom had managed to do was feed his family, that was still a good day in his eyes. He didn't even try to keep up with his former workout schedule or to plan major outings.
- **Remain calm.** Lucy cried less than Tom expected she would, in part because he didn't get upset at every peep. During long sleepless nights, he'd remind himself that Lucy was making steady progress toward better sleeping habits.
- **Establish bedtime routines.** Tom made it his goal to teach Lucy that nighttime meant sleep time. He'd experiment with different methods of inducing sleep, including the white-noise theory. "One night I ran the dishwasher four times, but it didn't work," he says. A trick that did: Tom would slip a heating pad into the baby's crib while she was being fed, then scoot it out when it was time to tuck Lucy back in. "She liked returning to a warm bed," he says.

putting superwoman pressure on herself and feels inadequate if she's not "doing it all." Sharing the baby—and the chores—is well worth the effort. Having two loving and competent caregivers benefits the baby and won't diminish Mom's special place in a newborn's heart.

Sex After Baby

We don't stop being sexual beings just because we've become parents. So why all the stereotypical stories about poor old Dad never getting enough sex? The truth is, it may take quite a while before the new parents get back into the sexual swing of things. And Mom *and* Dad may be too pooped to pop. According to a University of Wisconsin study of 570 new parents, on average the couples waited until about seven weeks postpartum before having sexual intercourse. When Mom was breastfeeding, couples waited until the eighth week. Only 17 percent of parents had intercourse the month following childbirth. That's not surprising given the physical hurdles—vaginal soreness, lochia discharge, leaking breasts, hormonal imbalances, sleep deprivation—facing new moms. Many women feel more comfortable waiting until after their six-week checkup before they even start thinking about resuming sexual relations.

That doesn't mean that you can't have a sexual relationship with your partner. According to the very frank Wisconsin study, during the first month after having a baby 65 percent of the women participated in petting with their partner; 34 percent performed oral sex on their partner. Just kissing, hugging, or giving each other a massage can help you feel connected. Even if you don't feel like making love, you can focus on loving.

Common Postpartum Concerns About Sex

• **Intercourse will hurt.** If you've had stitches to repair an episiotomy or tear, your vagina may still feel tender. Although the stitches typically heal within four weeks, it can be months before the soreness completely disappears. The missionary position can put pressure right where you're the most sore, so now might be the time to try some other positions.

Vaginal dryness can also cause painful intercourse. After delivery, your vaginal lining thins; breastfeeding further aggravates the situation by inhibiting natural lubrication. Using lubricated condoms, K-Y jelly, or a made-for-sex lubricant can help ease the dryness. So can prolonging foreplay to give your body a chance to respond. If pain during intercourse persists, tell your doctor.

• **My vagina will be stretched out.** Luckily, the vagina is a very elastic organ. It stretches during delivery and shrinks afterward. Kegel exercises will also help you rebuild and tone the muscles in your vagina.

• **I'll never find the energy to have sex.** Yes, you will. But give yourself some time. You deserve to be tired after the physical and emotional demands you've weathered. Try to conserve your resources and channel your limited energy. Which would you rather have—a clean house or an intimate night with your husband? Plan ahead for such time together.

• **My husband won't be attracted to me anymore.** Many women are turned off by their new nonpregnant body, but

HOW TO

Kegels

If you've been doing this pelvic exercise throughout pregnancy, you're probably already a pro. If not, to firm up your vaginal muscles, do the following in sets of three to five as often as possible.

1. Firmly tense your vaginal and anal muscles, as if you were trying to restrict the flow of urine.
2. Count to 5.
3. Relax.

To see how well you're doing, you can also try this exercise while urinating. Your goal is to stop and hold the stream of urine until the count of 5.

most husbands don't seem to find their wives any less sexy. If he's reluctant to have sex, he may be sensing your lack of interest or struggling with his own fatigue and the demands of new fatherhood. And he may still be in such awe of your birthing talents that he's a little intimidated. After all, you've become more than just his wife; you're now the mother of your child, and that's a big deal (for both of you). Talking frankly about how you feel about each other and about sex can help clear the air.

What You Need to Know About . . . Birth Control

Most women aren't ready to think about conceiving again (or even having sex) during the first weeks after birth. Still, it's not too soon to be thinking about what sort of contraception you'll want to use once you resume having sex. If you're nursing, don't count on that as your method of birth control. While nursing is commonly believed to be effective, most doctors don't recommend it. It's true that many breastfeeding moms don't get a period until months after they wean, but nursing's effect on ovulation varies greatly from woman to woman. And some women even ovulate without having a period.

Some breastfeeding proponents do argue that breastfeeding is at least as effective as the pill, but you have to follow the rules: have a baby who is less than 6 months old, exclusively breastfeed the baby (no formula at all), consistently breastfeed *at least* every five hours. But it's best not to count on this as your sole method of contraception.

Your gynecologist will probably ask you about birth control at your six-week checkup and may discuss the options with you. Any method of birth control is effective only if you use it consistently and correctly.

New parents who don't have the energy to make love can still concentrate on loving time together.

Birth Control Methods

METHOD	ADVANTAGES	DISADVANTAGES
Oral contraceptives	Most effective except for sterilization; great for spontaneity; diminished cramping and PMS; periods become very regular	Need to take every day to be effective; side effects may include bloating, weight changes, breast tenderness, hair loss; not OK to take during breastfeeding unless you use a progestin-only brand; not recommended for women over 35, smokers, or women with a history of cancer, heart attack, stroke, migraines, blood clots, fibroids; may inhibit fertility for a few months after you stop taking it; prescription needed

METHOD	ADVANTAGES	DISADVANTAGES
Norplant	Effective for five years; great for spontaneity; safe for nursing moms if milk supply is established (after six weeks)	Expensive: $500–$700; requires doctor visit for implantation and removal; some problems/pain with removal have been reported
Depo-Provera	Good for spontaneity; lasts three months; safe for nursing moms once feeding has been established	Requires an injection every 3 months in doctor's office; may have side effects: weight gain, irregular periods, fatigue; may take a year or more to regain fertility
Diaphragm	Effective barrier method when used with a contraceptive jelly; used only when needed; doesn't interfere with nursing; may help prevent pelvic inflammatory disease and spread of STDs	Must be reinserted with contraceptive jelly before intercourse each time; some women find inserting it messy and a turnoff; has to stay in 8 hours after intercourse but no longer than 12 hours for best results; increases chances of urinary tract infection and toxic shock syndrome; needs to be fitted by doctor and refitted after childbirth
Male condom	Available without prescription; reduces risk of STDs and AIDS; doesn't interfere with breastfeeding; doesn't	Not ideal for spontaneity; care must be taken when putting it on; not as effective without use of spermicide

METHOD	ADVANTAGES	DISADVANTAGES
Male condom (continued)	require refitting after childbirth; can be used with lubrication to increase post-partum comfort	
Female condom	Available without prescription; reduces risk of STDs and AIDS	Not widely available; not ideal for spontaneity; care must be taken when putting it on; not as effective without use of spermicide
Spermicides	Inexpensive; easily available; don't interfere with breastfeeding	Much less effective alone than when used with barrier methods; messy
Natural family planning	Free; sanctioned by some religious groups; totally natural; more reliable than calendar-rhythm method, which it has replaced	Work intensive (checking and charting consistency of vaginal mucus, color of cervix, basal temperature); lots of room for error
Vasectomy or tubal ligation	Permanent; safe; allows for spontaneity	Life-changing decision for men and women; expensive; can't count on reversing it, if you change your mind; involves surgery

Dealing with Unwanted Advice

Everybody—your mother, your mother-in-law, your great-aunt, the elderly woman in the checkout line behind you—wants to put in her two cents about how you should care for your newborn. The advice may be well-meaning but old-fashioned and inaccurate. Here's how to rebut the most common (and erroneous) beliefs from days gone by.

- **"You're spoiling that baby. You shouldn't pick her up every time she cries."** These days, few people believe you can spoil an infant. Picking up a baby every time she cries gives her the security she needs to grow and develop.
- **"All you're feeding that baby is breast milk?! That can't be enough."** A baby *can* live on breast milk alone. If your mother didn't breastfeed (and it was out of style for several decades, so she may not have), she'll be convinced that your baby's nutritional needs aren't being met. Tell her that breast milk is absolutely the best food for your baby and that your doctor and even the formula makers agree.
- **"Put another blanket on the baby; she's going to catch cold."** Babies (or adults) don't catch a cold from being cold. And too many blankets on a baby can cause him to overheat, which raises the risks of SIDS. Don't overbundle; if your baby feels cool, add a light layer.
- **"I always fed my babies water; you should too."** Babies don't need water. If they're drinking enough formula or breast milk, they're getting all the liquids (and nourishment) they need.
- **"Give him a little cereal to help him sleep. In my day, we never waited until six months to introduce solid food."** Introducing solids early can cause or aggravate food sensitivities and may not deliver the nutrition your baby needs (especially if he's not keen on eating from a spoon). Plus, there is no guarantee that a baby will sleep better. Wait until six months before beginning solids.
- **"I'd break her of that thumb-sucking right now before it ruins her teeth."** At this age, it's perfectly acceptable for a baby to use a pacifier or suck her thumb. She won't ruin her teeth or develop a permanent dependency. If you're lucky, she just may learn to soothe herself.
- **"You slept on your tummy when you were a baby and nothing bad happened to you."** Yes, but there's now strong evidence that back sleeping greatly reduces the chances of SIDS. Why take the chance?
- **"Just feed her every four hours. Don't let her push you around so much."** To ensure that she's getting enough milk, a baby should be fed on demand until he's at least 3 months old. Forcing a schedule on one so young can deprive him of adequate nutrition. Once he's a little older, he'll develop a feeding schedule. Not to mention that the more responsive you are, the more your baby will understand and begin to trust his environment.
- **"It's never too early to get started on toilet training. I had you trained by the time you were eleven months old."** It's more likely that it was your mom who was trained back then than you as a baby. Potty training shouldn't begin until a child shows signs of readiness, usually after she's 2 years old. Before then you're wasting your time and putting unnecessary pressure on your baby.

• **"That baby will grow up bowlegged if you keep standing him up like that."** Nope. Most babies have bowed legs because they were all curled up in utero. And a tendency toward bowed legs is sometimes inherited. Blame it on your baby's youth or on Great Grandma Edna, not on lap bouncing or the Johnny Jump-up.

Even when you have a quick comeback, child-rearing advice from relatives, especially your own mother (or mother-in-law), can make you feel thoroughly inadequate. Criticism that doesn't bother you when other folks, even your friends, say it may seem harsh and mean when it comes from your mom. Many of us are still looking for approval from our parents, even when we become parents ourselves, so it's painful to feel we're not measuring up.

To avoid constant hurt feelings and battles over your mothering skills, try to take the advice in the spirit it's offered. Explain why you're doing what you're doing. Say thanks and then do whatever *you* want. If Grandma won't take a hint and back down, try the empathic approach and see if she remembers the advice

THE BIGGEST THRILL WAS
Surviving the First 24 Hours at Home

Breastfeeding
"After nursing became easier, it was the most incredible experience. There is nothing like knowing that my daughter was growing because of me and only me! I knew I'd love my baby, but I wasn't prepared for the intensity of the feeling. I felt like my head and my heart would burst."

—*Carolyn Gruning-Jones, Blackwood, NJ*

That Sweet Smile
"When Grant first came home, my hormones were out of whack, and I got extremely depressed. For three days I felt helpless and lost. I'd cry all the time. But when he first smiled at me, it melted my heart. When my postpartum depression lifted, I was overcome with happiness."

—*Heather Goff, Memphis, TN*

Discovering the Baby's Personality
"I thought we'd be dealing with a blank slate, but Eva had a strong will right from the start—she absolutely refused to be held in the cradle position. She wanted to be propped up over the shoulder so that she could look around."

—*Rebecka Wright, San Francisco, CA*

⤳ A MOTHER'S VIEW ⤳

"My New Bond with Mom"

"**I**'ve always been very close with my mother, but after the birth of Vedika, I appreciated her even more," says Jyoti Gopal of Riverdale, New York.

She had read that the beginning of parenthood should be a time for husband and wife to be alone with their new baby, but Jyoti felt incredibly lucky to have her parents stay with them during Vedika's first six months.

"Even with a really supportive husband, having my parents there made everything so much easier," she recalls. Her parents cooked, cleaned, and took over all household responsibilities so that Jyoti could rest.

Jyoti's mom didn't just bathe, massage, and pamper the baby. "She gave me oil massages and pampered me, too," says Jyoti. "I was still her daughter even though I was a mother," she says.

Jyoti's tips for postpartum bonding with your mother:

- **Let yourself be helped.** Jyoti was very open-minded about letting her parents help in any way they could. She wasn't overly possessive of her baby, and was thrilled to have someone else take charge of her household.
- **Gain a new perspective.** Once Jyoti became a mother, she felt she better understood her own mother. "It used to bug me when she worried about me, but now I was worrying about my own daughter in the same way," says Jyoti.
- **Don't expect perfection.** Jyoti's greater connection with her mom didn't end the arguments that always characterized their relationship. "We just argue about different things, now," laughs Jyoti. "We argue about how much clothing to put on Vedika and how hot the water should be for her bath!"

she got as a new mom, and how that made her feel. If you remind her how important it was for her to feel good about her own parenting skills, maybe she'll better understand how her criticism is making you feel.

If all else fails, tell her that it's on doctor's orders that you're picking up the baby each time she cries or feeding on demand. She may respect her authority enough to keep her comments to herself. Or focus on the baby's development and avoid the kind of hot-button topics (feeding, crying, potty training) that usually end in a difference of opinion. Once you gain more confidence in your mothering skills, you'll care a lot less about what others think.

I WISH I'D KNOWN

About Disposable Panties
"I laughed when I first saw those ads for disposable panties—until I realized how much you bleed those first few weeks! Then I bought lots of them. I certainly didn't have time to change the sheets and wash loads of panties, and they put my mind at ease."

—Jo Anna Koreiba, Nashville, TN

About Postpartum Depression
"After about a week at home, out of nowhere I was hit with this uncontrollable urge to cry. And it wouldn't go away. I felt as if my life was over. I fought the feeling for three days and then broke down and called my mother. I answered her question of 'What's wrong?' with a teary 'I don't know!' She told me I had postpartum depression. I got through it by talking with a nurse at my OB's office for about half an hour. She put into words everything I was going through and feeling, and I finally felt like somebody understood."

—Sherry Robinson, Tulsa, OK

About Emergency C-Sections
"I was extremely disappointed that I had to have a C-section. I never considered the possibility that it would happen to me. And most of the ones I read about were planned. The hardest part was right after my daughter was born. I could hear her crying, but I could see nothing. It seemed like an eternity before the nurse brought her to me. I was so tired I could barely make her out, and then she was swept off to the nursery. After I went home with the baby, I talked to lots of moms who'd had emergency C-sections. They hadn't told me because they didn't want to scare me while I was pregnant. I think it would have been comforting to know that my C-section was not an unusual case."

—Virginia Sicari, Lake Parsippany, NJ

More than ever, your baby is learning to communicate her needs.

CHAPTER 3

MONTHS FOUR THROUGH SIX

It's amazing how much a baby grows and changes in his first months. The next time you see a newborn, you'll marvel at how large and grown-up your baby looks in comparison. The new baby appears curled up and content to look inward; your older infant is all roving arms and legs and eyes. At the ripe old age of 4 to 6 months, he would rather embrace the world than shut it out. Your job as a parent is to provide the novelty he needs to keep stimulated, without sacrificing the familiarity he needs to feel safe.

In spite of (or maybe because of) how much and how quickly your baby is developing, your life together is still quite a roller-coaster ride. Sleeping and feeding patterns may be settling down, but are still erratic. Your confidence level as a parent may be high one day and rock-bottom the next. Just remind yourself that although *regularity* is not a word used often to describe the first six months of a baby's life, later in the year you'll look back with fondness on those months before your little one began eating dustballs and scaling walls.

By the end of six months your baby will probably* . . .

- Sample his first food that's not white
- Roll from front to back and back to front
- Give you at least one baby-proofing scare
- Have doubled his birthweight
- Sleep five hours at a stretch at night
- Enjoy sitting in a high chair
- Have given you some pretty strong clues about his emerging personality

By the end of six months, you will probably . . .

- Still be catching up on lost sleep

*Every baby is different and has his or her own developmental timetable.

- Have found several hundred things to already feel guilty about as a parent
- Have changed more than 1,000 diapers
- Know the doctor's office phone number by heart
- Have developed a sense of humor about your baby's impeccable timing: he saves big spit-ups and blowouts for right after you've changed him
- Have noticed how you and your partner have different parenting styles
- Have lived through one major holiday with your baby

CARE AND FEEDING

You've finally mastered breastfeeding—or know just how your baby likes his bottle—and now you have to think about introducing cereal? You've learned to live with spit-up, but now he's started drooling? You've fallen in love with that gummy smile, and now he's getting a tooth? Life with baby keeps you hopping.

Demand and Supply

During the next few months, feeding—which may have felt like a round-the-clock exercise in the past—will ease into a more predictable pattern. At first, your baby will still have periods when she seems insatiable (possibly during growth spurts at around 3 months and again around 6 months), but after the introduction of cereal and fruit in months 5 and 6, the days of nonstop feeding should be history. And as your baby goes longer between feedings, it will be easier for you to schedule some of her meals to match the rest of the family's.

If you wish to evolve from feeding on demand to more scheduled feedings, it will be useful to learn the difference between the "I'm hungry" cry and the "I'm wet" or "I'm bored" cries. Some parents discover that their baby's hunger cry has its own distinctive cry-pause-cry-pause rhythm, which helps them know how to respond. If your baby's cries all sound alike, rule out other reasons she may be crying before you feed her. If she stops crying when you pick her up, and stays happy for a while, she probably wasn't crying out of hunger. If you can distract her with a little game or a diaper change, you'll know she's not starving. In that way, you'll begin to stretch the time between feedings. If she continues to cry, by all means feed her.

What You Need to Know About . . . Water

Drinking lots of water, which we know is one of the healthiest things an adult can do, is *not* recommended for babies. In fact, if your baby is 6 months or younger, she's probably getting all the fluids and nutrients she needs from formula or breast

YOUR BABY'S WORLD

In months 4 through 6, your baby's curiosity grows right along with her developing senses and skills. Now that she can touch and hold an object, she'll use her fingers and—as she gets more adept—her mouth to learn all she can about shape, texture, and taste.

What Your Baby Sees. Your baby's eyes should be in alignment now. She'll follow or track an object with both eyes as it moves. And she's now able to spy Mom from 4 feet away.

What Your Baby Tastes. Your baby still has her inborn taste for sweets and dislike for bitterness. Soon, she'll have her first taste of cereal, more of a texture than a taste sensation.

What Your Baby Hears. During months 4 through 6, your baby will turn toward the familiar voices she hears and appear to be listening. If you don't observe this behavior in your baby, consult the pediatrician (see "Do You Hear What I Hear," page 213).

What Your Baby Feels. Your baby is exploring what the world feels like with her mouth, as well as with her hands and feet. In fact, she's using her whole body.

What Your Baby Likes. It's time to play! Your baby is now fascinated with lots of playthings, including ring toys, rattles, your hair, and her own fingers. She likes a good view of the world, so turn her around in her sling so she's facing forward.

LIFE WITH ESTEBAN

Follow along with new mother Grege Lastra's month-by-month diary of her first year of motherhood.

MONTH 4

At Esteban's fourth-month well-baby checkup, he weighed 18 pounds and measured 27¼ inches. He was pretty irritable after his shots and was very protective of his little thigh. Every time I went near it, he growled to keep me away. He's teething so much now that I change his clothes at least four times a day. His drooling saturates everything.

At 6 months, Esteban grabs for a toy, plays with it, then demands another. When he wants something, he swings his hands and lets out a big squeal. His newest trick: kissing Mommy.

Esteban is so alert now. He looks over right away when someone walks into the room. He loves to be tickled around his neck. When our dog barks, he laughs. In fact, he laughs at me constantly—I'm like a big toy to him. He also loves to watch Knicks games on TV, sitting between his dad's legs. I have to perform for Esteban to get him to react to me. But he and his dad just seem to chill out together.

MONTH 5

Esteban really knows what he likes and what he doesn't. When he wants something, he swings his hands and lets out a big squeal. He gets really aggravated when I can't figure out what he wants right away. He grabs for a toy, plays with it, then demands another. He hates a dirty or wet diaper, so I'm constantly changing him. And he hates being on his stomach. When I place him tummy down, he immediately rolls over. He does a lot of rolling around, but he doesn't push up on his knees yet.

MONTH 6

Esteban is eating rice cereal, and loves peaches and pears—but we avoid bananas because they make him constipated. He's now starting on green vegetables. He's an eager eater, a bottomless pit. He's been a little piggie ever since he was born—and it all seems to go straight to his adorable chubby cheeks.

Esteban's new thing these days is "kissing" me. He opens his mouth, grabs at my face, and then gently gums me everywhere—my chin, my cheeks, my nose. It's so sweet. These are special mom kisses—he doesn't do this to anyone else.

milk. If she's formula fed, limit her water intake to no more than 4 to 6 ounces a day. Breastfed infants don't need any additional water.

Why limit water intake? Recent studies have shown that babies' kidneys can't quickly and efficiently flush water out of their systems. If they get too much water, it dilutes the sodium in their blood, which can cause a condition called *water intoxication*. Call your doctor if your baby experiences any symptoms of water intoxication: puffy face or body, seizures, irritability, or a change in sleeping patterns.

IS IT TRUE THAT . . .

Breastfed Babies Eat More Often than Formula-Fed Babies?
This is often the case, but not for the reason you may think. Infants who are breastfed don't dine more often because they're eating less at each feeding. The simple truth is that breast milk is digested more easily and quickly than formula. Once the digestion process is finished, a baby becomes hungry all over again. For this reason, the addition of a little cereal—which takes longer to digest—can really help breastfed babies lengthen the time they can go between feedings, and that's a happy day for many nursing moms.

HOW TO
Convert a Bottle-Hater

If you have a baby who turns up his nose at the sight of a bottle, try this:

- Serve breast milk in the bottle early on once breastfeeding is well established (after 6 weeks).
- If you're trying to wean from breast milk to formula, start out with breast milk in the bottle and make a slow transition to formula in the bottle.
- Have your partner or someone else do the bottle feeding. Your baby may associate you so strongly with a feeding from the breast that he's too distracted to try the bottle.
- Smear a bit of your breast milk onto the bottle's nipple.
- Try different kinds of nipples. You may find that your baby prefers a certain nipple shape or hole size.
- Introduce the bottle at different times: breastfeed for a tiny bit to take the edge off his hunger, then switch to a bottle. Or wait until your baby is so hungry that he'll care less about the delivery system.
- Try offering him breast milk or formula in a cup.

For more information about weaning a baby, see Chapter 4.

Once your baby is 6 months or older, it's OK to offer her an occasional cup of water. If she's dehydrated from diarrhea or vomiting, offer her a rehydration beverage (such as Pedialyte), or a Popsicle, instead of water.

From Liquids to Solids

The transition from liquids only to solids is a very big deal in a new parent's life. Maybe that's why they're so eager to get on with it. Or maybe it's owing to the continued influence of past child-rearing customs that encouraged rushing everything, from starting cereal to potty training. When we were kids, before doctors and nutritionists knew better, our mothers started spoon-feeding us long before the age that's considered acceptable today. Parental fatigue may also play a part in our eagerness: we think that if we feed our babies a few more calories, they'll be full enough that they'll sleep through the night (which sometimes does work).

As with so many other things, your baby won't jump on the solid-food bandwagon until he's good and ready. The transition from liquids to solids really takes more than a year, from about 4 months to 24 months. In the 4 months through 6 months period, it's more like a liquids-to-mush transition.

The American Academy of Pediatrics suggests that a baby be 6 months or older before you start him on solid food.

CHECKLIST
Is Your Baby Ready for Solid Food?

You'll know your infant is ready for solids if:

✔ He watches every bite you take. Babies show their developing interest in solid foods by hungrily eyeing the food on the table, on your plate, and on your fork.
✔ He wakes up in the night hungry. If he's been sleeping a solid block at night, reverting to an interest in a middle-of-the-night feeding could be a sign that he needs more to sustain him.
✔ He cries for more after a feeding. The baby who eats 32 ounces or more a day of breast milk or formula, and still isn't satisfied, is probably ready for solids.

So, how can you tell whether or not your baby is ready for his first bite of cereal? It's more than just a question of age. The American Academy of Pediatrics now recommends that a baby be 6 months old before you start him on cereal. Watch him for cues (see "CHECKLIST: Is Your Baby Ready for Solid Food?" page 186), and keep in mind the following:

- A baby won't be able to eat well from a spoon until he loses his tongue-thrust reflex. When you first start spoon-feeding your baby, you'll notice that his tongue pushes out anything solid (including the spoon) that tries to go in. This was an inborn reflex, possibly to prevent choking. If he continues pushing out the spoon and spitting out the cereal, give it a rest and try again in a few weeks. Don't try to overpower the tongue thrust.
- A baby's energy needs increase as he ages and grows, but his digestive system also has to be mature enough to tolerate solid foods. Even if your baby is guzzling down more than 32 ounces of milk a day before the 6-month mark, his system may not be able to handle the introduction of solid foods until at least 4 months and sometimes several months later.
- Although food allergies are relatively rare, some doctors believe that introducing new foods before a baby is ready may make him more susceptible. If you have a family history of food allergies, the pediatrician may recommend that you wait until your baby is a little older to introduce cereal.
- The better your baby can sit, the more comfortable (and safe) he'll be eating from a spoon. If he hasn't moved into a high chair (which usually happens around 6 months), make sure he's secure in an infant seat when you begin to spoon-feed. (A booster seat is not safe for this use; boosters are intended for a toddler who's too big for his high chair but too small for an adult chair.)

The Best First Foods Because your baby's tender taste buds aren't ready for a lot of flavor or texture (and his tummy can digest only foods that are easily broken down), you'll be living in bland-land for a while. And that makes rice cereal—the big daddy of bland—the perfect first food for your infant. Iron-fortified rice cereal also delivers a much-needed supplement and isn't likely to cause an allergic reaction. Mix a few flakes of the cereal with breast milk or formula and—voilà!—you have your baby's first solid-food feast. Actually it's more like a soup than a solid food; for beginners, the thinner the mixture the better.

That's not to say that he'll smack his lips and dig right in. Rare is the baby who doesn't have some trouble figuring out what that spoon is doing in his mouth.

CHECKLIST

High-Chair Do's and Don'ts

Do

✔ Buy a high chair that meets the standards of the Juvenile Product Manufacturers Association (JPMA). An approved high chair will carry a JPMA label.

✔ Make sure that your high chair of choice has all the necessary safety features: wide-spaced legs to make it stable, a safety belt with a crotch strap that's impossible for a baby to undo, and a tray that attaches firmly. Also be certain that it has no sharp edges.

✔ See that your high chair (if it's a folding model) has a locking mechanism that prevents it from folding up or collapsing while in use. These models are more lightweight, but still should be strong enough to support 100 pounds.

✔ Use the safety strap and tray every time your baby is in the high chair.

✔ Consider buying a high-chair pad if you have a wooden model. It will cushion your baby's back and bottom and may make him feel more secure.

It's a big day when your baby (6 months or older) can sit up in a high chair and join the family table. Just make sure he's belted in securely and you have a towel ready for the inevitable flying food.

Don't

✔ Put your baby into a high chair before she's ready. She needs to have the neck strength to hold her head up and the torso strength to stay balanced. Most babies are trying to sit up by the time they're 6 or 7 months old.

✔ Substitute a booster or other seat designed for an older baby. Infants in the 5- to 8-month-old age range need a true high chair that gives them lots of support.

✔ Leave your baby unattended in the high chair.

✔ Leave breakables, small items, or food you don't want your baby to sample on her high-chair tray.

And even diluted, the texture of rice cereal is a far cry from his liquid diet. After he spits out the first three spoonfuls, more than one exasperated new mother has wondered, *Now what?* Here are answers to common first-food questions:

• **How long before my baby catches on to eating from a spoon?** Give him several days to get used to the new experience. Use a spoon that's plastic covered, which may be less of a shock than hard, cold metal. If he remains totally uninterested or adamant about not wanting the spoon or cereal anywhere near him, put the spoon and cereal away for a few weeks and try again later.

• **Can I mix the cereal with water?** It's best to use breast milk or formula. For one thing, your baby is already familiar with the taste, which may make him more receptive to the cereal. For another, water doesn't provide the extra calories your baby needs to grow. Breast milk and formula also contain vitamin C, which will enhance the absorption of the iron in the cereal.

• **Does the cereal need to be iron-fortified?** It's a good idea. By 4 months and older, your baby has exhausted any stores of iron that he was born with. He relies on what he eats and drinks to provide essential nutrients.

• **How much cereal should he eat?** Follow your baby's cues. Even if he spits out most of it, or takes only one spoonful, that's fine. If he starts pushing away the spoon with his hand, or appears uninterested, he's telling you he's finished. Wait a little while, and follow up with a bottle or breastfeeding.

• **Should I serve cereal at every meal?** Doctors typically recommend that you begin by offering cereal at two feedings a day. First thing in the morning may not be wise, since your impatient baby may be very hungry. At bedtime he may be too cranky or tired. Cereal at lunch and dinner may help establish a sit-down-at-the-table feeding pattern. Serve the solid food first, before his usual beverage, so that he's not too full to try it.

• **How long should I wait before introducing another food?** The transition to solids is a slow introduction process that shouldn't be rushed. Offer cereal for a few weeks before moving on to anything else. Since this is your baby's first solid food, give her time to get the hang of spoon-feeding before you add more exotic fare. Many parents offer just cereal for a month and then move on to another pureed single-ingredient food after that. Wait three days to a week between new foods to make sure your baby isn't allergic (see "What You Need to Know About . . . Food Allergies," page 192).

• **What food should I offer after rice cereal?** You have a couple of options. Some doctors suggest that you try another single-ingredient cereal, such as oatmeal or barley. Or you could move on to fruits next. The fruit-first folks say that you'll be amazed at how your baby will chow down his rice cereal once a little fruit is added. The vegetables-first side claims that a baby introduced to fruit is likely to reject the less-sweet vegetables that follow. Most nutritionists say it doesn't much matter what you try next, although they agree that you should hold off on meats and poultry until your baby is 7 months or older. And you should always leave at least three days (and preferably a week) between new-food introductions. A rough schedule looks like this:

1. At 6 months: cereal. Mix 1 teaspoon of rice cereal with breast milk or formula. Wait several weeks and try another cereal, if you want. (Don't introduce wheat or mixed cereal until the end of the year.)

2. At 6–7 months: 1 teaspoon of pureed or strained fruit. Most parents start with applesauce, pears, bananas, or peaches. Wait a week or two between new fruits.

> ### Q & A
> ## "Can I feed my baby adult cereal?"
>
> Not a good idea. Although it's less expensive, adult cereal isn't a healthy substitute for infant cereal, which is iron fortified. Adult cereals don't have enough iron for little ones—and they don't contain the right kind of iron. Infant cereals are formulated such that the iron is easily absorbed.

3. At 6–7 months: vegetables. Start off slowly with a teaspoon of a yellow or orange vegetable (most babies love the sweetness of sweet potatoes). Other yellow or orange vegetables include carrots and squash. Follow with green veggies, such as green beans, peas, and avocado. Save mashed potatoes, thinned with breast milk or formula, for last. Don't offer corn and spinach, which are more likely to trigger allergies or cause gas.

4. At 7–9 months: pureed or strained meats, poultry, and beans such as lentils. Mashed egg yolks (don't serve the whites, which can cause allergies) are also a great source of protein. Don't offer them more than a few times a week, though.

5. At 6–9 months: unsalted crackers or teething biscuits if your child is teething. Babies love to gum these, but you should sweep up and discard the little bits that fall as your child is gnawing. The tiny pieces could cause her to choke. (For more on finger foods, see "Starting Finger Foods," page 252.)

• **Now that the baby is eating cereal and fruit, how much should I cut back on her liquid intake?** At first, you shouldn't cut back on fluids at all. Since it's a fairly minuscule amount of food that's actually making it into the mouths (and tummies) of babies this age, the solid food consumed isn't eliminating the need for breast milk or formula. Many babies continue to drink 32 ounces per day while they're slowly building their intake of solids. If you think your baby is rejecting solid food because he's full of milk, make sure you're offering the solid food first and the milk about an hour later.

If your baby seems to lose interest in the bottle or breast, make sure that he's still wetting enough diapers. It's rare, but a baby who fills up on solids may be taking in so few fluids that he's at risk of dehydration.

• **Is it possible to overfeed my baby?** Not if you follow his cues. If he's pushing away the spoon or bottle, spitting out his food, pursing his lips closed, or looking away from you, he's telling you he's had enough. Trust his instincts, even if he's eaten just a smidgen of food. If you're sneaking cereal into his bottle (which is a choking hazard and is not recommended), consistently ignoring his "I'm full" cues, or mistaking crying for hunger when it's signaling something else, you could be giving him more calories than he needs and helping to create a lifelong habit of overeating.

• **How do I know what sort of baby food to buy?** At this age, the simpler the baby food, the better (and you can always make your own). The fruits and vegetables that you introduce should be free of additives, sugar, and starch. They should be single-ingredient foods (not "combination" dinners). Here's what you can find out from a baby-food label:

1. *The main ingredient.* The item that's listed first is the main ingredient. If you're buying applesauce, this should be apples; bananas, if you're buying bananas, and so on. Sugar or water should not be a main ingredient (unless you're looking for a sweet dessert). Watch out for foods that list "modified tapioca starch." This isn't real tapioca; it's filler that's added to make the food smooth. It won't hurt your baby, but it also doesn't deliver any valuable nutrients.

2. *How much sugar the product contains.* Specifically you're interested in what kind of sugar the food has in it. Natural sugars from the fruit or vegetable are preferable to added sugars. By looking at the sugar information on the label, you can be sure that you're buying a fruit and not a fruit "dessert."

3. *The amount of fat in the food.* Fat count may be what you look at first when you're buying your own food, but it's not that big a deal when it comes to baby food. Babies *need* fat and cholesterol in their diets. In fact, to discourage weight- and

> **Q & A**
>
> ## "What's so different about 'organic' baby food?"
>
> For a food to be labeled organic, it must be free of chemicals. That means no fertilizers, hormones, or man-made pesticides can be used in its growth. Typically, that has also meant that the food will cost more.
>
> Some parents and nutritionists think that higher-priced organic food is worth it, especially for babies. Fans of organic baby food claim that during the first year of life children are especially vulnerable to potential carcinogens because their cells are growing rapidly and because, proportionately, they eat more than adults do.
>
> The alleged benefits of organic baby food, and organic food in general, are being researched. In the meantime, just consider organic baby food as another option, along with regular baby food and baby food that you make yourself.

fat-conscious parents from obsessing over this, only total fat counts (as opposed to breakdowns for saturated fat, cholesterol, and calories from fat) are printed on baby-food labels. Until your baby is 2 or older, don't worry about fat.

4. *Percentage of daily value.* The label will tell you how much of your baby's daily requirement of particular nutrients is provided by a serving (usually the full jar) of that food. This won't be that relevant to you at first, since your infant will begin by eating small spoonfuls (at best) of the food.

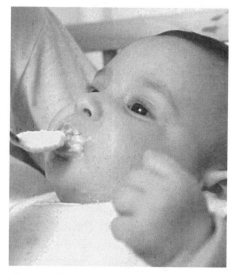

If your baby spits out his cereal and pushes out the spoon, he's telling you he's not ready for solids. Try again in a week or two.

• **What if my baby refuses to eat any solids?** Maybe your expectations are too high. Even if your baby appears to be spitting out three spoonfuls of every four, he's probably getting enough. A small spoonful or two of cereal constitutes a serving. Or maybe he's getting too much food in liquid form; a 6-month-old baby should drink about 32 ounces of formula or breast milk (four to five feedings for formula; five to eight feedings for breast milk) a day. If your baby is having more, cut back and offer a little cereal instead. Give him just a little to drink to satiate his hunger, then offer the solids. If he still refuses, don't force him. Try a few days later. If at 6 months old, he's still refusing cereal, is gagging on it, or seems to be in pain during or after a feeding, talk to your pediatrician.

What You Need to Know About . . . Food Allergies

Your baby's chances of having a food allergy are relatively slim; about 6 percent of children suffer from the problem. The foods most likely to trigger an allergic reaction are cow's milk, egg whites, strawberries, citrus fruits (including tomatoes), fish, spinach, wheat, peanuts, and corn. Since you're just at the stage of introducing cereal and pureed fruit, it's unlikely your baby will even encounter any of the foods with the highest allergy potential. (Egg whites and cow's milk shouldn't be given to a baby under a year old; it will be years before your child can safely eat peanuts, and even a spoonful of peanut butter is a choking hazard.)

Still, it's wise to get into the habit of introducing one new food at a time and keeping a food diary, so that if there is a reaction you can easily identify what may have caused it. Don't offer another new food for at least three days. Your

Baby's Daily Diet

A guide to what, when, and how much your baby should eat.

AGE	BREAST MILK OR FORMULA	CEREAL	FRUIT	BREAD	VEGGIES	MEAT/ PROTEIN
4–6 mos.	32 oz. (4–5 feedings of formula, 5-8 of breast milk)	1–2 servings (2–4 Tbs.)	1–2 servings (2–4 Tbs.)			
6–9 mos.	24–32 oz. (3–5 feedings of formula, 5–8 of breast milk)	2 servings (2–4 Tbs.)	1–2 servings (3–4 Tbs.)	teething biscuit, if necessary*	2 servings (3–4 Tbs.)	2 servings (1–2 Tbs.) Limit egg yolk to three times a week
9–12 mos.	16–24 oz. (3–4 feedings of formula, 6–8 of breast milk)	2 servings (2–4 Tbs.)	2 servings (3–4 Tbs.)	1/2 slice of bread or 1/4 cup of soft pasta	2 servings (3–4 Tbs.)	2 servings (2–3 Tbs.)

*Don't leave Baby alone with any sort of cracker or teething biscuit; to prevent choking, pick up and throw away any sharp corners or small pieces.

baby needs to be exposed to a potentially offending food a few times before she builds up antibodies to it (she may have "tasted" the food before via your breast milk, too). It's the antibodies that cause the allergic reaction, which can range from a skin rash or hives, to vomiting or diarrhea, to respiratory problems. To be linked to the food, the reaction should occur a few hours after it was eaten.

If you or your partner has a history of allergies—food, skin, or even hay fever—let your pediatrician know before your infant gets to the solid-food stage. Detecting and dealing with a food allergy is a complicated business. He may want you to take special precautions with your child or have her tested. Breastfeeding exclusively for the first 6 months is recommended for babies in families with allergies. After that, continue to breastfeed and introduce other foods per your pediatrician's recommendations.

Thankfully, kids often outgrow food allergies, although an allergy to peanuts or wheat may persist.

IS IT TRUE THAT . . .

Babies Shouldn't Have Honey? Yes, honey shouldn't be given to a baby until she is at least a year old. Besides being devoid of any necessary nutrients, honey contains spores that can cause botulism in babies. Though rarely fatal, infant botulism (which is different from adult botulism) can make your baby very sick, and may lead to a serious illness such as pneumonia. Symptoms of botulism include lethargy, lack of interest in sucking or eating, and constipation.

HOW TO

Make Your Own Baby Food

There's no real secret to making your own baby food, but there are a few tricks. Use high-quality fruits or vegetables (some parents choose to buy organic). And make sure that the food is smooth and lump-free.

For easy pureed apples
1. Peel, core, and slice 2 Red or Golden Delicious apples.
2. Cook the thin slices over low heat for 30 minutes in a tablespoon or two of water (just simmer gently, don't boil the water away).
3. Drain if necessary, and cool.
4. Mash the apples with a fork or puree them in a food processor or blender until smooth.

For sweet potato mush
1. Peel a large sweet potato and cut into small pieces.
2. Put in a saucepan with just enough water to cover; simmer for about 25 minutes.
3. Drain and cool.
4. Puree until smooth; add a little breast milk or formula if potatoes are too thick.

Tip: Spoon miniportions of homemade baby food into ice-cube trays and freeze for future use.

Preparing for the First Tooth

The addition of teeth can dramatically change your baby's appearance. One day your little one has that signature gummy smile; the next day he has a tooth and he looks so . . . grown up. *When* that first little pearl erupts all depends on your baby's personal timetable. Some babies' first tooth appears at 4 months; others (like my two late-bloomers) don't get one until they are a year or even 18 months old. That's OK. Either way, most babies have all their baby teeth between 28 and 36 months.

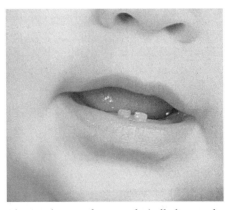

The two bottom front teeth (called central incisors) are usually the first to appear.

For some babies, sprouting a tooth is a cinch: they seem to experience no particular pain, don't fuss at all, and breeze through all 20 baby teeth. For other infants (and their parents), the whole teething process is one long, sodden, painful affair. There's no way of telling what sort of experience your baby is going to have (although if you got your teeth late, your baby may, too). There *are* ways, however, of telling if your baby is teething:

• Your usually cheery baby is really cranky and cries more than usual.
• His gums are swollen or red (or both), or have a small red or white sore spot (that's where the tooth will erupt).

DEFINITION
Baby-Bottle Syndrome

Some babies are so attached to their bottle, they suck on it day and night. The problem with using a bottle as a pacifier is that Baby's teeth are continually exposed to a bath of milk, which is an open invitation for decay. If he falls asleep drinking from his bottle, he may hold milk in his mouth all night long. This condition is actually misnamed, since breastfeeding babies may sleep all night long with milk in their mouths, too.

The solution is to remove the bottle or breast from baby's mouth and bring him up into burping position. This might encourage him to swallow or expel the unswallowed milk. It may also wake him up, so do it gently!

New research indicates that baby-bottle syndrome may not be the sole cause of such tooth decay. But until more is known, it's best to avoid letting a child fall asleep with milk in his mouth.

- He's drooling copiously. Although babies naturally begin to drool more after 4 months—when their salivary glands kick in—excess drool is produced during teething because the salivary glands treat the incoming tooth like a piece of food: let's get that thing really wet so we can swallow and digest it.
- He's waking in the night (after going through a period of sleeping for a longer stretch) in pain.
- Your baby is licking his lips or mouth a lot.
- He's sticking his fingers or whatever else he can get his hands on into his mouth.
- Your baby starts to gnaw like a dog. Putting any sort of pressure on the sore spot in his gum—from his fist to his favorite toy to a spoon—seems to make him feel better.

Fever, cold, ear infections, or diarrhea aren't usually symptoms of teething (although many parents swear that excess drool can cause diarrhea). If your baby has a temperature of over 100°F or appears to be ill, don't put off calling the doctor because you think he's teething.

When Do Baby Teeth Come In? Pediatric dentists are more concerned about how teeth come in (that is, in what order) than they are about when. They're not going to worry even if a child's first tooth erupts after he's 18 months old. Teeth that erupt out of the usual order are a problem because they sometimes get misaligned when the other teeth come in.

Estimated Time of Arrival for Baby Teeth	
Lower central incisors (2)	5–10 mos.
Upper central incisors (2)	8–12 mos.
Lateral incisors (4)	9–16 mos.
Upper cuspids (2)	16–22 mos.
Lower cuspids (2)	17–23 mos.
Upper first molars (2)	13–19 mos.
Lower first molars (2)	14–18 mos.
Upper second molars (2)	25–33 mos.
Lower second molars (2)	23–31 mos.

CHECKLIST

Teething Pain Relief Do's and Don'ts

Tips to help ease your baby's transition from toothless to toothsome.

Do

✔ Give your unhappy baby something to gnaw on—whether it's a teething ring or a washcloth.

✔ Provide cool relief. A cold, wet cloth or a refrigerated teething ring may help soothe swollen gums. (Check that the teething ring is filled with drinking water, just in case it breaks and your baby drinks some.)

✔ Apply a little pressure to the gum area with a clean finger or cloth. The pressure may feel good to your baby.

✔ Offer a teething biscuit (if your baby is 6 months or older). Always supervise biscuit eating and remove any large crumbs or pieces that break off that could cause a choking hazard.

If your baby gnaws on her own hand, she may have found her own smart way to relieve teething pain.

✔ Ask your doctor about salves that numb the pain. Some have stronger ingredients than others and need to be used very sparingly.

✔ Give your baby children's acetaminophen if she's been miserable for a while.

Don't

✔ Freeze teething rings or offer your baby ice cubes. Both can actually give your child's sensitive gums a case of "freezer burn," and ice cubes are a choking hazard.

✔ Offer cold or frozen bagels or carrots. Many parents swear by these, but as they thaw small bits can easily break off and become a choking hazard.

✔ Smear your child's gums with whiskey or other alcohol. Yes, our parents probably used this old "cure," but there's no medical proof that it works, and there are lots of good reasons not to give babies booze.

✔ Crush an aspirin onto the sore tooth. Another old custom, this one can burn your baby's gum and introduce toxic levels of aspirin into your baby's body.

1,000 New Questions

While so many things become easier as you and your baby get to know each other, new challenges, problems, and questions pop up every single day. Here are answers to some of the most common baby-care questions:

• **My baby's chin is always chapped from constant drooling. What can I do to prevent it?** You can't keep a baby from drooling; the best you can do is wipe off the drool as often as possible to prevent more chapping. To soothe the irritated area, gently apply a mild skin cream. Your pharmacist or doctor may have a recommendation.

• **I received a baby bath chair for a shower gift. When can my baby start using it?** If your baby is around 6 months old and can sit up by himself fairly well, go ahead and use the chair. You'll find it gives both you and your baby

---

IS IT TRUE THAT . . .

Babies Can't Get Cavities? Ah, if only it were so. Although the number of cavities in children is way down (thanks, in part, to fluoride), one-third of children still develop cavities before the age of 3. Even though the cavities are in temporary baby teeth, they can harm the developing adult teeth.

You should get into the habit of cleaning your baby's mouth even before she cuts her first tooth. Wipe her gums with a clean, soft cloth after each feeding. Not only will this help prevent future tooth decay, but it will get your baby used to having her gums massaged.

Once she has a tooth, clean it twice each day by wetting a piece of sterile gauze (most first-aid kits contain it) and wiping it across each baby tooth. Many parents find that this is best done by holding Baby on their lap, facing away from them. Toothpaste isn't recommended for babies under 3 years old because they're bound to swallow it. Once you're dealing with more than one tooth, try using a small, soft-bristled baby toothbrush.

To further safeguard your baby's dental health, avoid baby-bottle syndrome (see "DEFINITION: Baby-Bottle Syndrome," page 195), and make sure she's getting enough fluoride, which strengthens tooth enamel and bone, and can even help repair damage from minor decay. If your water supply isn't fluoridated, ask your pediatrician about other supplements. (Fluoride isn't recommended for babies under 6 months old.)

Recommendations about when to take your baby for her first dentist visit vary, depending upon whom you ask. A dentist will probably suggest that you bring the child in when she's about 1 (before she has time to develop dental phobia). Many pediatricians recommend that you plan a first visit around age 3. When it's time, get references and recommendations from friends. You'll be amazed at what a difference jungle wallpaper, bubblegum tooth cleaner, a jolly dentist, and a free toy can make in your child's early dental experiences.

∽ A MOTHER'S VIEW ∽

"Teething Woes"

Joseph Milner had all the signs: He was drooling and cranky, and had been sporting swollen gums for a month. So where was his first tooth? wondered his mother, Rene, of Sharpsburg, Georgia.

"His gums would swell up, then they'd go down again—and no tooth would come," she recalls. While she waited for the tooth that was causing Joseph such pain, she tried a variety of remedies.

She offered him a frozen washcloth, but Joseph gave it a big thumbs-down. She tried to massage his gums with her fingers, but he pushed her away. And he didn't like the topical anesthetic she applied on his gums, either.

What did the trick? "He liked cold teething rings the best," she says. At the height of his teething pain, he'd gnaw on the smooth ring for a good 10 to 15 minutes. "But once it started getting warm, he would throw it down."

And he loved his rubber toothbrush. "It's as if he had an itch, and he could use the brush to really scratch," says Rene.

Joseph's first tooth finally erupted around 6 months, followed by a second just-as-painful one a month later. Two more finally made an appearance after his first birthday, but not before totally disrupting his nights for months. Rene's not sure if she's going to make it through the next 16 teeth, but here's what's worked for her so far:

- **Find a favorite teething toy.** Rene (and Joseph) swear by a Nuk toothbrush with rubber bristles.
- **Buy several teething rings.** When one isn't cool anymore, you'll want to have another chilled one all ready to go.
- **Try painkillers.** Acetaminophen sometimes helped Joseph pass more restful nights.

added confidence. Many models have suction cups that keep the chair in place in the tub, and little foam seat cushions are available for making the hard plastic seat more comfy (wash and dry the seat cushion after each bath to prevent any bacteria from multiplying). Don't let the seat give you false confidence, though; it's still not safe to leave your baby in the tub alone (and won't be for several years).

The other great tub invention (which I still use on my preschooler) is the bath hat. This flat, stretchy rubber disk with a brim slides over a baby's head and keeps the shampoo and rinsing water from running into his face.

• **What kind of baby carrier is safe now that my baby is 5 months old? She seems way too big for a front carrier.** While some parents carry their babies in front carriers until they're a year old, you and your baby may be ready for a change. Try a backpack-style carrier or a side carrier. Before your baby can graduate to her new ride, she needs to be able to sit up.

A back carrier will give your baby a whole new view of the world, but keep in mind: your baby must always be completely and securely tied in, you need to remember to duck when walking through doorways, and your baby will be able to reach things she couldn't before (such as the hair on the back of your head, down the back of your shirt, and the antique vase on the top shelf). A side carrier keeps a less independent baby tucked in close to Mom, but still gives you two free hands. Warning: it's not safe to cook with a baby in any sort of carrier.

• **My baby loves his swing, and sometimes spends as much as two hours in it (including his morning nap). Is that too much time?** When a baby is enjoying something so much, it's often hard to know when it's too much of a good thing. A swing is incredibly handy when it comes to soothing a younger baby who's fussy, but you have to guard against turning it into a crutch—for you or for your child. When you're cooking and need to keep him in a safe spot, the swing works well for a short time. But once a baby is 5 months or older, it's best to have him nap in his crib and to encourage other more stimulating activities, such as playing on the floor with age-appropriate toys, or with you.

• **I've seen other parents in restaurants using baby seats that seem to snap on to the side of a table. Are they safe?** Some parents swear by these, but I didn't have a lot of success with them. My daughters always managed to push off a table leg, thereby tipping over all the food and scaring me to death. If you are going to use a hook-on seat, make sure it's in excellent working order. Use good judgment about what kind of table to attach it to; obviously glass table-tops, flimsy tables that'll tip over from baby's weight, and tables with lots of extra leaves aren't good choices. Test the seat and table before putting baby in.

And make sure that the seat has a strap so that you can buckle in your young diner.

• **Our dog is always licking our daughter's face, much to my mother's disgust. Should we be worried?** Dog kisses aren't anything to push the panic button over, but it wouldn't hurt to discourage them. At least clean your baby off as soon as possible after she gets slimed. Once your baby starts eating more solid foods, your pet will probably try to eat leftovers off her face, which will really gross out your relatives. So if it worries you, start the no-licking-the-baby drill with your dog now, before it gets out of control.

• **My baby has started biting my nipples. Does this mean she's ready to wean?** Not necessarily. It probably means a tooth is on its way and that nibbling on anything helps make her painful gums feel better. Say "Ouch, that hurts" to discourage the behavior. She also may just be signaling that she's done with her meal.

• **Our 6-month-old tried a jumping device at a friend's house and loved it. But can jumping hurt his legs?** There has been some talk that a baby's joints and bones may suffer from the repeated pounding, but there have been no formal warnings about the jumpers. If you do use one, make sure it's securely attached to the doorjamb, limit your baby's jumping time to just a few minutes, and don't leave him alone while jumping.

• **My baby started out with a full head of hair and now she's going bald. What's going on here?** At birth, hair stops growing. And yes, it's not uncommon for it to fall out during the first couple of months. Until the next cycle of growth starts, your little cutie may be a baldie. Not to worry: she *will* have hair—eventually. Infant hair usually grows at 1 centimeter a month, so don't expect monumental growth any time soon. And when it does come in, it sometimes grows in odd places, like on the tops of infants' ears or low on their brows. This, too, will right itself over time. (And as the new hair grows in, you may notice that it's nothing like your baby's first hair. It can differ in texture, color, and quantity.)

If your baby is just going bald in certain spots, she's probably losing her hair owing to friction, which sometimes happens to babies who usually sleep in the same position. The hair will grow back once she begins to move around more in her sleep. In

---

GOOD ADVICE

Fun Diaper Changes

"When my daughter Kayla started to roll, I put aside a few special toys that she could have only when I changed her diaper. These toys, like a special spoon or rattle, helped her stay still long enough for me to safely change her diaper."

—*Melissa K. Gajeton, French Camp, CA*

the meantime, if your baby's hair (or lack of it) is bothering you, go hat shopping.

• **My baby loves to be thrown up in the air and caught, and his daddy is more than happy to do it. But is it safe?** Definitely not. Aside from the fact that the baby may bump into something on the way up or down, all that jarring—even though it seems gentle—can be dangerous, especially at this age when her brain is still developing. Babies who are jarred or shaken even just once (see "DEFINITION: Shaken-Baby Syndrome," page 95), can suffer brain damage or bleeding around the brain. One out of four shaken babies dies from her injuries. Most parents decide it's not worth tak-

Always watch your baby while he's in a jumper, and limit his hopping sessions to 15 minutes. Check the stability of the device each time you use it.

ing a chance. For safer rough-and-tumble fun, get down on the floor with your baby and roll around.

IN SEARCH OF SLEEP

One of parents' biggest disappointments (and rudest shocks) is when they discover that their older baby still doesn't give a hoot about *their* sleep schedule. After three or four months of waking up several times a night to feed, change, and rock baby, fatigued parents are ready to move into the "no more Mr. Nice Guy" mode. Actually, the timing is right for your baby, too. During months 4, 5, and 6, she'll be more receptive to your efforts of "training" her to sleep than she will be later.

If you train your baby well now, there's a good chance you'll avoid bedtime battles later in life. I've often thought that if I'd been better at helping my second daughter get to sleep without me in her first year of life, bedtime in her fourth year wouldn't be such a struggle. Gracie is a big comfort seeker and has always had trouble getting to sleep—and getting *back* to sleep—without a favorite object (me) by her side. It wasn't until she was 4½ that I got her to hold her stuffed lobster's hand every night instead of mine. Hallelujah!—but several years too late. If you don't want to be in the bedtime boat that I was, try some of these gentle sleep-inducing techniques now.

Establish a Night-Night Routine Send your baby "it's bedtime" signals with soothing prebed rituals:

- Give him a warm bath and brush his teeth.
- Read a story.
- Sing a lullaby.
- Give your baby a massage if he likes it.
- Say prayers or good-night to favorite toys.
- Kiss him and tuck him in.

Some parents use music as part of their nightly routine. They turn on a favorite lullaby tape or wind up a musical mobile right before bed. That's fine as long as your baby doesn't holler for you the minute the music stops. And it's wise to vary your routine a little, so your baby doesn't become rigid in his expectations.

Promote Self-soothing The idea is to encourage your baby to put herself to sleep, whether it's at naptime, bedtime, or after waking in the middle of the night. You want to be able to put her in her crib when she's still awake but drowsy. That may mean that you have to separate feedings from sleep time, so she begins to disassociate your warmth and milk from sleep—otherwise, she may continue to fall asleep at your breast or with a bottle. If she gets a big comfort fix from sucking, encourage her to suck her fingers, or give her a pacifier (soon she'll be able to locate it when it falls out and put it back in her mouth by herself—a red-letter day).

Offer a Special Transitional Object Your baby may need a special blankie or "softie" during this time to reassure her that everything will be OK. Make sure this item is always handy, and make a ritual of handing it over at bedtime.

Get Dad Involved One way to help your baby break the breast-bed ritual is to have Dad put her to bed. He, too, can soothe, massage, and sing, and by doing so will broaden your baby's expectations of what happens before she's supposed to go to sleep.

Reduce Nighttime Waking Once your baby is 5 or 6 months old, you should be able to help her sleep through the night (defined as a five- to six-hour stretch).

- **Put her to bed with a full tummy.** Try waking your baby before you're ready for bed, and feeding her then. Don't feed her back to sleep, though, or you'll be encouraging the eating-sleeping connection that you're trying to break.

• **Enforce your own schedule.** One mom I know, whose 6-month-old baby was still waking up three times a night, decided to preempt the baby by waking her up first. She fed the baby on *her* schedule, not the baby's. By taking control of the night wakings (she'd wake her daughter up 15 minutes or so before the baby usually awoke), this mom was able to first eliminate one feeding, and then stretch the time between the two remaining feedings to four, then five hours. Many parents find this to be a pretty painless way to reduce feedings at night.

• **Keep nighttime feedings brief.** Give your baby the strong message that nighttime is for sleeping, not for fun. Make middle-of-the-night changing and feeding very businesslike and boring: keep the lights off or very low, don't sing or play any games, take care of his needs and quickly return him to bed.

• **Don't jump up at her first little whimper.** If you think your baby is waking because she needs comfort, not food, give her some loving pats without taking her out of her crib. Or wait it out and see if she falls back to sleep on her own. Many babies make noises or whimper during their transition from one stage of sleep to another. If your baby is doing this, patting her may wake her up.

If you're breastfeeding and you're willing to nurse your baby back to sleep every night, go for it. But know that she probably won't stop waking until you stop offering her the breast. Why would she want to pass up such a good thing?

Delay the Morning Wake-up Call You can begin to teach your little one to sleep a little later if you slightly delay your response to him each morning. You don't want to let him cry too long, but if he's rising at 4 A.M. and you want to move that toward 5, or even the more civilized 6, wait several minutes before you go pick him up. Over time, he may respond to your cues and learn to sleep a little longer.

How Babies' Sleep Patterns Change			
AGE	DAY SLEEP (HOURS)	NIGHT SLEEP (HOURS)	TOTAL SLEEP (HOURS)
1 week	8	8½	16½
1 month	7	8½	15½
3 months	5	10	15
6 months	3¼	11	14¼
9 months	3	11	14
12 months	2¼	11½	13¾

Limit Daytime Naps Even through the fog of sleep deprivation, most parents will admit that their baby has come a long way on the nap front. While newborns typically take four naps a day, the 6-month-old is down to two—usually one in the morning and one in the afternoon. For most babies, total daytime sleeping has gone from an average of 8 hours to 3.25 hours. If your baby is 6 months or older and is still napping four hours or more a day, consider reducing naptime. If you're lucky, she'll make up for the lost sleep at night. To keep her more alert during the day, make sure she's getting plenty of stimulation and playtime.

What You Need to Know About . . . Letting Baby Cry

When all else fails to get their baby to sleep at night, parents begin to play with the idea of letting their little one cry it out—a subject that even the childcare experts can't agree on. (What they do agree on is that no baby should be left to cry before he's 6 months old.)

Some parents feel so guilty at the very thought of letting their baby cry himself to sleep that they never try it. Others find that a technique known as *Ferberizing*—named after Dr. Richard Ferber—gives them the guidelines they need to muster up the courage to try it (see below).

There are varying degrees of the crying-it-out plan—it doesn't have to be an all-or-nothing proposition. Depending upon your resolve, and how and when your baby cries, you can find a method that works for you. Some plans to consider if your baby is 6 months or older:

• **Cold turkey.** The idea here is that if you know that your baby isn't sick and doesn't have any other pressing physical need, let him cry. This takes great courage (and good earplugs) on the parents' part. Most parents—and some experts—believe this technique is contrary to all parenting instincts and isn't worth the trauma.
• **Warm turkey.** In this technique, it's OK to check on your baby once after he's cried for several minutes. Make sure he's OK by giving him a visual check (don't pick him up). Then tell him good-night again, leave, and don't go back.
• **The Ferber method.** Dr. Richard Ferber, director of the Center for Pediatric Sleep Disorders, recommends this progressive-waiting technique to check in on your baby at preset times:

1. Go through your usual bedtime routine and put your baby in her crib when she's drowsy but still awake. (If she wakes in the night, check on her but leave the room while she's still awake.)
2. If she cries, don't go back for five minutes. When you do return to her room,

don't pick her up. Talk to her a little, pat her back, and leave after a minute or two while she's still awake.

3. If she cries again, wait 10 minutes before going back. Repeat the comforting routine.

4. If she cries again, wait 15 minutes. Repeat the routine.

5. If she cries again and again, continue to wait 15 minutes between visits—until she falls asleep.

6. The next night, wait 10 minutes before going back in for the first time. Then wait 15 minutes before visiting again, and 20 minutes for subsequent visits.

7. Start with a 15-minute wait on the third night and work up to 25 minutes.

8. As the nights go on, continue to extend the time between visits until you're up to 35 minutes before the first visit and 45 minutes between the third and future visits.

Ferberizing will only work if you're consistent, and you must stick with it—otherwise your baby will be miserable, confused, and unable to put herself to sleep. Some parents swear by this technique. Others find it excruciating. Some

Q & A

"The back of my son's head is flat from sleeping on his back. Should I be worried?"

Your son is probably suffering from what's called "positional molding," a condition that occurs when a baby spends a lot of time on his back. In addition to the back of the head being flat, sometimes a baby's forehead protrudes slightly, or his ears are misaligned.

Positional molding is harmless and can be corrected. Often, all that's needed is for you to vary your son's routine so that he's not spending so much time on his back. Cut back on the amount of time he's reclining in a car or infant seat, for instance, and make sure he gets plenty of playtime on his tummy. (But don't start to put him to sleep on his tummy; the American Academy of Pediatrics *strongly* recommends that babies sleep on their backs to prevent SIDS.) If your home remedies don't do the trick, talk to your doctor about a special headband or helmet that gently reshapes your baby's head.

And a word of warning: sometimes this simple flatheadedness is misdiagnosed as craniosynostosis, a very serious (and rare) condition in which skull bones fuse and limit brain growth. If your doctor thinks your son has this condition, make sure your child has a complete evaluation by someone knowledgeable about this problem. You may want to get a second opinion to avoid unnecessary surgery.

⌒ A MOTHER'S VIEW ⌒

"How I Got My Daughter to Put Herself to Sleep"

Like many babies her age, 4-month-old Annalise Schulman wasn't thrilled about bedtime. And her mother Lisa was becoming less and less thrilled with the complex antics required to get Annalise to drop off to sleep: breastfeeding, walking, rocking, swinging.

By the time Annalise was 5 months old, the San Rafael, California, mom decided to take the advice of her mothers' group and Ferberize her daughter (see "The Ferber Method," page 205). She tried it, but the technique of letting her baby cry for longer and longer intervals before going in to soothe her backfired. "Each time I would go in, Annalise would become angrier and angrier," says Lisa. "Eventually I think she started to like it. If she kept crying, she knew we'd come back."

Determined to find a bedtime routine that worked, Lisa decided to go cold turkey. "I put her down in her crib, walked out of the room, and just let her cry," she says. The first night, Annalise cried for half an hour. The next night she cried for half an hour. But gradually, over a two-week period, her cries dwindled to a minute or two. "Now, when I put her in the crib, Annalise will often just look up at me and then lay her head down," Lisa says. Her tips for bedtime bliss:

- **Avoid nursing your baby to sleep.** Lisa nurses Annalise about 15 minutes before bedtime, plays with her, and then puts her in her crib while she's still awake.
- **Don't cave in.** Know that babies this age are just learning to manipulate parents and will use bedtime cries as a way of practicing their skills. This is natural, developmentally appropriate behavior; your child isn't being "bad."
- **Whatever technique you try, stick with it and be consistent.**
- **Do a cry check.** Listen to your baby's cries closely to distinguish the "rescue me from my boring crib" cry from the "I really need help" cry.

IS IT TRUE THAT . . .

Adding Cereal to Baby's Bottle Will Help Him Sleep Through the Night? Most doctors don't recommend that you give a baby this age cereal in his bottle, but it has nothing to do with the sleep issue. It's more likely that your baby will consume more calories than he needs (which isn't good at any age), and he could choke on the thickened liquid, especially if he's drinking in a reclining position.

Instead, try serving your nonsleeper a spoonful or two of rice cereal diluted with breast milk or formula during his evening feeding. Start out by offering just a smidgen of cereal and work up to no more than a few tablespoons. It may be that your baby is going through a growth spurt and that this little extra bit of food will be just what he needs to fill him up and make him sleepy. If the cereal solution doesn't work, don't try feeding him more. His sleep patterns probably aren't connected to his tummy; he just hasn't yet learned how to sleep through the night.

Q & A

"When can I stop worrying about SIDS?"

If you're like most parents, you won't stop worrying until your baby is in college—and then you'll move on to other worries.

Statistically, though, the great majority of sudden infant deaths occur before a baby is 4 months old. Still, you should continue to practice sensible SIDS prevention (see "What You Need to Know About . . . SIDS," page 101). And until your baby is 1 year or older, make sure that you're not covering him with thick, heavy blankets, which can trap exhaled carbon dioxide when they cover his face. A light blanket is always best for an infant this age.

---

babies catch on in just a few nights; for others it takes several painful weeks. Occasionally, a baby will become more and more upset as the visits continue (in which case stop).

Dr. Ferber himself has said that he thinks the technique has been misused and that it's best as a last resort when a baby is very dependent on a sleep crutch, such as being nursed to sleep.

• **The softhearted approach.** Keep the door closed between your room and the baby's. Don't turn on the monitor. Don't run in every time he makes a peep. Do check on him each time he cries for more than 15 minutes, and decide—based on his cry and the situation—how you want to deal with it.

HEALTH AND SAFETY

By now, visits to the pediatrician may seem almost routine—except for the vaccinations, which most parents (and children) never seem to get used to. Your baby will get shots at her 4-month and 6-month well-baby checkups, so be prepared (see "CHECKLIST: Immunization Update," page 210).

Although she isn't zooming around the house yet, your baby's ability to roll, scooch, and sit should get you thinking about baby-proofing. And now that she's out and about more—and possibly spending some time in daycare or with other babies—she'll be exposed to more germs. More germs mean *more* visits to the doctor.

Well-Baby Visits

It's often quite a thrill to chat with the pediatrician about how well your baby is developing, and it's reassuring to have an authority to talk with about the little things that may be bothering you. The 4-month checkup, for instance, is a good time to ask questions about the transition to cereal and about teething.

When it's time to compare your baby's growth to the standard growth charts found in the doctor's office, here's a word of warning about their accuracy: a recent study reported that the charts are typically based on data gath-

---

CHECKLIST
Safety Update

At this stage, your baby may be more like the tortoise than the hare when it comes to moving around, but you'll be surprised at how much trouble he can get into while rolling or sitting.

✔ Make sure electrical cords are out of his reach. Not only can he pull a heavy lamp down on himself but he also might be tempted (especially if he's teething) to chew on the cord. Babies have been electrocuted this way.

✔ If your baby has graduated to a high chair, don't assume that your worries are over because he's buckled in. Pay special attention to how far he can reach, and make sure that dangerous items—things he could choke on, hot beverages, and sharp knives—are out of his reach.

✔ Because he's rocking and rolling, don't ever leave him unattended on a bed, couch, or changing table. Not even for a second.

✔ It's particularly important, now that your baby is bigger and stronger, to place his infant seat only on the floor. By bouncing it, he can rock it right off a table or counter.

CHECKLIST
Immunization Update

Your baby will receive routine immunizations during her 4- and 6-month well-baby visits. If she skips a shot owing to illness (fever is usually the only reason a vaccination might be delayed), be sure to note it in her health record. It's easy—and dangerous—to fall behind on vaccinations, so as soon as she's well, make a follow-up appointment (often it's just a nurse visit) to get the missed shot.

	DTP	Hib	Hep B	Polio
4 months	•	•		•
6 months	•	•		
6–18 months	•	•	•	•

ered primarily from formula-fed babies. If your breastfed baby's weight falls into a very low percentile on the chart from 4 months on, don't be alarmed or make any rash decisions about weaning your baby (see "Weaning from the Breast," page 255). Because from 4 months old, breastfed babies often gain weight at a slower rate than formula-fed babies, your baby's growth may be right on schedule in spite of what the chart says. (Breastfed babies' length is usually equal to that of formula-fed babies.) Talk to your doctor if you're concerned.

In addition to the other routine examinations, your pediatrician may pay special attention to your baby's eyes and hearing. He will also check your baby's soft spots and may tell you that the posterior fontanel (which is in the back) has closed. This milestone typically occurs between baby's second and fifth month. The front fontanel doesn't close until the second year.

The Eyes Have It Your baby will be checked to make sure that he is tracking objects with his eyes (you can do this at home, too; see "PLAYTIME: Vision Games," page 211), and that he isn't experiencing any of these common infant eye disorders:

• **Blocked tear duct.** A baby with a blocked tear duct may look as if she's crying all the time. For months, people would look at my daughter, Gracie, and say, "Oh, why is she crying?" when she was as happy as a clam. Her problem: blocked tear ducts. Tears flow down a baby's face, even when she's not crying, because they have no place else to go: the little opening at the inside corner of her eye isn't open enough to drain the tears. If the duct stays closed, her eyelids may become irritated, pus may build up, and an infection could develop.

PLAYTIME

Vision Games

From 3 months on, your baby's vision will have improved enough so that she can track a moving object. This new ability can be a great source of fun, especially since her eye-hand coordination is also much improved and she's developing an interest in colors. Try this:

- Hold a colorful object in front of your baby and move it horizontally from right to left and then back again. Your baby's eyes will track the toy from side to side. When you stop moving, her eyes will stop—and she'll wait with anticipation until you move the object again. She may even kick excitedly during this activity or try to swat at the object with her hands.
- Babies usually master horizontal tracking before being able to follow vertical movements. Move a toy down in a straight line (not out of sight) and back up again. With practice, she'll be able to follow the up-and-down action as well as the side-to-side.
- Diagonal tracking is the last to develop. Make interesting sound effects as you swoop the object up and down at a 45-degree angle.

Q & A

"When will I know what color my baby's eyes will be?"

By 6 months, you can usually get a pretty good idea of baby eye color, although it may continue to darken or evolve for a little while.

Caucasian babies are typically born with gray-blue eyes, often described as a slate color. During baby's first six months, eyes that will end up being blue or gray will lighten and become a clearer color. Eyes that are destined to turn brown, green, or hazel will darken. The shade and intensity of color can continue to change as time goes by. At 6 months, my daughter Halley Rose looked as if she'd have dark hazel eyes. Years later, her eyes are much more green than brown.

Non-Caucasian babies usually have brown eyes, which stay brown, but which may also darken over time.

To treat the condition, your doctor will probably show you how to massage the area between the bridge of your baby's eye and her nose. This painless procedure often opens up the duct and works out any pus that's built up. If that doesn't work and your child still has the problem by age 1, your physician may use a special instrument to open the duct.

- *Conjunctivitis (also known as pinkeye).* Usually caused by allergies or infection, pinkeye shows up as irritated eyelids, bloodshot eyes, and a sticky discharge. It can range from mildly irritating to painful. Medicated drops or ointment are usually prescribed. Because it is highly contagious, other family members should be careful to wash their own hands frequently and avoid rubbing their eyes.
- *Strabismus (also known as crossed eyes or lazy eye).* Babies' eyes can look crossed or appear to be wandering during their first three months without causing any worry. But from 3 or 4 months on, their eyes should be aligned and work together. Treatment—ranging from glasses, an eye patch, eye exercises, or medication, to surgery—is required to correct the problem.
- *Amblyopia.* There are two types of amblyopia: obstructive and exanopsis. In both cases, one eye is weaker and the condition is treatable. Both are difficult for a layperson to recognize, however, so it's very important that your baby have a

HOW TO
Give Ear Drops and Eyedrops

Wash your hands before and after administering eye and ear drops. Warm up the bottle of drops in your hand so that your baby isn't startled or scared by cold drops.

Ear Drops
1. Wrap your baby in a blanket with her arms at her sides, or have another adult help hold her (otherwise she'll bat your hands and the medicine away). Position her so that the affected eye or ear is facing you.
2. Hold her head with one hand while you position the dropper with the other. (Again, get a helper if your baby is actively resisting.) Squeeze out the drops.
3. Wiggle her earlobe a bit to encourage the drops to disperse. Hold your baby still for one to two minutes to keep the drops from running out, and before you start on the other ear (if necessary).

Eyedrops
1. Wrap up your baby so that she can't swat away the drops, and place her face-up on a comfortable surface.
2. Use one hand to tilt her forehead back. Position the dropper with the other hand about an inch above the inside corner of her eye. Squeeze out the drops. (Don't attempt to hold her eye open, which will only upset her and make the job more difficult.)
3. For shaky beginners, consider leaning the top of the dropper against baby's nose to get it into the right position for dropping (the tip should never touch the skin, which could cause the drops to become infected; sterilize the dropper after each use).

vision screening by the time he's 6 months old. Treatment varies, but sometimes consists of glasses, or using a patch to encourage the weak eye to work harder.

Do You Hear What I Hear? By 4 months, your baby should be turning his head in the direction of your voice. By 6 months, he should start to babble back to people who're talking to him, and his babbles should include four distinct sounds. If your baby doesn't pass the above tests, tell your doctor.

Thankfully, modern testing techniques can uncover hearing problems earlier and earlier these days—which is good news since hearing loss can affect a child's speech development. A new device, called an Audx, bounces sound waves into a baby's ear and is now being used to test some newborns. Traditionally, though, your pediatrician will check your baby's hearing at the 4-month or 6-month checkup.

If he suspects a problem, he'll first rule out an ear infection (see "The Inevitable Ear Infection," page 264), and then may refer your baby for further testing by an audiologist.

Common Infant Health Problems

Although your baby seems to have grown by leaps and bounds, she's still an infant who can be knocked for a loop by any number of diseases or problems.

Q & A

"My son has a hernia that requires surgery. How did he get it?"

Hernias are pretty common in baby boys 6 months old and younger. There's nothing you could have done to prevent your son from developing a hernia. Basically, part of an intestine has bulged out in his groin or lower abdomen. When your baby cries or is active, the bulge is more noticeable.

The hernia will heal after simple surgery, which usually requires a day or less in the hospital. Some doctors suggest that the surgery be done right away; others think it's OK to wait until the child is older. If the hernia is strangulated, meaning that the bulging intestine is getting in the way of blood flow and digestion in the intestines, the surgery will be done immediately. (This condition sometimes occurs when a hernia is undiagnosed.)

Symptoms of a strangulated hernia include severe pain and vomiting. A baby may also stop having bowel movements. If this happens to your child, head to the emergency room as soon as possible. Once corrected, hernias usually don't recur.

- **Croup.** There are two kinds of croup; both have the characteristic (and scary) cough that sounds like a seal barking. Regular croup is triggered by a virus. When a baby catches this virus, it can cause her voice box or small airways to swell or spasm, making it hard to breathe. Spasmodic croup is usually caused by dry air or allergies, or may occur at the tail end of a viral infection. Call your doctor if you suspect your baby has croup. Sometimes she may just need a spell in the bathroom with the hot water turned on or a drive in the car to ease her breathing; other times, a hospital visit and oxygen and oral steroids may be needed.
- **Tummy troubles.** Diarrhea and vomiting are usually the result of a stomach or intestinal infection. Often they go away on their own. If you've just made the transition to baby food, they also may be the result of a food sensitivity.

In any case, if your baby vomits or has diarrhea more than twice in a 24-hour period, call your doctor. Although he may only recommend that you push fluids to avoid dehydration, he may also want to examine the baby to rule out a more serious illness. Vomiting, for instance, can be a symptom of strep throat, meningitis, appendicitis, a hernia, or pneumonia.

Constipation isn't nearly as serious a problem, but it can be uncomfortable for your baby. Don't mistake natural changes in bowel activity and consistency for constipation. When your baby begins cereal, for instance, her bowel movements may stop for a while as she learns to digest this new fare. Or her movements may be hard and dry. (Constipation, actually, refers only to the consistency of the feces, not to the frequency.) Formula-fed babies suffer more than breastfed babies, since formula is harder to digest.

What You Need to Know About . . . Emergency Rooms

Not all emergency rooms are created equal (nor are all ambulances). The truth is, most medical emergency equipment is designed for adults, and most personnel are trained to work on adults. That's why it's smart to research your local hospitals and find one that specializes in caring for children. Ask your pediatrician for a recommendation.

I learned this lesson the hard way when my daughter Gracie fell on a sharp point of woodwork and punctured her forehead. We'd moved to San Francisco only two months before and hadn't a clue where to go. While she was gushing blood, we called 911 and asked for directions to the nearest hospital. When we got there, the staff wasn't very enthusiastic about stitching up a 1-year-old. In fact, I think they would have turned us away if they could have.

We found out later that the hospital we went to was well known for its

A MOTHER'S VIEW

"My Real-Life Visit to the ER"

Karin West, mother of twin boys, had the misfortune of landing in the emergency room twice within four months.

Gregory was 5 months old when he spiked a fever of 103°F one Friday night. He'd suffered with a cold for a few days, so Karin called her pediatrician, who suggested she go to the emergency room. Within a half hour of their arrival, a pediatrician took a history, examined Gregory, and confirmed that he had a double ear infection. He was sent home with antibiotics.

Karin's second visit was more dramatic. The other twin, Derek, was 9 months old when he hit his head on the leg of a table, and then on the floor. He cried a bit, then stopped. Thirty minutes later, Karin noticed a squishy bump on the side of Derek's head where he'd fallen. She checked his pupils for dilation and woke him every few hours during the night to make sure she could rouse him. Everything seemed fine until she got an urgent call from her baby-sitter the next day. Derek was crying and wouldn't stop. Karin picked him up and headed to the urgent care center.

Because it was a head injury, five different medical personnel asked Karin how Derek hurt his head. She told them how he'd been cruising around a table and fell, but she was a little unnerved by what seemed like their disbelief. "I'm a corrections officer, so I know they have to ask the questions and watch your reactions," says Karin, "but knowing it's routine didn't make it any easier for me."

An X ray revealed a 1- to 1½-inch skull fracture. The squishy bump Karin had felt was a hematoma—blood that had seeped up between his skull and the skin. The neurosurgeon and doctors agreed that Derek's skull bones will heal on their own.

Karin is hoping that she's seen the last of the emergency room, at least for this year. Her tips for surviving a visit:

- **Be prepared.** Admit to yourself that it could happen, and decide which hospital you'll go to and how you'll get there.
- **Don't panic.** It's hard to calm a sick or injured child—and to hear and understand the doctors—if you're not in control of your emotions.
- **Expect questions.** Know that if your child has suffered any injury (and a head injury in particular), medical personnel will ask you lots of questions in order to rule out child abuse. Remind yourself that they are just doing their job.

HOW TO

Be Prepared for an Emergency

1. Know which emergency room you'll go to.
2. Map out the fastest route to get there.
3. Have all emergency numbers posted by your phone (doctor, 911 or other local service, number of children's hospital, poison center).
4. Post a copy of your child's medical history on the bulletin board or carry it in your purse.
5. Always know where your insurance cards are.
6. Keep a bottle of syrup of ipecac in the house. (But don't use it unless the poison center says you should; Poison Control Center: 1-800-POISON1.)
7. Make sure your caregiver, daycare center, relatives—anyone who is caring for your child—know where to reach you in an emergency. And give them written permission to have your child receive emergency care without you if necessary.

thoughtful and innovative care for AIDS patients; the children's hospital we *should* have gone to was 15 minutes away.

When it's a life-and-death situation, it's even more important to know you're in an ambulance or at a hospital that's equipped to deal with infants. A children's hospital (or one that has a special unit for children) is more likely to have child-sized cervical collars, breathing tubes, IVs, or oxygen masks. And their staff is more likely to have recently tended a seriously ill or injured child. So, do some research, and be prepared.

Another thing to think about is whether or not you want to stay with your child if she's undergoing some sort of invasive procedure—having blood drawn or having an IV or catheter inserted, for instance. Some medical personnel prefer that parents get out of their way (and some parents would prefer to not have to watch). I've even heard the theory that parents shouldn't be around when their children are getting painful procedures done because the child will associate pain with the parent. But a recent study at Boston Hospital found that parents were actually *less* anxious if they stayed with their child, and that the child seemed to experience less discomfort.

I once let medical staff take Gracie away to have blood drawn; they asked me to wait outside. I did and almost had a heart attack listening to her screaming. The procedure took forever and when they came out, Gracie was hysterical and the two nurses—who said she was a "tough cookie" with hard-to-find veins—weren't in much better shape. Gracie was mad at me, bruised, and to this day she looks at her arm and has an apoplectic fit if you even mention the word *blood*. I'm certain she would have screamed had I been there, too, but I'm also sure she would have been somewhat comforted or calmed by my presence.

OTHER BIG DEALS

A parent's newfound confidence can quickly flee when faced with baby's first long-distance trip or holiday celebration. The twin pressures of travel and family have been known to spoil the most festive affair. But it doesn't have to be that way. The best advice: be prepared, and relax.

Have Baby, Will Travel

Whether you're going on a vacation or a visit to relatives, traveling by car or by plane, getting there can be a chore. How to make life easier?

Air Travel

- Try to book a flight that isn't crowded. This is desirable for a number of reasons. First, there may be a spare seat for you to install your baby's car seat. Not only is it infinitely safer for a baby to be in her own seat, but it will also give your arms a break. (If there isn't a seat right next to you but there are free seats, ask someone to switch with you, or ask the flight attendant for help.)

  Second, flight attendants will be a lot happier to see you if they're not overstressed by a full plane. In my experience, even the nicest airline staff are *not* thrilled when they see a family get onboard. On an emptier flight there'll be fewer annoyed people if your baby cries constantly.
- Consider a red-eye flight if you think your baby will sleep. If he won't, or if you have an older, active baby who'll want to be walked up and down the aisle 40 times an hour, avoid these flights. Other passengers are even more annoyed by a crying baby when they're trying to sleep.
- Be prepared for a grouchy baby during takeoff and landing. The changes in air pressure may hurt her ears. Nurse or feed her during these times. Swallowing relieves the pressure.
- Choose a nonstop flight on a bigger plane, if possible. It's easier than having to get on and off several planes, and it means fewer painful pressure changes.
- Find a seat that suits you. Parents with babies seem to end up sitting way in the back or in the very front. There are pluses and minuses to both. Front seats with a wall in front of them are called bulkhead seats. They provide extra space for your legs and for diaper changing (if you must).

Bulkhead seats don't have anywhere to store your diaper bag, however, so you have to stow it above your seat. This may be a problem if you need it in a hurry. The seat arms usually don't raise up (giving you more room or allowing you to be closer to your baby) because they have the little tray table folded up inside of them (instead of on the back of the seat in front).

Seats in the back are often closer to the lavatories and to the flight attendants. They're usually noisier (since they're closer to the engine), which is good if you need the noise to cover up your baby's crying or if noise soothes her.

- If you're going to use a car seat, it has to be buckled into a window seat. That's so it doesn't interfere with anybody's ability to exit during an emergency. Some airlines are stricter about this than others.
- Don't carry too much onboard. The less stuff you have to keep track of (and cart around), the less harried you'll be. Along with an infant car seat, a sturdy carry-on bag is essential. Your carry-on should hold your purse and all the baby gear (or you can keep your wallet in a fanny pack). You also might want

CHECKLIST
Don't Leave Home Without . . .

✔ Your insurance cards and baby's medical history. If he should get sick while you're away, you'll need both.

✔ Enough diapers for the plane or the car trip, plus a few extras. If you're traveling light, you can buy a big package of diapers at your destination. Bring Ziploc bags to put the dirty diapers in until you get to a trash can.

✔ Your baby's favorite blankie or stuffed animal for comfort—and a favorite toy for stimulation. Plus, it's helpful to bring along an interesting new toy to introduce when the going gets rough.

✔ Plenty of spit-up cloths and wet wipes.

✔ A few bibs and spoons.

✔ If your baby is formula fed, several bottles containing prepared formula powder.

✔ Pacifiers.

✔ A changing pad.

✔ Any medicine your baby may be taking. If it needs refrigeration, keep it in an insulated bag with ice in it. Bring along your baby's favorite medicine spoon or dropper.

✔ Baby-food jars or finger foods, depending upon your baby's stage of development. Bring a few baggies of food with you on the plane if you're flying; pack the rest or buy it when you get there.

to bring along a baby sling or a lightweight umbrella stroller. Most flight attendants will let you bring the umbrella stroller right on the plane and will stow it for you nearby. A big stroller or carriage will need to be checked (and won't be handy for flight connections).

- Do be the first to board if you're invited. It's nice to settle in (especially if you have a car seat to install) before everybody else crowds on. Unfortunately, many airlines are no longer doing the "parents of small children or those needing a little extra time may board now" announcement. So much for family-friendly travel.
- Don't change your baby's diaper on your seat on a full plane (at least if you want to get off alive). Use the lavatory. Some planes have flip-down diaper-changing stations. If you have to change your baby on the closed toilet seat, pad the area with a blanket or cloth diaper first. This isn't easy or comfortable, but it can be done. If your plane is *very* empty, you can change the baby in a remote seat.
- Don't forget to bring along plastic baggies (the kind that seal shut) for diaper disposal.
- Don't give a flight attendant the diaper to throw away; this seems above and beyond the job description and is a health hazard, since attendants spend most of their time serving food and beverages. Also, try not to bombard attendants with too many special requests to chill or fill bottles. Come prepared (see "CHECKLIST: Don't Leave Home Without . . . ," page 218).
- If your baby is fussing or crying a lot, give her to Dad to hold or comfort. It's a sad but true fact that Dad holding a crying baby will be viewed by most with sympathy, whereas Mom with the same fussing child will be viewed as a failure and a nuisance. I've seen it happen time and time again with my own babies, and my attitude has become, "Hey, if Dad and Baby are so charming, fine. I'll hand over the howler and get out my paperback."

In the Car

- Be certain that your baby's car seat is in good working order.
- Make sure you have an emergency kit in the car.
- Buy one of those fancy rearview mirrors so that you can see what your baby's up to even though she's facing backward.
- Don't overdress your baby. She should wear comfortable clothes that are easy to change. A blanket over a sweater or light jacket is a better choice than a warm snowsuit if you're going a long distance. Unless it's extremely cold, cars are usually warm inside. Put on a hat to keep her head warm.
- Pack as much as you want and have room for, but make sure it's secured well.

Gear that's stored next to your baby or in the back of a station wagon can shift and fall on your child.

- Plan frequent stops in advance. Pick out family-friendly restaurants or rest stops that are well lit and populated. Your baby will need feedings, diaper changes, and a change of scenery now and then.
- Play soothing music on the car's tape player.

At the Hotel or Home of a Relative

- Arrange in advance for a crib or playpen and a high chair. Relatives can often borrow these items. Inspect them carefully before you let your baby use them.
- Try to stick to your baby's routines so that she's not totally out of sorts. But be aware that jet lag can strike babies twice as hard as adults. Her routines may be shot for a while.

GOOD ADVICE

Surviving the Holidays

"My advice to new moms: don't spread yourself too thin. Delegate authority if you're in charge of the meal, reduce your expectations, and you'll avoid a lot of stress."

—*Kathleen Gaffney, Boston, MA*

"Remember that if things don't go well the first year, it doesn't mean that all your family celebrations are destined to be that way. It's not like your sweet baby even notices."

—*Susan Kostal, San Francisco, CA*

"If you want to have a big, extended-family holiday with a new baby, make it Thanksgiving. It's much more manageable than Christmas. You have a lovely meal, which is what you really care about, and then everybody goes home."

—*Pat Reynolds, Bethesda, MD*

"When my daughter, Stephanie, was ten months old, I must have spent $200 on her Christmas gifts. I liked them for me, so I bought them for her. But babies that age don't care about these things. She was overwhelmed and I was disappointed.

"With my son, Kevin, I was smarter: He was five months old, and basically I bought him three balls. He loved them."

—*Carmen Cecilia Giron, Pittsburgh, CA*

ꭢ A MOTHER'S VIEW ꭢ

"On the Road with Emily"

Emily Savrin was 8 weeks old when she boarded her first airplane. "That was my easiest trip with her, because she was so light," says Emily's mother, Patti Sims. As her daughter has gotten older and heavier, Patti's philosophy of traveling comfortably with a baby has shrunk to one word: minimize.

"I dress as minimally as possible. I only carry on an umbrella stroller and a knapsack. Everything else gets stuffed into my checked baggage," Patti says.

Providing plenty of entertainment and distraction is key to keeping a lap baby occupied and happy during a long flight, the Yardley, Pennsylvania, mom has found. "I bring new board books, extra pacifiers, some favorite toys, and a few new ones." She also packs plastic baggies stuffed with dry cereal, and a light sweater for Emily.

So far, Patty and Emily have had one bad experience: "We had to make an emergency landing in Phoenix to transfer to a new, smaller plane," says Patti. Naturally, the plane they were being transferred to was on the other side of the airport. When Patti stepped off the plane, she expected to have her umbrella stroller handed to her as usual. This time, however, the flight attendant couldn't get it for her and had only these words of advice: better hurry over to the new gate before all the seats get assigned.

Usually, Patti's experiences have been more positive. "On one trip, a flight attendant even offered to hold Emily while I used the bathroom." Patti's travel advice:

- **Practice walking (or rushing) with your carry-on luggage and your baby.** If something is too heavy, check it.
- **Find a spot to keep your wallet and tickets handy.** If your hands are full with a baby, and your tickets are in the zippered compartment of your backpack, which is out of reach on your back—you're not going to be a happy camper.
- **Plan how you're going to get through the airport crowds.** An umbrella stroller can be convenient, ditto a baby backpack.
- **Don't pack toys with small parts.** You want to avoid groping around under three airplane seats to retrieve them. Likewise, attach a pacifier to baby's sweater with a pacifier holder and pack extras.
- **Make a car-seat plan.** Patti uses a bungee cord to attach the seat to the umbrella stroller, leaving her hands free to push the stroller.

- Do a quick baby-proofing check wherever you're staying: outlets should be covered, stairs should have a safety gate, windows should be kept closed and locked or have guards on them, drapery cords should be tied up and out of the way. Be extra vigilant if your baby is cruising: he can pull down a table-cloth filled with a holiday meal or swipe everything off a coffee table in a flash.
- If your baby seems cranky, consider letting him sleep with you until he gets used to his new surroundings.
- Discuss with your host where you're going to dispose of diapers. Don't surprise anybody!

Baby's First Holidays As much fun as holidays are, they can be incredibly crazy making. A few things to keep in mind:

- It's the thought that counts. Don't drive yourself nuts trying to make everything perfect for an under-1-year-old who won't remember it. Sounds like harsh advice, but you'll have more fun (and your baby and everyone else will, too) if you can relax and concentrate on what matters: being together and enjoying the holiday.
- Your baby doesn't need lots of gifts. Go ahead and splurge if it pleases you, but don't expect him to notice (except for toys, if he's older).
- Try to schedule big events—the Thanksgiving meal, lighting the menorah, religious services, opening presents—during his naptime (to make it really easy on you), or right after he has rested and is in a good mood.
- If your baby seems overstimulated, take him outside for a quiet walk or to a guest room for a cuddle.
- If the thought of having relatives stay with you, or you staying with relatives, gives you a headache, make reservations at a hotel. Cramming a group of people you only see once a year into a too-small space won't be enjoyable.

What You Need to Know About . . .
Holiday Baby-Proofing

Candles
- Keep them away from anything flammable and out of reach of little hands.

Fireplaces
- Use a sturdy screen to keep sparks in and Baby out.
- Keep matches in a safe spot.

Christmas tree	• Use a sturdy stand. • Keep it watered to avoid a fire hazard. • Use only indoor lights and put only three strings on one extension cord. • Put up a gate to keep Baby from toppling the tree or eating decorations. • Vacuum needles often (babies will try to eat them). • Hang breakable ornaments and those with small pieces up high.
Presents	• Put away wrapping paper (which may contain lead) and ribbons (which can strangle Baby) after you unwrap each present. • Tie plastic wrapping in a knot and throw it out. • Don't burn the paper in the fireplace. • Before opening, make sure all toys are age appropriate and don't have small pieces.
Plants	• Keep all holiday plants out of Baby's reach. • Poinsettia, Christmas cactus, holly berries, and crown of thorns can all make Baby sick if ingested.
Food	• Keep chokables—nuts, hard candies, foil-covered gelt, cocktail hot dogs—out of Baby's reach. • When baking, recap and put away bottles of vanilla and almond extract; they're heavy in alcohol content.

YOUR GROWING BABY

Can a baby grow overnight? It certainly seems so to parents of 4- to 6-month-olds. By the end of this stage, your baby will probably have doubled his birthweight and will be able to sit, either propped up or by himself. As you watch how fast he grows—mentally, emotionally, and physically—you realize once again how important it is to provide a safe, stimulating, and loving environment for him.

With new developments come new challenges: Your baby is becoming an expert in a couple of "M" words—*manipulation* and getting *mad*. Trying to get what he wants and becoming frustrated when it doesn't happen fast enough is healthy, normal behavior. Your job is to continue to respond to his needs no matter how demanding he is.

Physical Development

Height and Weight

Average Growth*			
AGE	4–6 MOS.	7–9 MOS.	10–12 MOS.
Height	+2 in.	+2 in.	+2 in.
Weight	+4 lbs.	+4 lbs.	+3 lbs.

*There is a wide range of normal; every baby has her own growth timetable.

Motor Skills It's a milestone a minute during this three-month period. Your baby is perfecting her push-up, rolling over, and polishing all the skills she needs to be able to sit up by herself. What's more, her movements are becoming far more deliberate, instead of reflexive. She knows what she wants—and is learning how to get it.

• *The push-up.* Although your baby may have started to push up during her third month, now she's doing it with more style and grace. She has improved head and trunk control, which allows her to stay in this position longer. She has also learned that if she cranes her neck, she can see more. She may resemble some sort of alert forest animal as she pushes up and cranes her head around to see what she can see.

• *The airplane.* With her newfound trunk strength, your baby may enjoy what looks like an advanced yoga move done on speed: she raises her head and chest off the ground and rocks back and forth with legs and arms extended and flapping. Whee! Somebody's ready for takeoff.

• *Rolling over.* The first couple of times a baby rolls over, it's usually by accident. Somehow she rotated her spine and shifted her weight enough until the momentum carried her right over. Tummy-to-back is usually easier for babies because they can use their arms (albeit accidentally), and their round tummy sometimes helps with the mo-

MILESTONE

BABY PUSH-UPS

"At five months, Joseph is doing something new every day. His favorite activity is lying under an activity gym and batting at things. He stands (with help) in my lap, and does a great baby push-up."

—*Shailah Kuo,
New York City*

MILESTONE

SITTING UP

"Rebecca, at seven months, sits up perfectly, with the posture of a ballerina. If a toy is slightly out of reach, you can just see the intense concentration on her face as she tries to inch her way toward it."

—*Carol Smith, New York City*

Reaching for a toy takes concentration.

mentum. Soon they're rolling both ways at will, and building the muscle tone they need to move on to more complex moves.

• **Sitting up.** At 4 to 5 months old, your baby may be able to sit, propped up, for several minutes. Make sure the area around her is padded and doesn't contain any sharp objects she can fall on—make it a sort of topple-zone. When she gets tired, or momentarily distracted, she'll most likely demonstrate what looks like a slow-motion tim-*berrrrr* that lands her on her side on the floor.

Over the next three months, she'll begin to hold her back straighter and her head steadier, until her posture is quite impressive. Often, a baby will lean on her hands if she's feeling unsure of herself or if she's eyeing a toy that's a few inches away. By the end of 6 months, she may be sitting unsupported for a moment or two. And as her confidence in her sitting abilities grows, she'll use her hands less and less for support—and more for playing with toys.

• **Scooting.** Also called worming, creeping, or wiggling, this slithering form of locomotion is a precursor to crawling. Don't be taken by surprise by how far and fast your little one can go, especially since all this movement is generated without using her hands to pull or her feet to push. Don't leave her alone—even on the floor—for a second. That lamp cord is only 2 feet away.

• **Standing.** When you pull your baby up to a standing position now, she may have the control to support some of her weight on her own legs. She'll like to stand on your lap, bouncing up and down or dancing a little change-foot jig.

As your baby's motor skills improve, yours will have to, as well. Changing and dressing her will become a wrestling match. Whatever anyone else has, she'll want. She'll grab your nose, Dad's glasses, the dog's dirty ball, your cup of

"Can my baby get sick from all the stuff she's mouthing? Yesterday I found her chewing on a magazine I'd left on her high-chair tray."

Now that your baby has the ability to pick up an object and the desire to stick all such objects in her mouth, the subjects of germs and cleanliness rear their ugly heads. Since mouthing objects and exploring them orally is a normal part of your baby's development, you should encourage it, not discourage it. It is important, though, to monitor whatever is heading into her mouth.

It's unlikely any of the germs or dirt your baby is swallowing will do her any serious harm. Sometimes the dangers aren't obvious, though: a magazine isn't a safe chewy toy because the ink used in its printing may contain lead.

Other items that regularly make it into your daughter's mouth can be easily washed. Put plastic toys in the dishwasher and stuffed animals in the washing machine and dryer. A swipe with a baby wipe will clean the mess off larger or awkward-size toys. Do wash with a very mild soap (not a strong household cleaner, which could be toxic if ingested), and make sure everything has been rinsed and dried well before letting your baby at them.

hot coffee. Redirect her to safer pastimes: passing a block from hand to hand, grabbing a ring toy or her own feet, learning to hold her bottle. Give her plenty of time in a safe place to roll and show off her new tricks.

Mental Development

Cognitive Watch your baby grab a small block, and you'll notice something interesting: his hand will reach out with the palm wide open. As he gets closer, he'll process the size of the block and adjust his grasp to match its size. This is an amazing cognitive development. He's also beginning to figure out that a dropped toy doesn't cease to exist (this development is called *object permanence*). At 4 to 7 months, he may look down and around to try to figure out where

MILESTONE

RECOGNITION

"When Paige started to sleep in her own room at three months, every morning she would give me the biggest, most beautiful smile. She remembered me. When she was four months old, I went back to work. The first day, when I came to pick her up at the baby-sitter's, she flashed a big smile, and I knew everything was going to be OK."

—Kim Waggoner,
Manassas, VA

Mirror, mirror on the wall,
your 6-month-old knows
who's the fairest of them all:
He is!

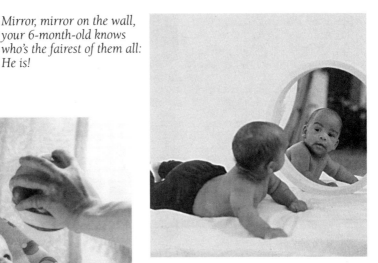

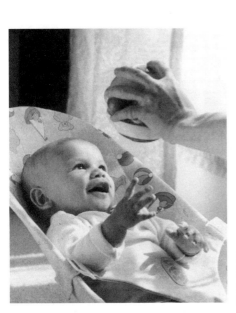

Your baby is learning to use
his hands to signal "gimme"
when he sees something he
wants.

it went. At 7 months or older he'll want to get right down there and find it.

This knowledge that something out of sight may soon reappear, combined with his developing understanding of cause and effect, makes for all sorts of great playtime possibilities. He's just beginning to be interested in peekaboo and Where's the _____? (fill in the blank: ball, toy, and so on) games that can stimulate his brain and his funny bone. By 8 to 9 months old, he'll be an ace at them.

In addition to using his hands to grab and to signal "gimme," your baby will begin to use them to tell you "no way"—as in "No way am I going to eat that mush you're trying to serve me." He'll push away the spoonful of cereal, the medicine dropper, the post-dinner washcloth.

Your little smarty-pants has also caught on to manipulation and will become adept at knowing the best way to get a response from you, whether it's with a particular body movement or cry. He now can recognize your voice and face, and other familiar faces. And he's fascinated by mirror images. By the end of 6 months, he'll have figured out that the guy in the mirror who looks just like him *isn't* him.

It's never too early to start reading with your baby. Babies love to look at bright pictures and hear the sound of your voice.

Social Development

Emotions Your baby has already made some amazing progress in learning to express his emotions. At first, he was able only to demonstrate that he felt distress (wet, cold, hungry) by crying. Later he showed he was content by peacefully gazing at his mobile. He showed excitement by waving his arms.

During his second three months of life, his displays of emotions become more sophisticated. More than just contentment, he's actually learning to feel happiness—and to show it with smiles and laughs. The reverse of happy is sad, of course, but it will be months before your baby understands what sad is, and how to express it. Instead, he'll get mad before sad.

Part of what's happening here involves a huge developmental leap: your baby has learned that he has some control over his environment. Not only is he feeling happy and mad but he's showing you how he feels in hopes that he can shape the situation to his liking. You hug him and kiss him, he smiles to persuade you to continue. You put away a favorite ball, he gets mad. How does he show it? By kicking, screaming, arching his back, or waving his arms at you. "Hey you," he's saying, "give that back *this instant*." Your baby is pitching his first intentional fit, one of many you'll experience in his first year of life (and beyond).

Language When it comes to communication, your baby has gone beyond crying to cooing, gurgling, shouting, laughing, giggling, growling, fussing, screeching, and, now, babbling. He may make a different sound to express each different need. His "Yippee, we're going on a swing" squeal, for instance, may be quite different from his vocal "I don't *want* to give Mommy her glasses back" reaction. His babbling may be all vowel sounds or begin to include some consonants.

A baby this age recognizes his mom's voice (and often pauses in his babbling when he hears it), and responds most often to female voices. If you pause long enough in your conversation, he may babble back and wait expectantly for your response.

Although you may not understand what he's trying to say, he's become more adept at understanding *you*. In fact, by the end of 6 months he may begin to recognize the sound of his own name, and a few months later he'll recognize simple words such as *baby* and *bottle*.

Give your baby plenty of opportunities to talk to you and to hear new words. This is incredibly important for his language and general development. Provide a running monologue, with plenty of pauses for him to chime in, whenever you're driving somewhere in the car, pouring a bottle, changing his diaper, or shopping in the supermarket. Name things as you go along and repeat words often.

If you haven't already done so, now is a great time to introduce books to your baby. He'll like the bright pictures and the sound of your voice. If it's an animal book, all the better; he may not be able to imitate the animal sounds now, but he'll love listening to you do it.

You may notice that your baby is fascinated by your mouth as you speak (even as you eat). His own eating may be interrupted if he's at the family table because he wants to talk, talk, talk (or, in his case, squeal, babble, and jabber).

Interaction Your baby is alert now for half of her waking hours—which gives you all sorts of time to talk, to socialize, and to play.

CHECKLIST
Best Books for Babies

The very best books for babies are ones parents will enjoy as much as their child. The magic of reading will rub off if you pick simple stories that have rhymes or pictures that appeal to you, too. Choose cuddly soft books that will feel good to baby's hands, and smooth, sturdy board books tough enough for baby teeth. Some suggestions:

✔ *All Fall Down; Clap Hands; Say Goodnight;* and *Tickle, Tickle,* by Helen Oxenbury (Little Simon/Simon & Schuster)
✔ *My Cloth Books,* by Lucy Cousins (Candlewick Press)
✔ *Let's Eat; Let's Go; Let's Make Friends;* and *Let's Play,* by Patrick Yee (Viking)

Since she is going through a social period and hasn't yet become overly anxious around strangers, get her out and about with other babies, families, and friends. She may be particularly attracted to other babies her size. Even when no other infants are around, your baby may try to join in your adult conversation by squealing or making an attention-getting noise. That's her way of saying, "Look at me! I want to talk, too."

Get down on the floor with her and play as often as possible. She'll have a special penchant for squeeze toys that make a noise (now that she can squeeze it herself), so you'll be very popular if you provide her with a squeaky or musical toy and a few minutes of your time.

> ## *MILESTONE*
>
> ### INTERACTION
>
> "At four months old, Kaitlyn is more fun than ever. She's easier now, too, probably because I'm more in tune with her. It's great to give a smile and get one back. Whenever she starts babbling, I just stop everything to talk to her because it's such a joy."
>
> —*Karen Liu,
> New York City*

Another enjoyable activity for parents and babies is listening to music. It makes no difference whether it's Raffi, the Rolling Stones, or Rachmaninoff, a musical interlude gives you the chance to rock and sway baby, dance and swing her around, or teach her how to clap to the beat. She may even hum along. (Don't play the music too loud or it may damage little eardrums.)

More than just a way to connect and play, researchers now believe that early exposure to music may actually strengthen the developing connections between brain cells. Other research has shown that children who get a steady diet of music are better at math. Your goal now, of course, isn't to raise the next Einstein or Elvis, but to make interaction as much fun and as satisfying as possible.

A Parent's Life

Sleep is still as precious as gold, but for the 50 percent of women who head back to work before their baby is 6 months old—so is time. Dealing with the home-to-work transition can be tough. You may feel guilty—or relieved—about leaving your child. Both are common and normal reactions. After all, you may have been working for years, but you've been a mother for only a couple of months. There are also worries about childcare, pumping breast milk at work, and juggling what suddenly feels like *two* full-time jobs.

⸎ A MOTHER'S VIEW ⸎

"My Life as a Single Parent"

Laura McCormick has been a single mom since the day her baby was born. Laurance's father wasn't interested in having a child, so Laura—who had wanted a baby for a few years—decided to go it on her own.

She lasted six weeks before she decided she needed help. "Being a mother was such a big change," admits the Tucson mom. "I wasn't comfortable doing it on my own. I got very stressed out." She moved in with her grandmother.

At her grandmother's house, Laura could forget her financial obligations for a while and focus on the baby. As Laurance became easier to care for and Laura became more confident, she began to work from home.

When Laurance was 6 months old, Laura felt able to take care of him without family help. She got her own place and has a roommate who exchanges childcare for reduced rent. "I'm calmer now," she says. "I can be nursing him or bouncing him on my knee while I'm working." Laura also works when Laurance naps. Her advice for single moms:

- **Don't let yourself get isolated as a new mother.** Ask your family or friends for help.
- **If you feel you're so stressed out that you're losing control, get help.** During the first month with her baby, Laura made the mistake of trying to do it all: she ended up losing her temper and feeling mad at the baby.
- **Connect with other single parents.** Try support groups, computer bulletin boards, the pediatrician's office, or wherever you can find help. "I don't care how small your town is, there's always some support available," Laura says.
- **Treasure the time you have with your baby.** It may be hard as a single parent, Laura says, but never lose sight of your blessings.

⌒ A MOTHER'S VIEW ⌒

"Easing the Guilt of Going Back to Work"

After five months of staying home with her baby, Kylie, and her 4-year-old, Tommy, Lisa Martine of Vineland, New Jersey, knew that D-day had arrived. Her maternity leave was over.

"In a way, returning to work was bittersweet," says Lisa. She finds her work interesting and fulfilling, but she also loved staying home with her children. "Emotionally it's harder to be at work," Lisa says, "but in a way it's less demanding. Being a stay-at-home mother is a very hard job."

Here are Lisa's tips for doing the best you can for your children, and still getting to work on time:

- **Find excellent childcare.** Lisa was lucky that her son's daycare center also accepted babies, allowing Kylie to be with her brother for three days a week. The other two days, Kylie stays with her grandma.
- **Make the effort to pump your breast milk.** "Pumping makes me feel I'm doing something for my daughter during the day," says Lisa. "And it eases my working mother's guilt."
- **Get organized.** "I'm very disciplined about my getting-out-the-door routines," says Lisa. "I have to be or I'm late for work." She prepares bottles and lunches the night before, and sets out breakfast dishes. She puts Kylie to bed in an outfit that she can wear to daycare, and lays out clothes for herself and her son.
- **Don't forget to button your blouse after pumping at work.** (Lisa learned this the hard way.)

Back to Work

One of a working mom's first (of many) worries is about the quality of care her baby will receive while she's on the job. Nailing down decent daycare is critical if you expect the home-to-work transition to go smoothly. (For childcare options, see "What You Need to Know About . . . Infant Childcare," page 124.)

One of the very best situations, although it is rare, is to have your child in a childcare facility that's connected with, or near, your work. The company I worked for when my second daughter was born had its own corporate daycare center. The facility wasn't in the building, but was only two blocks away, so I could run over at a moment's notice to nurse Gracie. For months I visited her every day at lunch.

Once you have your childcare situation set up, think about ways to ease into work. Consider starting on a reduced or part-time schedule. Your employer may be more open-minded than you think. Some women start on a half-day schedule or four days a week; others telecommute or work from home for a couple of days a week. If that's not an option, go back to work in the middle or near the end of the week, so you're not too overwhelmed or exhausted.

Be clear with everyone that you intend to pull your weight, but that you need to do it within set work hours. Be firm about the parameters of your workday: this is not the time to take on extra assignments or to work longer hours. Even though you may want to prove that you're still a dedicated, career-oriented employee, you'll do yourself a favor if you wait until you're more settled and less tired. And if your pay isn't full-time, make sure your work isn't, either.

To ease any sore feelings about the extra work that your absence created, make sure to thank those coworkers who helped out while you were on maternity leave, and try not to bore them to tears with tales of your labor and wonderful child.

Get a Grip on Guilt You're bound to feel some conflicted feelings about leaving your baby, even if you like your job. "Guilt" and "working mom" seem to just naturally go hand in hand. So do "working mom" and "supermom," another deadly combination.

It's often been said that to feel good about themselves, women need to do everything 100 percent. They feel they have to be a 100 percent wonderful mother, worker, wife.

Why are women so hard on themselves? Part of the guilt stems from the fact that society still isn't entirely comfortable with the notion that mothers have to—and often want to—work. So it's an external pressure. But a lot of guilt and feelings of failure stem from working mothers' own inability to acknowledge

A MOTHER'S VIEW

"Why I Work at Home"

For Kathy McCleary, going back to work after the births of her daughters Emma and Grace meant walking down the hall to her at-home office. She didn't even have to take off her pajamas if she didn't want to.

The mother of a 6-month-old and a 3-year-old, Kathy telecommutes full-time to an office on the East Coast. After each baby was born, she was back at her computer within 6 to 12 weeks.

Because she lives in Portland, Oregon, which has a three-hour time difference from her employer in Virginia, her workday is unorthodox. "I start at 6:30 A.M., right after I get up, and work until 3:30 P.M.," she says. Her husband cares for the children in the morning until the nanny arrives at 7:30 A.M.

"When I'm working, I'm really working," Kathy says. That means no chores or exercise breaks during working hours. When she spends her lunch break with her daughters, she doesn't get to relax and read the newspaper as she would if she were in an office. But for Kathy, that's a small price to pay. She likes her job, the commute is great, she can nurse her baby at lunchtime, and she's done by 3:30, in time to play with her girls for a few daylight hours before the hectic dinner hour sets in.

"Working at home allows me to give what I need to my job, and give what I need to my family," she says. Her tips for juggling work and family at home:

- **Get a nanny you love.** "My older daughter usually understands that when I'm working, she can't interrupt me," says Kathy. Still, there are times when Grace isn't so cool: "I've gone into my office with her screaming at me not to work. I just have to close my door and know that I have a wonderful nanny."
- **Know yourself and love your job.** If you're not self-motivated and very self-disciplined, and if you only feel so-so about your work, you won't be able to keep the office door shut when you hear your baby cry, or the doorbell ring, or Oprah is on TV.
- **Set parameters.** Under what circumstances will you come out of the office? Kathy gives her nanny full authority to comfort her children or solve disputes. "But of course I'll come out, if there's an injury," she says.
- **Set work limits.** Make it clear to your employer that when work hours are over, you're done.

how much they really are doing—and doing well. With all the running around from job to childcare to home to doctor's appointments, it's hard to see the forest for the trees, and easy to blame yourself for not having dinner on the table when your partner gets home, or your best dress ironed when you need it.

For a quick reality check, get together with other new moms and talk about how you're feeling. The point isn't to compare yourself with others (which can add to your guilt), but to empathize and learn from each other's successes and mistakes. Mothers are good at reminding each other why they work in the first place: not just for the money but also for the self-esteem and contact with the outside world. And they're often more than willing to swap tales about the intense joys of parenthood, which on bad days can help you remember why you had a baby in the first place.

If you can't shake your feelings of guilt or your frenzied efforts to be supermom, maybe you *are* doing something wrong. Pick out some legitimate ways you could accomplish a task better. If you're late relieving the baby-sitter three nights in a row, you're obviously not leaving on time. Ask yourself how you can solve that problem: being stricter about leaving work? putting your partner in charge of evening pickup? admitting that you need an adjustment in the hours your childcare provider works? going to work an hour earlier? You need to acknowledge that you're out of control before you can fix any of the problems—or get rid of the guilt.

Most working mothers eventually find the right work-family balance, although it may take years. Some find that they have to make a dramatic change to get their new lives back on track; they scale down to a part-time job for a while, or find employment where they can work from home. Some just finally learn how to say no to too-high demands at work, to their supermom tendencies, and to guilt.

What You Need to Know About . . . Pumping at Work

Just because you're going back to work, doesn't mean you have to stop breast-feeding your baby. Besides the obvious benefits for your infant (especially if she's in a daycare situation where the extra immunities may help her stay well), nursing at night and before work, and pumping during the day, may help you stay connected to your baby.

Pumping at work takes a bit of planning. You need to rent or buy a good pump, have a place in which to comfortably pump, and have a way to keep the pumped milk cold. And you should alert your employer (and possibly your co-workers) that you'll be pumping at work.

• **Telling your boss.** Reassure your supervisor that'll you'll be using your scheduled breaks or lunch hour to pump, and that pumping won't affect the quality or quantity of your work. Many women can pump and work—opening mail, reading reports—at the same time; use your judgment about whether that's something your boss will believe. Be firm about the fact that you're going to pump but that you have no less of a commitment to your job. If you think it will help, you can mention the study that claims that mothers who continue to breastfeed their babies after they go back to work lose less time from work because their children are sick less often.

• **Finding the right pump.** If you want to express your milk as quickly as possible, it's best to rent or buy a high-quality pump (see "HOW TO: Use a Breast Pump," page 83), which often comes in an easy-to-carry case so you can lug it from home to office. Many women just leave it in the office and take it home for weekend pumping.

• **A place to pump.** I've pumped in all sorts of rest rooms, from offices to airports to restaurants. It's not something I'd highly recommend, but you can use a bathroom in a pinch. Some bathroom stalls have outlets in them so you won't be pumping in front of everyone, but it's not the most sanitary of surroundings.

GOOD ADVICE

"Why I Pump at Work"

"Pumping really makes me feel connected to my son when I can't be with him. I have occasionally gotten curious looks while I'm washing my equipment in the kitchen sink, but I don't let it bother me."

—*Leah Hennen, Brooklyn, NY*

"It's nice to have two brief times during the day when I think about my baby and remember that I'm a mom as well as a working person."

—*Melanie Haiken, San Raphael, CA*

"I had terrible asthma and allergies as a child. There's evidence that breastfed babies are less likely to develop these problems, so there was never any question about continuing to breastfeed or pumping at work."

—*Valerie Fahey, Piedmont, CA*

With the right equipment and a little planning, you can continue to breastfeed after going back to work.

When I was expressing milk for my second daughter, I was lucky to have an office with a door—but it also had windows to the hallway and windows to outside. Neither had curtains. I'd simply put a note on the door, turn my back to

---

For More Help: Going Back to Work

Organizations

- 9 to 5 National Association of Working Women
  800-522-0925
- New Ways to Work
  415-995-9860

Books and Other Resources

- *Breaking Out of 9 to 5,* by Maria Laqueur and Donna Dickinson (Peterson's)
- *Divided Lives,* by Elsa Walsh (Anchor)
- *The Working Woman's Guide to Managing Stress,* by J. Robin Powell, with Holly George-Warren (Prentice-Hall)
- *Working Parents' Help Book,* by Susan Crietes Price and Tom Price (Peterson's)

the hall windows, and pray that nobody across the street had binoculars. The staff got used to hearing the whoomp-whoomp of the pump and seeing the breast milk in the fridge.

If you don't have a private office or a private lunchroom in which to pump, consider hanging a curtain across your cubicle door. When I was the editor of PARENTING magazine, we put up blinds for those staffers who had window offices and wanted to pump in private. Curtains made of sheets were hung across cubicle entries. Workers with cubicles were welcome to use empty offices. Make sure you ask first, of course, before you move your pumping paraphernalia anywhere but into your own work space.

• **Stimulating let-down.** Understandably, some women have a hard time achieving let-down in an office situation. They may be embarrassed because of the proximity of others or be stressed out from being back at work. Try these tricks:

1. Drink a big glass of water right before pumping.
2. Look at your baby's picture, or hold a piece of her clothing.
3. Call the baby-sitter and talk about your baby.
4. Play a tape recording of baby sounds.

• **Where to store the milk.** Breast milk needs to be kept cold. It shouldn't be left at room temperature for more than four hours. If an office fridge isn't available, store it in a cooler with ice or in an insulated bag with gel ice packs.

• **Wearing the right clothes.** Given the inherent awkwardness of pumping at work, it pays to wear clothing specifically designed for nursing or that provides easy access to your breasts. Keep extra nursing pads in your desk for leaks and dribbles.

HOW TO

Relax for a Minute

- **Run away.** Leave the office and take a five-minute trek around the block. Or run up and down the stairs in your house for a minute.
- **Breathe deeply.** Breathe in slowly and hold your breath until the count of 10. Release to the count of 10.
- **Stretch your back and neck.** Gently bend over from your waist with your arms relaxing at your sides. Roll up slowly and rotate your neck in one direction, then the other.

If you can't or don't want to pump at work, it's still possible to continue nursing your baby before and after work and before bed (see "Weaning from the Breast," page 255). This is a revelation for many women who think nursing is an all-or-nothing proposition. Instead of being a hassle, limited breastfeeding provides some surprising benefits: it's a pleasant transition time for many moms, and your baby is still receiving important nutrients and immunities even when he's not being nursed full-time. Part-time nursing does, naturally, lead to a reduced milk supply. Make sure your baby is getting enough additional formula to satisfy his appetite and stage of growth.

Taking Care of Yourself

In surveys where new moms are asked what suffers the most—your baby, your job, your spouse, your housework, or yourself—you can probably guess the answer. Working moms often cheat themselves of the time and attention they need to stay healthy and happy. They eat on the go, they don't exercise, they don't get enough sleep, they even forget to breathe correctly. It's not long before all that stress can make a person sick.

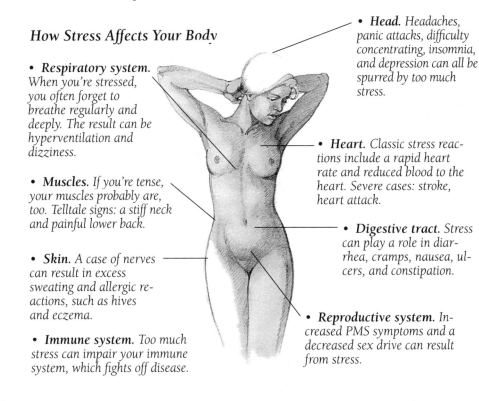

How Stress Affects Your Body

• **Respiratory system.** *When you're stressed, you often forget to breathe regularly and deeply. The result can be hyperventilation and dizziness.*

• **Muscles.** *If you're tense, your muscles probably are, too. Telltale signs: a stiff neck and painful lower back.*

• **Skin.** *A case of nerves can result in excess sweating and allergic reactions, such as hives and eczema.*

• **Immune system.** *Too much stress can impair your immune system, which fights off disease.*

• **Head.** *Headaches, panic attacks, difficulty concentrating, insomnia, and depression can all be spurred by too much stress.*

• **Heart.** *Classic stress reactions include a rapid heart rate and reduced blood to the heart. Severe cases: stroke, heart attack.*

• **Digestive tract.** *Stress can play a role in diarrhea, cramps, nausea, ulcers, and constipation.*

• **Reproductive system.** *Increased PMS symptoms and a decreased sex drive can result from stress.*

Give Yourself a Break

"I remind myself that I don't have to be perfect. My children just have to know that I love them."

—*Dawn Lee Adams, Burien, WA*

"Keeping a daily journal—even if I only write for 15 minutes before I go to bed—helps me release some of the day's stress and gives me time to focus on myself."

—*Sonia Barlow, Mishawaka, IN*

"I make sure my baby is safe. Then I go into the bathroom with a couple of magazines and lock the door. Just five minutes works wonders."

—*Debbie Pedersen, Sarasota, FL*

"Waking up at 5:30 A.M. to work out isn't easy—some mornings, I literally have to crawl out of bed—but then I have uninterrupted time to myself, before the baby has even thought about getting up."

—*Lynn Browning, Edinboro, PA*

"Joining a mother's group really helped me. It's very calming just to talk—whether it's comparing our children's development or moaning about our husbands."

—*Julie Rogers, Orlando, FL*

"My son has been very independent and headstrong from the beginning. When I start to lose my cool, I've learned to remind myself (sometimes several times) that he was sent here to bring out the best and the worst in me. And I've realized that there are some things I need to work on (like not always having to be the one in control)."

—*Shawn Trego, Simpsonville, SC*

The Importance of Being Dad

Although Dad is often the first person an infant sees, gazing down at her in awe, he often has what's considered a secondary role in raising and rearing his child. That's been true for centuries and in most cultures. But no one should under-estimate the importance of what a baby learns from a dad who's involved in her care.

It's interesting that within the first two months of life, a baby can already begin to distinguish Mom from Dad—and reacts differently to each. She is more likely to calm in her mother's presence and become stimulated when her dad is around. Experts who study the interactions between young children and parents say this may be because of some differences in how moms and dads typically play with and watch over their children.

Mom	Dad
Picks up and holds baby the same way each time	Uses a variety of techniques to pick up and hold baby
Won't let crawling baby out of her sight	Will give baby a little more chance to explore
Will hover and offer reassurance during a new situation	Will stand back and let the child decide how to proceed (unless it's obviously dangerous)
Will play with baby quietly	Will roughhouse with baby
Is gently encouraging	Encourages risk taking
Is more serious	Goofs around more

This combination of reassuring and challenging parenting styles seems to be just what children need to grow up smart and independent. Studies

Dads' special way of playing helps babies develop an independent spirit and a love of fun.

A FATHER'S VIEW

"Diary of a Stay-at-Home Dad"

"**H**ow nice. You must have so much free time." Don't say that to Scott Bokun after he tells you he stays home full-time with his daughters Abby and Lilly. He's likely to respond: "I don't get time to myself until 10:00 at night!"

Scott, a former New York City film editor, decided to make the move to stay-at-home dad when Abby, now 3, was 6 months old. His wife, Michele, had been offered a job in Boston, and they were discussing future job moves when Scott surprised his wife (and himself) by offering to stay home. "I had always thought it might be fun," Scott says, "but I never thought I would ever get the chance." Because the Bokuns could get by on one income in Lexington, Massachusetts, Scott's new career was born.

In addition to caring for the girls, now 3 years and 8 months old, Scott runs the household. "I'm doing the typically manly jobs like mowing the lawn, and I'm also cooking all the meals and cleaning the bathroom."

Scott is still a little uncomfortable with strangers' assumptions about his life. "It's hard meeting fathers who work outside the home because nobody looks at staying at home as a job," says Scott, "yet it's the hardest job I've ever done." And the most meaningful. "Your children are only going to be this young once," he says. "Once they don't need you anymore, there'll be plenty of time for other pursuits." His tips for dads at home:

- **Always shower before the kids get up.** "If you don't," says Scott, "you'll never get another chance."
- **Don't be afraid to be silly with your kids.** The sillier you are, the happier they'll be.
- **Lower your expectations.** Don't expect to accomplish life projects while you're at home with young kids. "I don't get much of a chance to read past the first page of the newspaper," Scott says.
- **Find like-minded souls to bond with.** Scott put up flyers in his neighborhood and posted messages on the Internet soliciting members for a dads' play group. Now 12 fathers meet every Friday for a play date, and go out once a month to see a movie or play cards.

have only scratched the surface on this very complex and complicated subject, but some reports have said that children whose fathers have been involved in their care:

- Have higher IQs.
- Can control themselves better.
- Are less violent later in life.

Of course, a baby attaches to Mom *and* Dad, and learns from both. And babies thrive when they have just one parent or two parents of the same sex. There are all sorts of other factors that affect a child's intelligence, self-esteem, and self-control. But if there is a dad in the family, there's good reason to encourage him to get involved with the baby's care early. Mom and Dad aren't interchangeable. A dad who *doesn't* wait until his baby is old enough to play ball before he gets involved will be doing his infant a huge favor.

Being able to crawl gives your baby a newfound sense of power.

CHAPTER 4

MONTHS SEVEN THROUGH NINE

It's like falling in love all over again. That's what many parents say about the intense period in the middle of their baby's first year. Of course, you loved your baby from the second you saw her. And she loved you (well, she loved being fed and kept warm and dry).

But during this magical time you and your baby really begin to speak the same language—whether it's a shared giggle over a favorite game, a quiet snuggle as you gaze into each others' eyes, or just the special way you come to the rescue when she holds up her arms to be picked up.

And even while you're growing closer, she's growing away from you. Shaking her head "No." Pushing away the spoon. Crawling to the other side of the room. And skedaddling right back to you when she pushes herself too far or when a stranger enters the picture. This push-pull is just as it should be: it's what growing up is all about.

By the end of nine months your baby will probably* . . .

- Have surprised you (and himself) with his loud voice
- Be crawling faster than the speed of light
- Be independent one minute, clingy the next
- Have pitched more than one major hissy fit when he didn't get his way
- Show an interest in feeding himself
- Add dustballs and pieces of lint to his diet (thanks to mastering the thumb-and-forefinger pincer grasp)
- Be better at letting you know what he wants (as in "ba . . . ba . . . BA . . . BAAAAA!!!!!!" accompanied by frenzied arm movements, meaning "get me my bottle and get it *now*")
- Recognize his own name (and other names you use often, the dog's name, for instance)
- Recognize the word *no*, but choose to ignore it

*Every baby is different and has his or her own developmental timetable.

By the end of nine months, you will probably . . .

- Be able to play peekaboo and pat-a-cake in your sleep
- Have lowered the crib mattress two or three times (now that your baby is standing up in bed)
- Have lost touch with a few friends (who don't have children) and made a few new ones (who do)
- Have said no 100 times in the past three months
- Have gained an appreciation for how stain-removal products work on baby food
- Have lost your sense of humor about that last 10 pounds you can't lose
- Have spent more than you care to admit on baby toys, baby safety products, and baby pictures
- Have had more than one backache from picking up your eating machine
- Fondly remember the days when your baby just sat there and looked pretty
- Have had sex, at least once

CARE AND FEEDING

Months 7 through 9 are a big transition time for your hungry baby, who is now more than happy to sit in his high chair and eat with the rest of the family.

New Feeding Experiences

In addition to sampling a wider variety of baby foods, including strained meats and poultry, your baby will soon be ready for a few finger foods. If he's bottle-feeding, he may also be giving you signals that he's ready to try a cup or give up his bottle. With change come new messes!

Saying Good-bye to the Bottle As with most things, weaning your baby from the bottle can take quite a while. It needn't be rushed. Many parents aim to wean their baby from the bottle by the time she's 1 year old. In months 7 and 8, your baby will still be very attached to her bottle. By 9 months, she may be less interested but still need the comfort that sucking on a bottle offers. This is a good age to watch for signs that she's ready to give up her bottle for a few feedings a day.

Now that your baby is sitting up, she may show an interest in holding her own bottle. This is when those plastic bottles with the hole in the center come in handy; they're very easy for little hands to grasp. (Your child will also show a great interest in throwing her bottle. Don't take this as a sign of bottle rejection; it's more a sign of playful independence.)

YOUR BABY'S WORLD

In months 7 through 9, your baby's world is full of new sensations: the texture of a soft rug or of scratchy grass under her knees, the taste of something thick and smooth on her tongue, and the feeling of power derived from getting across the room under her own steam.

What Your Baby Sees. With her 20/50 or 20/60 vision, she can see 12 feet or more away. That means she can see you coming, she can see that toy across the floor that she wants, and she can see out the window. Hello world!

What Your Baby Hears. She hears you—even from the next room—and is comforted by your voice. She hears you say 'no' and gives you a lesson in what selective hearing is all about (and how early it kicks in).

What Your Baby Feels. She's developed quite a taste for independence and wants to get her hands on everything. Her pointer finger and thumb get a good work-out as she learns to pick up pea-sized objects. Choking is a real threat: now's the time for extra-careful baby-proofing.

What Your Baby Likes. She likes everything—as long as it was her idea! But when her new big world seems scary, she likes Mom and Dad best.

What Your Baby Tastes. As your baby joins the new-baby-food-a-week club, she's experiencing a taste and texture extravaganza. She still prefers sweet over sour (fruit over veggies), but she's broadening her horizons every day. The love affair with the Cheerio begins.

LIFE WITH ESTEBAN

Follow along with new mother Grege Lastra's month-by-month diary of her first year of motherhood.

At eight months Esteban is a real speed demon, but he bolts right back to Mom or Dad when a stranger enters the scene.

MONTH 7

Esteban has practically bypassed crawling. He's much more interested in pulling himself up on anything that allows him to get upright. He's actually walking around the edge of the bed. I'm not ready for this!

Esteban loves mashed stuffing, thinned with milk, or sweet potatoes straight from his dad's plate. He's a master at spitting food—but that's not his only trick. Every button or knob attracts him. I need roller skates to keep up.

MONTH 8

When Esteban started crawling, he sort of dragged one leg behind, but now he's up on all fours. He falls well, sort of catching himself with his arms to break his fall.

He now weighs 24 pounds and is 30 inches tall. He still doesn't have any teeth, but he's always drooling.

Esteban hates being dressed and undressed. When his crib sheets need changing, I put down a pad and let him wriggle around without his diaper for a while.

This kid really knows what he likes and doesn't like. He can really be moody—and maybe he's getting a bit spoiled. He loves when his dad holds him up to "dance." He makes us all laugh.

MONTH 9

Esteban takes off and goes for everything—everything he shouldn't get into or touch. We childproof, but it's never enough. Some days it seems impossible to keep even one small step ahead of this little mover.

Esteban seems fussier now than he ever was before. He gets really frustrated when he can't do something. Sometimes he even pulls a temper tantrum.

Lately he's been suffering from stranger anxiety. And he really hates crowds. In any situation with strangers, he looks to Steve or me to be held.

On the talking front, we've only noticed a little movement. Esteban will often say a long string of "babababababa's" or "dadadadada's." The "dada" sound doesn't really seem to be connected to Steve, although I certainly can't tell his father that!

HOW TO
Remove Stains, Take 2

As your child grows, your stain-removal challenges increase. Spit-up and feces stains (see "HOW TO: Remove Spit-up and Other Stains," page 77) are nothing compared to this new batch of clothing wreckers.

Stain	Removal Tip
Baby food	Pretreat stain with liquid nonchlorine bleach for 30 minutes
Fruit juice	Pretreat with hydrogen peroxide if garment can be bleached; if not, use white vinegar
Tomato sauce/ ketchup	Rinse in cold water, then soak in nonchlorine bleach and water for 30 minutes
Grass	Pretreat stain with rubbing alcohol (test alcohol on garment first)
Grease	Pretreat heavily with stain remover or soak in enzyme detergent
Crayon	Pretreat spot with water and detergent, rubbing until crayon outline is gone. Then wash in hot water and chlorine bleach (if garment allows)
Egg	Pretreat with a stain remover

As your baby gets more mobile, you'll have to decide whether or not you want her bottle to travel around with her. This is when many parents decide that the bottle should be reserved for morning and evening comfort feedings, and to use a cup the rest of the time. If you don't mind the bottle going where your baby does, just make sure to remove the bottle once it's been out for more than 20 minutes. It doesn't take long for bacteria to breed.

Now's a good time to take a moment to study what your baby is doing and to decipher what she's really trying to tell you: Is she leaving your lap with her bottle because she wants to move around with it? Or because she's more interested in exploring than drinking? If she's simply finished, but has forgotten to put down the bottle, take it from her. If she just seems bored with the bottle, she may be ready for a cup at her high chair. Try it and see.

HOW TO

Hold an Older Baby

Their necks are strong, they're sitting up, but they still like to be held. They weigh more than 20 pounds! What's a mother to do?

Hip Straddle. This is surely why you have hips: so your bigger baby can ride around with you. One arm holds your baby's bottom while the other arm rests on his back to hold him in place. Swap sides often to avoid back strain.

See the World. Baby faces away from you. One arm serves as a bench for baby to sit on, the other arm crosses his chest to hold him securely.

Q & A

"Is it safe to save what's left in the baby-food jar for the next feeding?"

Babies this age are unlikely to eat a whole jar of food at one sitting, so it makes sense to refrigerate the remainder for a future meal.

To avoid introducing bacteria into the jar, however, always serve the food to your baby from a plate or bowl. A spoon that goes directly from baby's mouth to jar and back again may taint the food with bacteria. If you've spoon-fed your baby right from the jar, throw out the remainder of the food.

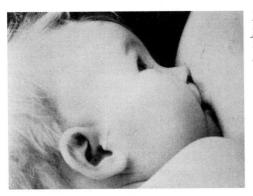

Many babies begin to wean themselves from the breast around 9 months, when they become interested in solid foods and in activities not related to sucking.

Starting the Cup The transition from bottle to cup is a major milestone for parents and baby. For some parents, the bottle is a symbol of babyhood that's hard to give up. For babies, the pleasure of sucking, which the bottle or a breast delivers, can be hard to live without.

Don't sweat it. A cup can be slowly introduced over time, so that your baby doesn't associate it with the removal of her beloved bottle or the breast. And for several months, she will be drinking from both a bottle and a cup. Or from bottle, breast, and cup. Whatever you do, don't turn introducing the cup into a battle with your baby. It should be a fun (although messy) experience for both of you. Some things to consider:

• **Timing the introduction.** Once your baby can open and close her fingers in a grasp, she may be able to hold a cup—usually around 8 to 9 months. If she's not ready, try again later. Introduce the cup—using a dribble-proof model—at a time when you're both relaxed and in a good mood. She shouldn't be dying of thirst and you shouldn't be in a hurry (or dressed in your best).
• **Demonstrating cup use.** You've probably noticed your baby eyeing you as you drink your morning cup of coffee. Her own sipping skills may not match her level of interest. A more formal demonstration may help her catch on to cup drinking. Show her how you take a little sip, and then help guide her own cup to her lips.
• **Preparing for the mess.** Your baby is likely to immediately turn the cup upside down (as she would a block or other plaything) and examine it from all angles. Even the best dribble-proof cup is going to leak when it's shaken furiously while held upside down. So cover your child with a waterproof bib, place her in her high chair, and cover yourself, too, if you're worried about your clothing.
• **Making a gradual transition.** Try the following:

1. Reducing the number of bottle feedings; usually the pre-nap and night-night bottles are the last to go.

CHECKLIST

The Right Cup

Baby cups come in all sizes, shapes, and colors. It may take a few weeks of trial and error before you find your baby's cup of choice. Since it will be launched across the kitchen a few times, you'll want to choose one that's made of unbreakable plastic and that has a lid. Other features to consider:

Introduce the cup slowly. For several months your baby will be drinking from a cup and bottle or breast—or all three.

✔ **The spout.** This facilitates the transition from nipple to cup. Some babies prefer one kind of spout over another.

✔ **Handles.** A cup may have two handles, one handle, no handles. Only your baby will be able to tell you her preference.

✔ **Weighted bottom.** This feature prevents the cup from tipping over easily.

✔ **Spill-proof.** Some cups have built-in valves that prevent the liquid from backing up and out through the spout. Others have snap-down spouts that allow you to carry a full cup in your purse (preferably in a clean baggie) without leaks.

✔ **Decoration.** Name a cartoon character and you'll probably find it staring at you from a baby cup. Will your child take a cup faster if Winnie-the-Pooh is on it? You'll have to decide.

2. Filling the bottle with a less desirable beverage; if your baby loves juice, for instance, serve a little of that in a cup at first and give only bottles of water. Her drink of choice should be saved for the cup, but don't overdo the juice (See "The Truth About . . . Juice," page 254). Give her lots of praise every time she uses her cup.

3. Fulfilling your baby's need for comfort sucking with a pacifier or her fingers.

4. Using the cup during her "best" meal. If she's happiest and hungriest at breakfast, use the cup then. If she's still thirsty after drinking a little from the cup, try more; if she wants the bottle then, go ahead and let her have the bottle. Increase the amount of formula or breast milk in the cup each time until you're able to skip the bottle or breast altogether at this meal. (Keep the bottle out of sight for this to work!)

Starting Finger Foods Given a baby's messy eating habits, almost anything you feed her—including spoonfuls of strained meats—could be considered a

CHECKLIST

Finger Foods to Avoid

Don't give these foods to your child until she's at least 4 years old. They're common choking hazards.

- ✔ hard candy
- ✔ popcorn
- ✔ nuts
- ✔ grapes or cherries
- ✔ hot dogs
- ✔ raw carrots or vegetables

- ✔ uncooked, hard fruit
- ✔ peanut butter
- ✔ chunks of soft cheese
- ✔ raisins
- ✔ whole peas

finger food. She'll certainly get her fingers into it! But by 9 months old, your baby may also be interested in the more literal definition of finger foods: tidbits she can actually pick up and eat by herself. What a feeling of pride and excitement your baby will experience when she navigates that first O-shaped bit of cereal into her mouth. In one simple action she's showing off her pincer skills, eye-hand coordination, and independence, not to mention getting a taste treat.

The self-feeding baby is demonstrating all sorts of new abilities including pincer skills, eye-hand coordination, and independence.

Although you and your child may both be tired of baby food, finger foods should be introduced slowly and cautiously. Don't be overeager to have her make the transition to regular table food. Food allergies are still a possibility and choking is always a big concern. She may be able to pick up the food and mash it into her mouth but not be able to swallow it.

While your baby is gumming Cheerios and teething biscuits (both of which will melt in her mouth and give her practice at self-feeding), you can begin feeding her one of the chunkier baby foods that come in a jar. These lumpier entrées introduce your baby to new textures, and teach her to mash the food inside her mouth before swallowing it. She may gag even on these soft lumps, so give her plenty of time to experience and master these foods before moving on to mushy table foods—such as scrambled egg yolks, soft pieces of fruit, mashed potatoes—or other finger foods (see Chapter 5).

Baby's Daily Diet

AGE	BREAST MILK OR FORMULA	CEREAL	FRUIT	BREAD	VEGGIES	MEAT/PROTEIN
6–9 mos.	3–5 feedings or 24–32 oz. (may be more frequent if breastfeeding)	2 servings (2–4 Tbs.)	1–2 servings (3–4 Tbs.)	teething biscuit*	2 servings (3–4 Tbs.)	2 servings (1–2 Tbs.). Limit egg yolk to three times a week
9–12 mos.	3–4 feedings or 16–24 oz.	2 servings (2–4 Tbs.)	2 servings (3–4 Tbs.)	½ slice of bread or ¼ cup of soft pasta	2 servings (3–4 Tbs.)	2 servings (2–3 Tbs.)

*Don't leave your baby alone with any sort of cracker or teething biscuit.

Don't offer your baby anything that can be inhaled in one piece (peas or raisins, for instance) or that is stringy (certain fruits and vegetables, such as mangoes or string beans), which can cause choking. Also take special care with teething biscuits. A baby who is teething may enjoy gnawing on a biscuit (found in the baby-food aisle of your supermarket) and have no trouble swallowing the mushy bits in her mouth. She could choke, however, on the sharp corners or bits that may fall off the biscuit as she gums it. Keep an eye on your baby at all times when she's eating.

Now that your baby is nibbling on a few crackers, smushing a mashed-up piece of fruit in her mouth, and tossing her cup on the floor, it's even more difficult to figure out whether she's eating enough, and enough of the right foods. See the chart on this page to determine what and how much your older baby should eat each day.

The Truth About . . . Juice

Juice seems like a healthy alternative to formula or breast milk, so it may come as a surprise to hear that it's not a good beverage choice for babies this age. In fact, juice of any kind isn't recommended for infants 6 months or younger. And a baby 6 months to 1 year old should have no more than 4 ounces of juice a day. This is bad news for parents who may have been planning to wean their baby from bottle to cup by offering them the sweet juice in the cup as an enticement. If you use juice, limit the amount and make sure she's getting plenty of formula or breast milk.

MILESTONE

FIRST FINGER FOODS

"If the refrigerator door opens and she's across the room, nine-month-old Faith will crawl over to it in a heartbeat. She loves Cheerios, but for her, *all* food is finger food—even pancakes and scrambled eggs!"

—Anne Welch,
Long Island, NY

A happy baby fingers her favorite food: those tasty O's.

There are many reasons to limit your baby's juice consumption, especially of apple juice, which has commonly been the juice of choice for babies:

- It contains lots of naturally occurring sugars—such as fructose and sorbitol—that are hard for a baby to absorb. These sugars can cause bloating, diarrhea, and excess gas.
- Juice isn't a naturally good source of vitamin C (although the vitamin is added by some manufacturers).
- Babies often fill up on juice, which means they skimp on more healthful milk, or if they're older, on vegetables and grains. Since juice lacks protein and fat, babies who drink a lot of it may suffer poor growth. One study found that juice drinkers were more likely to be overweight or short.
- Too much juice—especially in a bottle at naptime—can cause tooth decay.

A better choice for your baby might be white grape juice, which has less of the offending sugars and is easier to digest than apple juice. Make sure that any juice you give your baby is pasteurized. Juice that hasn't gone through the heating process may contain *E. coli* bacteria, which is especially dangerous to babies.

Weaning from the Breast

The American Academy of Pediatrics recommends that for the best start in life, a baby be breastfed for a full year or more. If you're able to breastfeed for a year or

⁓ A MOTHER'S VIEW ⁓

"When to Wean"

Cathy Myers of Concord, California, weaned her first baby at 8 months. She stopped offering Timothy her breast during the day, and pretty soon he gave up asking for it. Then one night he went to sleep without nursing, and that was it. Timothy was weaned.

A great success story for a mom who was ready to wean—but Cathy was not. Her decision to wean, she now realizes, stemmed from being uninformed and from peer pressure. "All the books I read recommended weaning before the child's first birthday," she says. Cathy didn't know anyone who'd breastfed for as long as she had. Even her family would ask her, "Are you still doing that?"

With her next child, Samantha, Cathy decided to wean when she—or Samantha—decided the time was right. So far, that time hasn't come. Now 14 months old, Samantha is still happily nursing. "When she comes up to me and asks to nurse, I feel as if we're working together as a team," Cathy says. She doesn't know if Samantha will be interested in nursing until she's 2 years old, as the World Health Organization recommends, but she does know she isn't going to force weaning this time.

The fact that Samantha is nursing now more for comfort instead of out of hunger doesn't bother Cathy a bit. "If she's learning that Mom is a source of comfort," she asks, "what's wrong with that?" Her advice for weaning on your own terms:

- **Get both sides of the story.** A woman's attitude toward breastfeeding is largely molded by what her friends' and her family's attitudes are, and by the books she reads, says Cathy. If you're uncomfortable with one friend's advice or what one book says, ask someone else, or buy a different book. (She recommends *The Womanly Art of Breastfeeding*, La Leche League International [Plume].)
- **Feel good about what you decide, whatever your choice.** "The decision to wean is very personal," says Cathy.
- **Stop worrying.** Don't be concerned that by letting your child dictate when to wean you'll be nursing a 5-year-old. Toddlers can be taught to wean and often self-wean as their world and skills expand.

longer, that's great. If you can't, rest assured that *any* amount of time you spend breastfeeding is time well spent. And the decision to wean, like the decision to breastfeed, is a very personal one. Weaning can take place anytime from a baby's first few days to her first few years. Some moms and babies wean early because they've had trouble feeding. Other women give themselves a weaning deadline—they decide to stop nursing before they go back to work, for instance, or when their baby turns 2.

The subject of weaning is being discussed in this chapter (instead of earlier) because at around 9 months of age many babies begin to start to wean themselves. As they become more interested in solid foods and in activities not related to sucking, they turn to the breast less often. Moms often choose to begin weaning during the 9- to 12-month

GOOD ADVICE
On Surviving Weaning

"One day when my son, Zachary, was eight months old, he wouldn't allow me to nurse him. I thought maybe I had some soap or something around the nipple area. I wiped the area several times, but he still wouldn't latch on. When I tried again the next day, he tightened his little lips and started to whine. My feelings were quite hurt because I wasn't prepared to wean him until he was a year old. I'm going to miss that special time we shared. But I decided he knows best when to stop, and he and I will always have a special bond."

—*Theresa Guillen, New Orleans, LA*

"At first I felt terrible when I weaned my daughter at five months. I would watch her drink her bottle of formula and think that I wasn't needed anymore. But it didn't take long for my sadness and regret to go away. I decided to give myself credit for nursing in the first place and for so long, and realized that this was just one milestone—out of many more to come—that we've reached."

—*Erin Martin, Inver Grove Heights, MN*

stage, when their baby can go from breast right to cup (and avoid the weaning-from-the-bottle stage altogether).

Whenever you decide to wean, adopting a gradual process (as opposed to going cold turkey) is usually more comfortable for you and for your baby. Just as your breasts filled up to accommodate your baby's growing hunger, they'll shrink as demand for milk decreases. Doing this over the course of a few weeks will minimize any pain from engorgement, and will give your baby the time to make an easy transition. As you eliminate a feeding at a time, you may discover that you're able to nurse on a part-time basis. Many women are excited to find that they can continue a morning or nighttime feeding schedule without any trouble at all, and without any need to express milk during the day.

Common-sense advice for weaning:

- Start by eliminating the feeding that your baby is least interested in—usually a midday feeding.
- Replace the eliminated nursing session with a bottle or cup of formula.
- If your baby is old enough, it's often convenient to begin to offer a cup of formula at every sit-down meal and save nursing for lap times, usually morning and evening.
- Crotchety or sick babies may need more nursing rather than less. Put off weaning until your baby is feeling better.

DEFINITION

Vegetarian

Vegetarian is a term used loosely to describe folks who don't eat meat, but there are several categories of vegetarianism. An asterisk indicates the food groups each category will eat.

TYPE	Red Meat	Poultry	Fish	Eggs	Dairy	Vegetables & Plant Foods
Vegan						*
Ovo-vegetarian				*		*
Lacto-ovo vegetarian				*	*	*
Pesco-vegetarian			*	*	*	*
Semi-vegetarian		*	*	*	*	*

For More Information
The Vegetarian Resource Group
410-366-VEGE
A nonprofit organization that provides information on vegetarianism.

The Physicians Committee for Responsible Medicine
800-875-4837
Provides a free "Vegetarian Starter Kit."

~ A MOTHER'S VIEW ~

"My Baby Doesn't Eat Meat"

Renee Wheeler, of Bowie, Maryland, became a vegetarian at age 19 and a vegan at age 29—not long before becoming pregnant with her first child. In addition to not eating meat, a vegan doesn't eat animal by-products, such as milk or cheese.

Since dairy is a mainstay of a pregnant woman's diet, Renee's eating habits worried her obstetrician—but not Renee: "I wasn't concerned about my health or about my child's health because I believe that being a vegan is healthier," she says. Renee was a vegan throughout the pregnancies and births of her three healthy children, and is raising them as vegans, too. Her youngest is just starting on solid foods.

Renee has found that it's helpful to have friends who are vegetarians, too. "It's important for my children's self-esteem that they think of themselves as normal," she says. They spend holidays with other vegetarians so that they don't have to explain to the children why others celebrate holidays by sitting around a table with a dead bird.

When her family is invited to a nonvegetarian's house for dinner, she explains how her family eats and offers to bring food along. "The parents often end up asking me for recipes," Renee says. Her tips for raising a vegetarian family:

- **Talk to other vegetarians or vegans about finding substitutes for milk, meat, cheese.** There are lots of tasty alternative foods available at food co-ops, farmers' markets, and even in the supermarket.
- **Keep explanations simple.** Although Renee believes not eating meat is healthier, she's found that it's easier to introduce kids to vegetarianism by talking about animals' families and feelings.
- **Involve your children in the whole process of choosing and preparing food.**
- **Practice what you preach.** Renee thinks all of her kids love vegetables— even her baby, who's just starting sweet potatoes—because they see their parents enjoying vegetables. "You have to serve them often," says Renee, "and you have to like them and eat them."

- Just because you're weaning your baby from your breast doesn't mean you won't be offering her all the comfort she needs. Continue to cuddle and be close and loving as often as possible and during bottle feedings.
- If you suffer from engorgement, express a little milk to decrease the discomfort. Apply ice to your breasts and take a mild pain reliever.
- Know that it's OK to feel sad about weaning. Breastfeeding can be a very rewarding and intimate experience that mothers miss as much as babies at first.

Raising a Vegetarian

Vegetarianism has been around for centuries and is thought to be a healthy way of life. But there are some concerns when it comes to raising a vegetarian baby. Although there are many benefits of a vegetarian diet—lower cholesterol, more fiber, less fat, and fewer calories—these aren't of critical importance to babies and young children, who need fat and protein to grow and develop.

Until a vegetarian baby is 9 months old, he'll do just fine being breastfed and eating cereal. But when it comes time to begin eating baby food and table food, raising a vegetarian can be more of a challenge.

If your diet includes dairy and eggs, those foods will help meet your baby's protein requirements. (Babies need plenty of protein, which is required for building muscle, blood, and antibodies.) If you're a vegan, your baby will need lots of pureed beans with avocado, hummus, or nut butter. As with all babies, don't feed yours peanut butter (which can cause choking) or gas-producing vegetables, such as broccoli and cauliflower. In fact, fiber, which is so important for adults, can cause digestive distress in babies.

SLEEPING

There's a wide range of normal when it comes to the sleep habits of 7- to 9-month-olds. Most will sleep about 13 or 14 hours a day, but some do sleep less, others more. Most parents are just pleased that the majority of their baby's sleep hours occur at night. And they're thrilled when they're greeted each morning by their baby's smiling face peeking over the crib slats: time to lower the mattress again!

Common Sleep Disturbances

• **Hunger.** A baby who is going through a growth spurt may wake up in the night and ask for an additional bottle. He may be very hungry for a few days

	DAY SLEEP	NIGHT SLEEP	TOTAL SLEEP
How Much Babies Sleep			
AGE	(hours)	(hours)	(hours)
6 months	3¼	11	14¼
9 months	3	11	14
12 months	2¼	11½	13¾

and nights, and then go back to his regular eating—and sleeping—schedule.

• **Teething.** The pain of erupting teeth can wreak havoc on your baby's sleep patterns. A baby who had slept six or seven hours in a row may suddenly wake up screaming in pain several times a night. This can happen just once or recur each time your baby sprouts another new tooth. You might want to try a teething remedy, such as a topical analgesic or a mild pain reliever (see "CHECKLIST: Teething Pain Relief Do's and Don'ts, page 197).

• **Inability to put herself back to sleep.** A baby who hasn't learned to put herself to sleep, or to soothe herself back to sleep in the middle of the night, will still be a challenge for her parents. Consistently using the techniques described in Chapter 3 should bring positive results. In addition, as your baby matures and eats more solid foods, she should develop a sleep schedule that's more predictable—and more to your liking.

• **Separation anxiety.** Even babies who've always been good sleepers can run into a patch of trouble when separation anxiety hits. An infant who's suddenly fearful of being alone will resist being put to bed and may panic if he wakes in the night (see "The Age of Anxiety," page 277).

CHECKLIST

Crib Safety

Once your baby can pull up and stand in her crib, it's time to:

✔ Lower the mattress again so that at least two-thirds of your baby's height is below the crib railing when standing.

✔ Make sure that there are no stuffed animals or other toys she can use to boost herself up onto the railing and over.

✔ Do a double-check that there are no curtain or blind cords nearby.

✔ Remove any mobiles that she could pull down.

✔ Check that any nearby furniture is stable and clear of reachable objects.

HEALTH AND SAFETY

Sometimes a parent's job boils down to one thing: protecting Baby from herself. At this age, your child is more likely to fall down, eat something she shouldn't (sand, pennies, dog food), or pinch her fingers than she is to get sick. When you're not in the doctor's office to rule out serious injury from your baby's latest escapades, expect to be there for the inevitable ear infection (the second most common childhood illness, after a cold) or for your regularly scheduled nine-month checkup.

Keeping Your Baby Well

Your baby's memory may be developed to the point now that she will recognize the doctor's office and remember her last visit. Don't be surprised if that memory makes her howl (those shots!).

Nor should you be surprised if, the half-dozen times you're certain your baby has a respiratory infection, she's sent home from the doctor's office with a clean bill of health. Or the time you take her in for her well-baby checkup, she's diagnosed with an ear infection. It's often very difficult to read a baby's symptoms, and some babies seem perfectly well when they're sick, or are out of sorts when they're well.

My mother used to tell me that diagnosing a problem that warranted a doctor visit was easier when I was a baby. In those days, if a child under a year old had *any* sign of fever—even a temperature of only 100°F— you immediately went to the doctor. *Any* greenish or yellowish discharge from a baby's nose was a sure sign of an infection and a signal to ring the doc.

Today, it's well known that a fever is only a symptom of the body's fighting off what could be any number of minor problems—and that green mucus isn't necessarily a sign of an infection. Most parents understand the difference between a bacterial and a viral

> **DEFINITION**
>
> ### Febrile Convulsions
>
> Some children with high fever experience uncontrollable shakes, called febrile convulsions. This occurs in about 5 percent of children between the ages of 6 months and 5 years and is thought to run in families. It's rare for a baby under 6 months old to have a febrile convulsion.
>
> Although the seizures usually last just a few seconds and are generally not dangerous, they can be very frightening. Call the doctor to rule out the possibility of serious illness.

infection (the former can be treated with antibiotics; the latter cannot). All this knowledge, though, isn't much help when it comes to deciding whether or not a baby is sick enough to warrant a doctor visit. What if your baby has green mucus *and* a fever? A fever and a cough?

If you have *any* question about your child's health, call the doctor. Many offices have nurse lines where you can describe the problem and get a call-back if you're unsure about what to do next, or if you're reluctant to make an unnecessary visit. Many common childhood ailments, such as strep throat or ear infection, can't be ruled out without a doctor's visit and can become dangerous if undiagnosed and untreated. If your baby is unusually sleepy or irritable, not taking liquids, having convulsions (see "DEFINITION: Febrile Convulsions," page 262), or breathing fast, call the doctor. An unnecessary doctor visit may cost a little money and a little time, but it's worth it in peace of mind.

The Nine-Month Checkup At this month's well-baby exam, your baby's doctor will do the now-familiar checks of your child's growth and development. She'll be weighed and measured, and will have a standard physical exam. Your baby will get immunizations this visit if she's missed any previously scheduled shots, or if your doctor likes to spread out the shots so that she's not getting as many at once (see chart on page 264).

This time your baby's developmental assessment may include exercises that let her doctor see how well she can pick up different-sized objects, whether she looks for an object that's hidden or has been dropped, and whether she re-

At the 9-month checkup, the pediatrician may play peekaboo or other games with your child to assess her development.

Immunization Schedule

	DTP	HIB	HEP B	MMR	POLIO	TB TEST	VARICELLA
6 months	•	•					
6–18 months	•	•	•		•		
12–15 months		•		•		•	•
12–18 months	•						

sponds to her name. The doctor also may play a game of peekaboo or pat-a-cake with her. In addition, she'll discuss your baby's eating and sleeping patterns with you, and will review any past problems your baby has had.

Some pediatricians recommend a lead screening test and an anemia test for 9-month-old patients. This requires a finger stick (called a venopuncture) to draw blood. If your child is diagnosed with anemia, she may need iron supplements. The lead test will determine whether your child has lead poisoning, which can cause a number of developmental problems (see "What You Need to Know About . . . Lead Poisoning," page 268). Iron deficiency anemia can also cause developmental problems.

The Inevitable Ear Infection About one out of every four pediatrician appointments concerns an ear infection—what doctors call *otitis media*, or OM. Typically a cold works its way up through a baby's eustachian tube and parks in the middle-ear space.

Otitis media takes two forms. Acute otitis media (AOM) often causes pain and fever. When the pediatrician looks in your child's ear, he'll see a bulging red eardrum with fluid behind it. AOM typically requires a ten-day course of antibiotics.

Otitis media with effusion (OME) occurs when the middle ear doesn't drain properly (common in children whose immature eustachian tubes are too short and too horizontal to drain well), so that fluid is trapped behind the eardrum. OME doesn't usually cause any pain and can clear up on its own.

When a child has recurring ear infections of either type, or has required antibiotics more than three times in four to six months, your doctor may try pro-

Q & A

"Our pediatrician sent home literature about children taking too many antibiotics. Is this something I need to worry about?"

In recent years, the use (or overuse) of antibiotics has been a hot topic. More than 100 million antibiotic prescriptions are issued each year for a variety of ailments. They do a great job clearing up many bacterial infections, but bacteria are constantly evolving, and more and more drug-resistant strains are showing up. One study, in fact, showed that 50 percent of the bacteria found in the middle-ear fluid of children under 2 was resistant to penicillin.

Some say the problem is that antibiotics are being prescribed when they shouldn't be, for colds or for otitis media with effusion (an ear condition with fluid buildup but no bacteria), which often clear up on their own. It's also a commonly held misconception that antibiotics can fight a virus; they're effective only against bacterial infections.

Whether or not your baby has had a lot of antibiotics, you should still be concerned about their overuse. If your baby gets a bug that's antibiotic resistant, it won't matter if he's had antibiotics before. There won't be an antibiotic that can easily fight it.

The solution, many experts say, is to use antibiotics only when they're absolutely needed. Don't pressure your doctor to give your baby a prescription when what's needed is just a few days' rest. You may also want to talk to your doctor about homeopathic treatments for common childhood ailments.

phylactic antibiotic treatment—that is, giving the child a small amount of antibiotic once a day to see if that prevents a recurrence. If that doesn't work, she may suggest that your child have an operation to put small drainage tubes in her ears (called a tympanostomy). This surgery, which is performed under general anesthesia, should be considered only for chronic ear infections and as a last resort. The tubes fall out on their own, usually after 9 to 12 months.

Keeping Your Baby Safe

There's a fine line between being too protective of your baby and keeping him safe. As time goes on, you'll find a healthy middle ground.

The Inevitable Head Bumps You don't want to discourage your child from exploring and from testing his newfound motor skills, but you do want to prevent any serious injuries, especially to his head. Try these common-sense precautions:

- Pad the surfaces of his play areas with a rug or rubber play mat.
- Pad all table corners and hearths.
- Remove some furniture from the area to make a wide-open space, if possible.
- Gate all stairs at the bottom and top, and any rooms you don't want him getting into.
- Make sure he can't climb out of his crib or high chair.
- Put gates on all windows and never open a window more than 5 inches. (Caution: a screen is not strong enough to keep a baby from falling out of a window.)

If your baby does bump his head, put ice on it immediately and check the following:

- **How he cries.** If your baby cries a little and stops after he calms down and gets a cuddle, and if he checks out in all other ways, he's probably all right. If he cries continuously or in sharp shrieks, go to the emergency room.
- **Whether his head is bleeding.** Head wounds, even little ones, tend to bleed profusely because the veins are close to the surface. If you can't stop the bleeding after applying pressure for 10 minutes, or if you have stopped the bleeding but can see that the wound is deep or jagged, go to the emergency room. Your baby may need stitches. (Babies don't have as much blood as adults do, so if yours is bleeding, apply pressure to the injury with a cloth to slow the flow of blood until you get to the hospital.)
- **What kind of bump he gets.** There are good bumps and bad bumps, and no bumps. Typically, swelling is a positive sign that blood is rushing to the spot to heal the damage. If the bump is very squishy, though, or unusually large, call your doctor. It could be blood leaking through a crack in the skull. It's also smart to call your doctor if there's no bump where you think there should be one.
- **How his eyes focus.** If your baby's eyes don't seem to be focusing, or one pupil is larger than the other, call the doctor or go to an emergency room.
- **If he gets sick to his stomach.** If your baby vomits more than once, go to the emergency room.
- **If he gets a fever.** Go to the emergency room.
- **How he behaves.** If your baby immediately gets sleepy or is unconscious or has a seizure, go to the emergency room. Watch your baby's behavior for any other signs that things aren't quite right. A baby this age can't complain of a headache, so it's your job to figure out how he's feeling. Severe crankiness may be a sign that his head hurts. When in doubt, call the doctor.

Other Safety Questions . . . and Answers

• **Are walkers safe?** Not if you ask the American Academy of Pediatrics. If you're thinking of using a walker to improve your baby's walking skills, don't. There's no proof that the device speeds up a baby's ability to walk; in fact, some experts say it impedes a baby's progress.

More important, a walker isn't a safe place to plunk a baby (like a play yard is) because walkers, obviously, move. A baby in a moving object is not safe, as I can attest firsthand. In spite of my superior vigilance (or so I thought), my first daughter flew down our steep basement steps in a walker when she was 9 months old. She landed facedown on the steps, and the walker landed on top of the washing machine, several yards away. She turned out to be fine (once her black eye healed); I will be traumatized for life.

There are activity centers available today that don't have wheels and do provide a fun, safe place for a baby to play for short stretches of time.

CHECKLIST

Toy Safety

The best way to guarantee that a toy is appropriate for your age child is to check the label. If it says "For children 3 and up," that toy is likely to have small parts that a baby could choke on. Some other toy safety hazards to avoid:

✔ **Stuffed animals made out of beanbags.** These little critters are all the rage right now and they are cute. But what makes them so cuddly is exactly what makes them so dangerous: the beans they're stuffed with are a choking hazard. One brand of the popular beanbag animal does provide two layers of material between the beans and your baby, but there are so many versions these days, it's hard for a parent to know which beanie is better than the other. If you must collect them, wait until your child is 3 to give them to him.

✔ **Metal or hinged toys.** Any toy made of metal is likely to have sharp edges; hinged toys can pinch or cut a small hand (so can toys with springs).

✔ **Batteries.** Your big hands may have trouble inserting the small batteries into a toy (and some require a screwdriver to close the lid), but baby hands are surprisingly agile. Avoid any toys that contain batteries, and don't throw old ones away in wastebaskets where little ones can discover them.

✔ **Small parts.** Anything that can be pulled off—a stuffed animal's nose, a doll's buttons, a toy truck's rearview mirror—poses a choking danger.

✔ **Strings.** Any cord, ribbon, or string longer than 8 inches can strangle a baby.

✔ **Older child's toys.** Be especially vigilant if there is an older sibling in the family, who undoubtedly will leave toys lying around. At this age, your baby certainly can't distinguish between his "safe" toys and any others.

• **How worried should I be when my baby eats the sand in her sandbox?** A little sand or a dead bug or two probably won't do any harm, as long as she doesn't choke on it (and as long as no dogs or cats have been messing in the sand). There have been some safety concerns about inhaling certain types of sandbox sand, however. Any sand that's too dusty can cause breathing problems, and some sand has been found to be contaminated with toxins. Real sand (from the beach, and carefully cleaned of any foreign objects) is less likely to cause any problems.

• **If I see my baby put something yucky in his mouth, how can I get it out without scaring him?** Don't poke at it, which might force it down his throat. Instead, squeeze his cheeks with your thumb and forefinger to open his mouth. If you can see the object, sweep it out with your hooked finger. If your baby appears to be choking, do the Heimlich maneuver.

• **I worry every time I put my son in a shopping cart. How can I make sure he won't unbuckle his seat belt and fall out?** You can't be sure, which is why you hear about lots and lots of shopping cart injuries. My youngest daughter undid her seat belt and landed on her head on a concrete floor. She got by with an emergency room visit and a bad headache, but other children have suffered skull fractures and more serious problems.

If your baby is small enough, the built-in reclining baby seats attached to shopping carts are a safer option than the standard shopping cart seat. More carts now have seat belts and many of them are difficult for even nimble fingers to unfasten. Still, it's not an ideal setup for a rambunctious baby. If you must put him in a shopping cart seat, be extremely vigilant.

What You Need to Know About . . . Lead Poisoning

Exposure to lead can have a dramatic effect on a baby. It can inhibit physical growth, impair hearing, and cause developmental delays. It can harm the kidneys, central nervous system, and blood. It can cause anemia, mental retardation, shortened attention span, learning disabilities, and aggressive behavior.

• **Who's at risk?** You and your family are, if you live in a home that was built prior to 1960 or have recently renovated an old home, or if you or your spouse work in an occupation in which you're exposed to lead.

Lead-based paint was banned in 1978, but it still exists in more than 60 million American homes. Paint chips can be ingested, paint dust can be inhaled. Lead can even leach into the dirt in your backyard where your children play, and be present in old pipes, contaminating the water you drink.

• **How are you tested?** A blood test is given, in which the amount of micro-

Lead-based paint still exists in more than 60 million homes. Keep your baby away from peeling or chipped paint.

grams per deciliter of blood is measured. In 1991, the Centers for Disease Control and Prevention (CDC) lowered the level considered a health hazard for children from 20 to 10 micrograms.

• **What can you do if your child has it?** Many cases of lead poisoning can be decreased to safe levels with no lasting effects. You'll need to institute a major cleanup if the source of the lead is in your home (or move away).

Eating certain foods may also help prevent or reverse the effects of lead poisoning. A diet rich in calcium and iron may help children's bodies block the ab-

---

For More Information

• The Environmental Defense Fund
  800-684-3322
  Provides a brochure about lead in dishes.

• National Lead Information Center
  800-532-3394
  Publishes a free brochure, "Lead Poisoning and Your Children."
  To speak to a specialist, call 800-424-5232.

• National Paint & Coatings Industry Center
  202-332-3194
  Offers a free brochure, "Dealing with Lead-Based Paint."

sorption of lead (chewable vitamins can help, too). Fat, on the other hand, may increase lead absorption.

For children whose levels exceed 20 micrograms, your doctor may recommend chelation medicine, which binds to the lead and is eliminated through the kidneys or liver.

OTHER BIG DEALS

It seems ridiculous to have a conversation about who's the boss when your child is less than 2 feet tall and barely able to get from one place to another. But power struggles start young, and your baby will benefit (and be safer) if you set ground rules for acceptable behavior now. In addition to learning that the stove is hot and shouldn't be touched, she'll be learning self-control, the difference between right and wrong, and how to get along with others—all lessons that will serve her well in the future.

Can You Spoil a Baby?

During a baby's first 6 months, it's impossible to spoil him. At that age, he'll cry and fuss for a legitimate reason: he's wet, or hungry, or has a sore ear or a tooth coming in. Or because he has unspent energy that he needs to release. You can't hold him or pick him up too much. Before you can set boundaries for your child, he has to know that he can trust you to be there for him.

But from 6 months on, your baby gets a little smarter, and it behooves you to get just a little tougher. Now, not every cry is a distress signal that needs immediate attention. In many cases, your baby has learned how to get what he wants. He cries to be picked up after you just put him down. So you pick him up. He fusses when you put him in his crib for a nap. You pick him up. He's learned that tears are a powerful tool. That's OK; it's how he communicates.

But instead of always picking up your baby when he cries for your attention, deal with him in a loving but firm way. Tell him you can't play with him right now but that he can play with his squeaky rattle or drum while you make lunch. If you're upbeat and positive about it, he'll begin to understand from the tone of your voice that everything is all right and that it's OK for him to play on his own for a while. This is an important step in his growing independence.

If you're consistent and kind, he'll tire of trying to get your attention with no results. He'll learn to entertain himself, and to save his tears for times of true distress. And, of course, he'll know that you love him because even though you're firm, you're affectionate and even-tempered. You react to his demands, but you don't overreact.

Parents who work outside the home and have limited time with their child understandably don't want to spend all their time with their baby teaching him that he can't always get what he wants. Just remind yourself that a parent who's firm and kind (and who's the boss) offers a baby the structure and affection he needs to thrive.

Of course, we're talking about a baby here, not a foot-stomping toddler or preschooler who is willfully disobeying a parent. Don't forget that babies need massive amounts of attention during the first year.

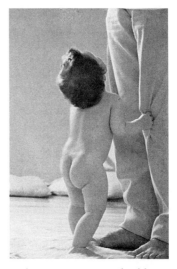

Pick me up! A 9-month-old baby knows exactly how to get a parent's attention.

Smart Discipline from the Start As your baby gets more mobile, you'll need some gentle techniques to remove him from dangerous situations and to direct him to more acceptable behavior. You'll also have to take a hard look at your own expectations. Most of a baby's so-called bad behavior isn't fueled by a desire to annoy you. Babies get into trouble because it's their job to explore every cranny, to poke every button, to grab every interesting thing they see. It's your job to keep them safe without squelching their natural curiosity. And it's also your job to repeat, repeat, repeat yourself. It's only through repetition that your child is going to learn what's off-limits, what's OK, and just how far he can test your (or his caregiver's) limits. Repetition isn't cruel; it's necessary. (Besides, what seems obvious to you—pull the cord and the lamp will fall on you—hasn't dawned on your little one.)

What You Need to Know About . . . Saying No In his second 6 months of life, your baby will begin to make the connection between his actions and the word *no*. (Before this age, he didn't have the memory to make the connection; your best bet was just to remove him from the dangerous situation.)

Use no to get his attention and make him stop during dangerous or hurtful antics—for example, when your baby is about to pull that lamp down on himself or has just hit another baby. Again, you'll need to repeat the reprimand when your baby ignores you or repeats the undesirable act. Eventually, he'll learn from the repetition.

Until he tries something dangerous, your baby may have never heard you say no before. More than the word itself, he'll probably be shocked by the tone of your voice or the look on your face. Your firm no should be accompanied by a frown on your face or a shake of your head. He may cry in reaction to your reprimand, mostly out of surprise. He'll soon catch on to your message.

Save your no for true transgressions. Much of what's considered baby's bad behavior isn't really bad at all—and certainly doesn't require a reprimand. Think about what your baby is doing when he throws his food off his high-chair tray or tosses all the toys out of his play yard. Yes, there's a remote possibility that he's trying to test you to see how much you'll let him get away with. But that's usually toddler behavior; more likely, your baby is just trying to get your attention or has found a fun new game. A baby who pulls your glasses off your head for the tenth time is probably fueled by natural curiosity and isn't intent on driving you crazy. In those cases, redirect him to more acceptable pursuits. And make sure you're giving him enough positive attention. You don't want your baby's world to suddenly be dominated by no.

Some Alternatives to No

• **Remove the object that's causing the problem.** If you don't want your baby gumming your coffee-table books, put them away. You get the idea.
• **Keep your baby away from the problem situation or area.** Gate off your office if you don't want your baby to test-drive your computer. Don't expect him to know it's an adult toy.
• **Redirect your baby's attention.** If you don't like him yanking on your glasses, give him a favorite toy to play with.
• **Give him a baby time-out.** Standard time-outs aren't appropriate at this age, but by the time he's 10 months old you can firmly (and briefly) hold your baby with his arms down at his sides to make the point that it's not OK to yank on the dog's tail until he yelps. This can be very effective when combined with a firm "no," and "hurts."

As with most child-rearing issues, consistency is essential in discipline. Set your limits and stick with them. And don't forget to praise all of your baby's wonderful behavior and give him lots of loving positive attention.

Raising a "Good" Child

If lessons learned in infancy truly do last a lifetime, then it's more important than ever to begin teaching your baby right from wrong during the first year of life. Of course, your little one isn't going to sit still for a daily lecture on morals (and it's never the child who is right or wrong, good or bad; it's her behavior).

Still, you can send her cues every day by how you interact with her. Here are some of the simple, and surprising, ways you can begin your baby's moral training:

- **Provide lots of affection.** By tending to your baby's emotional needs with hugs and cuddles, you're teaching her caring behavior. A baby who hasn't received enough loving early in life may be unable to learn how to be compassionate later in life.
- **Set limits.** By not letting her stand on the couch, by not letting her repeatedly throw her bottle out of her play yard, you're helping your baby learn restraint and how to delay gratification.
- **Teach yes and no.** Children who are taught the meaning of *no* will learn to control their own impulses and desires. Babies need to learn that there is a higher authority, whether that's you or some other person.
- **Play games.** By playing peekaboo and pat-a-cake, you're teaching a baby how to take turns. Responding to her babbling with your own babbling teaches what's called social reciprocity.
- **Demonstrate gentle touches.** By showing your baby how to gently touch a pet or another baby, you're teaching empathy early on.

Your Growing Baby

Your baby will make developmental leaps and bounds during the next three months that are likely to change his—and your—life. He'll go from being barely mobile to well on his way to crawling, cruising, and standing. He may add those magic words you've been waiting to hear—"Mama" and "Dada"—to his babbling repertoire. He'll also be entering the age of anxiety, a period where being separated from you or seeing an unfamiliar face can really upset him.

Height and Weight

Average Growth*			
AGE	4–6 MOS.	7–9 MOS.	10–12 MOS.
Height	+2 in.	+2 in.	+2 in.
Weight	+4 lbs.	+4 lbs.	+3 lbs.

*There is a wide range of normal; every baby has her own growth timetable.

Motor Development

At the beginning of this 3-month period, it was probably all your baby could do to sit unsupported and reach forward for a toy. By the end of 9 months, her back muscles and body control will be such that she may be able to sit, rock, reach for a toy, and wave at you all at the same time. Actually, she may be so busy learning how to get around, she has no time for sitting at all.

At 7 months, your baby was learning to gauge the size of a block and adjust the size of her grasp to pick it up. At 9 months, she'll pick up a pea-sized item without any trouble at all. In fact, she'll have discovered that the thumb-and-index-finger pincer grasp is very useful for trying to pick up the tiniest crumb or teeniest dead bug. And if that dead bug is across the room, no problem. Her improved vision will allow her to spot it, and her developing locomotive skills will get her there—faster than you can imagine. And if the bug is on your coffee table, watch out: holding on for balance, your baby may be able to pull herself up to take a closer look. At first she'll fold up and fall if she lets go, but by the end of 9 months she may be able to let go briefly or even take a step before relaxing into a sitting position.

In no time at all, she'll put several side-by-side steps together and will be cruising for a bruising. Time to put away the coffee-table knickknacks and pad everything that's hard or pointed.

Anatomy of: Crawling

Your baby has been working toward crawling since the minute he was born. All of the previous milestones—holding his head up, rolling, pushing up, and sitting up—were part of his basic training for the physical adventure of crawling.

Most babies begin to crawl between 7 to 10 months, but every baby has his own timetable. And there are as many ways to crawl as there are to dance.

Regardless of the crawling technique, many babies figure out how to go backward before forward. This can be very frustrating for them, but they eventually figure out how to get where they want to go. And some babies come to crawling late or skip it altogether. If your baby is big, his muscles may take a bit longer to strengthen to the point where he can crawl.

Don't worry too much if your baby isn't crawling. As with all other development, he has his own timetable. Look for signs that he's making progress toward crawling and give him plenty of opportunities to play on the floor. If he's very precocious on the language front, he may be using all of his energy in the communication department right now. Crawling may come later.

If you're very concerned about his motor development, discuss your worries with your baby's pediatrician at his 9-month appointment.

Crab crawlers scuttle around using a one knee/one foot technique.

Combat crawlers stay low to the ground and pull forward with their forearms instead of their hands.

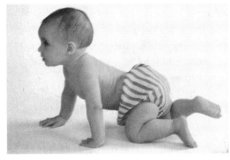

Cross-crawlers take the classic approach to crawling: When one hand moves forward, so does the opposite leg.

Bottom crawlers use a bouncing motion to move forward and sometimes skip the hands completely. (Thank heavens for good padding!)

The knees never touch the ground for this crawler.

⮜ A MOTHER'S VIEW ⮞

"My Son Isn't Crawling"

When James Larsen hadn't started crawling by 9 months, his mother, Marque, started worrying. "I know every child is different and develops at his or her own pace," she says. "But I couldn't help comparing him to my other children, who had crawled by then. I wanted him to be developing normally."

Marque's pediatrician tried to calm her fears. "But a doctor's reassurances can only go so far. Until a child actually shows you that he can perform a particular skill, the question 'Will he do it?' is always in the back of your mind," says the Escondido, California, mom. The pediatrician pointed out that James's motor skills were bound to be affected by his size. Born weighing 12½ pounds, James was off the height and weight growth charts. It's not uncommon for larger babies to take a little longer to get around.

James began inching forward at 10 months old, but still Marque couldn't stop worrying. She compared him to the younger babies in his play group who were already crawling and walking. She called the grandparents to see if she and James's dad had been slow walkers (they hadn't). She tried various strategies to get James interested in walking: "I'd take his hands and lead him around. I'd encourage him to walk between his dad and me. None of it did any good."

Finally, she gave it up and—lo and behold—at 13½ months James was taking little steps on his own. Marque's advice, which she admits she herself had trouble taking:

- **Don't rush your child.** Most parents feel that their baby is growing up too fast. If yours is taking a little longer, enjoy it. "Now that James walks," Marque admits, "I'm never going to have a moment of peace again."
- **Avoid comparisons.** Resist comparing your child to other babies or rigorously holding him up to developmental schedules. Babies really do develop at their own pace.
- **Discuss worries about your baby's development with the pediatrician.** Babies who are premature or extra heavy often develop at a slower rate, but your baby may have a problem that hasn't been diagnosed.
- **Admit that maybe you're just a worrier and leave it at that.** Now that James can walk, Marque has moved on to worrying that he can't pull himself up on his own! "I know he'll do it eventually. I know he will," she says. "But it does concern me some."

Mental Development

During this period, your baby will figure out the whole in-and-out concept. Once he catches on that he can fit one object into another, an entirely new world of play will be opened up to him. He may be quite absorbed with his in-and-out games and you may be surprised at how long this sort of activity pleases him and keeps him occupied.

He'll also be quite happy to spend a long time examining objects and moving them from hand to hand, a skill that usually develops by month 8. By month 9 he may be trying to hold more than one object at a time in one hand.

He's learned that if he points at something you'll figure out that he wants it, just as he knows to look when someone else is pointing at an object. Along with pointing, he'll continue to enjoy labeling games, where you name different objects as you're moving through the grocery store or around the house. He'll understand simple requests—"wave bye-bye" and "all fall down"—and will begin to anticipate the action even as the words are being spoken.

This is when your baby may develop a fear of heights, as his abilities to perceive depth improve. He'll also begin to learn that his actions have consequences. If he's a fearless baby who gets into everything, he'll soon connect your no with his latest bit of exploration.

Although your baby has figured out that a dropped or hidden object is still there, he doesn't quite believe that when *you're* gone, you're just somewhere that he can't see. This can cause him (and you) quite a bit of angst.

The Age of Anxiety The baby who at 3 months old would giggle and wiggle with delight when a stranger picked her up, and who responded with cautious curiosity at 6 months, now shrieks in terror and buries her face in her mom's shoulder if somebody she doesn't know even looks in her direction. If she strays too far from Mom during play group or sees her parents preparing to go out for the night, the baby cries as if her heart's been broken.

These are classic examples of stranger anxiety and separation anxiety (now sometimes called "awareness" instead of "anxiety"), which can start as early as 5 months, but typically kick in between months 7 and 9. The age of awareness can last throughout your child's second year to varying degrees. Although it's a perfectly normal period in a baby's development, it can be tough on parents and children alike.

What triggers this phenomenon is your baby's realization that she is a separate person. Even as she's learning to be independent—she's able to motor away from you under her own steam—she's realizing how dependent she truly is on you for her welfare and safety. So she freaks out when you're not in the room or

A MOTHER'S VIEW

"Separation Anxiety Strikes"

Heather Anderson had just finished a grueling year of internship in internal medicine, in Durham, North Carolina, when her son, Matthew, was born. She spent her time off hoping to give her son a secure foundation in life so that the return to her residency wouldn't be too traumatic for him.

"I was with him almost every minute for nine months," she said. That's when separation anxiety began to strike—for both of them. Heather returned to work part-time, but found herself cooling on the idea of finishing her seven-day-a-week, 24-hour-a-day residency.

"I really enjoy medicine, but my priorities have totally changed. I didn't expect to have all the feelings about Matthew that I do," she says.

And she didn't think he'd cry the minute she left the room. Up until Matthew was 16 months old, he had a very hard time separating. "He cried if I got too far away from him at the play group; he cried when I left him to go to work." It wasn't extraordinary separation anxiety, but it did tug at Heather's heartstrings.

Here's how she learned to cope with his (and her) anxiety:

- **When you have to leave, keep your good-byes short.** Don't linger. Drawn-out good-byes only extend the agony for everyone involved.
- **Provide comfort.** If your baby has a comfort object, give it to him when you're about to leave. If he doesn't have a cuddly for these times of transition, try to encourage such an attachment to a blankie or stuffed animal.
- **Create a short bye-bye ritual.** Offer a quick hug and kiss, and make sure to tell him you'll be back. He may not understand your words, but he'll like your comforting tone.
- **Leave your child with a familiar baby-sitter.** Matthew is sometimes watched by his 16-year-old stepbrother, with whom he's very comfortable.
- **Give a little extra one-on-one attention.** If your child is clingy at a play group or in another social situation, reassure him. Once he realizes you're not going away, he may feel secure enough to crawl a little farther away.
- **Recognize that this is a normal stage—for both of you.** Separation anxiety isn't your fault.

out of her sight. Because her memory isn't sophisticated enough to remember that in the past when you left her, you really *did* come back, she panics whether you're gone for three minutes or three hours. And because she's become a creature of habit, an unfamiliar adult or child can really throw her for a loop.

Some ways to ease the anxiety:

Rx for Separation Anxiety

"Whenever I'm out of sight, Adam gets fussy and starts hoop-hollering until he sees my face. I try talking to him from the next room—hearing my voice soothes him."

—*Debbie Ziervogel, Ballwin, MO*

"If we make a big deal out of leaving our son, Jacob, he gets agitated. So we stick to simple good-byes when we walk out the door. If we plan to be gone for a few days, we make sure that he sticks closely to his daily routines."

—*Marlene Speelman, Mansfield, OH*

"I went back to work when James was two months old. He wasn't really bothered by my absence then, but now, at eight months, he throws a fit every time I leave the room. I usually let him cry a little, and then he calms down on his own. If he gets hysterical, I pick him up or distract him by handing him his favorite toy."

—*Iris Whitaker, New York, NY*

- If your baby is afraid of strangers, warn visitors to your home that she needs a little time to warm up to them. If they come swooping down on her with hugs and kisses (as so many adults do), she's likely to dissolve before their eyes. Encourage your visitors to keep their distance while she checks them out. Then let them approach her when she seems comfortable with their presence. Or, if she can crawl over to them, let her make the first move.
- Slowly introduce your baby to other adults who can become familiar caretakers: grandparents who visit often, a regular baby-sitter, or a neighbor.
- To reassure your baby when you're in another room, hum or sing a little tune so she knows you're nearby, even though she can't see you.
- If your baby seems especially afraid and timid, encourage her to explore more, first in the safety of her own home where she can roam from room to room, and then at a playground.
- Take her often to places with other adults and children, so that she can get used to seeing lots of different people. A playground is a good choice because she can sit back and watch from afar and then decide if she wants to join a group at the sandbox or not.

- Create good-bye rituals that are quick but meaningful. Don't sneak out on your baby.
- Encourage her to cope with her fears with a comfort object, if it helps. A familiar object held close may make a morning at daycare seem more bearable to her.

Social Development

Although your baby may have developed stranger awareness, she's still an incredibly social animal at this age—as long as she feels safe and secure.

She'll enjoy dinnertime a great deal and will appear to be following your conversation as her head goes back and forth in the classic Ping-Pong motion. She'll make her own communication contributions, sometimes sounding as if she's speaking in complete sentences—in her own language, of course. Strings of vowel and consonant sounds punctuated by passionate gestures and changes in pitch sound like gibberish to strangers, but parents can sometimes catch their baby's drift.

She's gaining more control of her tongue and is able to make the "n" sound, and—send out the press release—she not only recognizes her own name, but she can say yours. "Mama" and "Dada" usually come springing from a baby's lips around month 9. And, yes, most of the time she really means you. (By around 12 months, she definitely means you.)

Although your baby will be crying less, she'll still be quite vocal when it comes to letting you know she wants your attention or doesn't like what you've planned for her. Through sounds and signals, she can say "pick me up," "put me down," "hello," and "good-bye."

Sometimes you'll see your baby looking to you to help her figure out how she should react or feel in a certain situation (and to check if she's about to get

---

CHECKLIST
More Good Books for Babies

Babies this age like books that are playful, reflect the huge world around them, and invite participation. A few favorites:

✔ *Goodnight Moon* by Margaret Wise Brown (HarperCollins)
✔ *Pat the Bunny* by Dorothy Kunhardt (Western Publishing Company)
✔ *Anno's Peekaboo* by Mitsumasa Anno (Philomel)
✔ *Boats; Planes; Trains; Trucks* by Byron Barton (HarperCollins)

into trouble). She uses your facial expressions and tone of voice to figure out her next move or reaction.

Play continues to be a most enjoyable time for your baby, so plan lots of time for games, blowing bubbles, and reading books. She'll get a real kick out of it if you record her babbling and play it back for her.

Getting to Know Your Baby's Nature Some parents say they can figure out their baby's temperament from day one. A few character traits that emerge during this 3-month period give you even more clues about who your child is.

• **The focused baby.** This baby has a long attention span and can amuse herself. She'll practice her skills again and again and will enjoy putting the block in a box, taking it out, putting a block in a box, taking it out. This trait will work to her advantage when she's at the stage where she can build a tower of blocks. She's not easily distracted, and may put up quite a fuss when you try to drag her away from whatever she's doing.
• **The easily distracted baby.** This baby is just the opposite. She'll move easily from activity to activity but won't have a lot of stick-to-itiveness. She's easily frustrated by things she can't master immediately and tends to give up easily. The challenge here is to teach her some persistence and to ease her frustrations when she doesn't catch on right away.

By this time, many parents can also determine whether their baby is happiest with strict routines or is more of a "whatever goes" sort of child.

A PARENT'S LIFE

"I just can't believe this," a mother said to me a few years ago as we stood in the corner and checked out the guests at a New Year's Eve party. "I still think of myself as a black-leather-skirted woman who could work all day and stay up all night. Look what's happened to us!" she lamented.

The celebration *was* very low key; it included eight children, six of them under a year old. Two of the women were wearing short skirts, but they were also wearing their babies (one in a sling, the other in a backpack). The fare was mostly breast milk and finger food of the nonchoking variety. The conversation was equal parts *Goodnight Moon* and "How much is your baby sleeping?" The champagne bottles were popped at 9 P.M. (although no one was drinking very much; the nursing moms, not at all), and the party was over by 10.

The funny thing was that everyone—including the mother who no longer

A MOTHER'S VIEW

"Bonding with an Adopted Baby"

After traveling for two days to Luoyang, China, Lisa Gibbs finally met her daughter, Basya Xiaoshan Kasinitz. She didn't feel an immediate bond. "The orphanage staff put her in my arms and I thought, 'She's a nice baby,'" Lisa recalls, "but she wasn't my daughter yet. It takes a while to love someone."

Lisa and her husband were very careful to make their 9-month-old baby's transition as easy as possible. They didn't try to change all of her routines or "Americanize" her right away. "We put a diaper on her but we kept her in her Chinese clothes," Lisa says. "We wanted to give her time to get acquainted with us and to trust us." When they bathed Basya, Lisa got in the tub with her. "She loved it and I'm sure the skin-to-skin contact helped us bond." Because no cribs were available in the hotel room in China, Basya spent her first nights with her new family sleeping in their big suitcase.

"The orphanage dubbed her the 'easy baby' because she had no eating or sleeping problems in the hotel with us," says Lisa. That wasn't the case, though, when Basya arrived at her new home in New York. "She had terrible jet lag," Lisa says. "Suddenly she wasn't sleeping at all."

Basya was also making up for lost developmental time. "She was going through a new developmental stage almost every day," Lisa says. Basya learned to roll over, sit up unsupported, and crawl all within one month of her arrival in New York.

Lisa found it difficult to find information in baby books that was relevant to her situation. Most chapters on 9-month-olds were talking about budding independence; Lisa was more interested in helping Basya feel attached to her new family. Now, she believes she has succeeded: "She is one of the family now," Lisa says. "She's become a part of us." Her advice for adoptive parents:

- **Take time to develop a trusting relationship with your adopted child.** This is not the time to let the baby cry it out or to teach her independence.
- **Don't strip her of what few traditions she may have already learned.** Basya kept her Chinese name and continued to enjoy some of her favorite Chinese foods.
- **Don't force your child's development.** She may have some catching up to do.
- **Don't hesitate to get help if you suspect your child has developmental delays.** Federally funded early intervention programs are available in every state.

wore a black leather skirt—had a great time. We reveled in the joys and challenges of new parenthood and could think of no better way to ring in the new year than with our new babies, surrounded by new friends, happy with our new lives.

Of course, that was one of the better days of new parenthood. Although the second half of the first year of parenthood is much calmer than the first half, your life may not be running particularly smoothly. The baby is a joy but your sex life is the pits, you're fighting with your partner about the chores, your friends aren't calling you back, and you can't shake that last 10 pounds no matter how you torture yourself. It's not unusual to have many, many other days that set your head spinning with big-deal questions, such as "Where did my life go? What's happening here?"

What's Happened to *Me?*

What's happened is that you've had a major life change that's affected your physical and emotional health, your sex life, your relationship, your sleep patterns, your social life, your career, and every minute of every day. Cut yourself some slack! You simply cannot be the same person you were before you became a mother. Not after six months, not after six years. The earth has shifted in ways you never imagined (and in ways you've yet to discover).

But now is a good time to take a harder look at how you're feeling, to make time for interests other than your child, and to reconnect with friends.

Your Friends As the dust settles and new moms begin to feel ready to spend more time away from their babies, they notice something: they haven't heard from their friends lately. It's not uncommon to lose touch with old friends, especially friends who are single or childless. You may feel more comfortable with women who have also recently had babies, or you may have made lots of new connections at a mothers' group or with a group of moms at work. Because your lives are so similar, you have lots to talk about with these women.

But don't write off all of your old friendships. You may have to look harder to find common interests with childless friends at first since you're so caught up in motherhood (try not to bore them to tears with stories about your child), but maintaining a few of these special relationships will enrich your life. Remember why you were friends in the first place. At the least, these friends will remind you that there are rewarding, interesting things to do that have nothing to do with being a parent.

✑ A MOTHER'S VIEW ✑

"Maintaining Friendships"

Stephanie Barsness used to see her best friend, Pam, every day. When she got pregnant, she knew that daily contact was going to come to an end. But she was determined not to let the impending change in her life overwhelm her friendship.

"Going into both my marriage and my pregnancy, I talked with my husband, Greg, about how important my friends were to me," says Stephanie, who lives in Durham, North Carolina. And her friend Pam understands how important Stephanie's family is to her. "Pam keeps current on events in Greg's life," Stephanie says, "and she's very involved with our son, Samuel. In fact, for a long time he said 'Hi, Pam' to everybody."

Now that Stephanie is a mother and Pam isn't, it's more difficult to empathize with the issues that are important to each of them, but they both make an effort. "Continuing a deep friendship involves adjusting to the changing roles in a friend's life," says Stephanie. When they get together twice a month for dinner and a movie or just to hang out at Pam's house, "we always talk about everything. She's a great support for me," says Stephanie. "We still have that old-girlfriends feeling in our relationship because we work hard to understand each other's perspective."

Even when maintaining a friendship is difficult, Stephanie keeps at it. "A friendship is a wonderful thing for a child to see," she says. "I want to model for Samuel what a true friend is really like."

Her tips for maintaining friendships:

- **Make it a priority.** Stephanie's husband works long hours but sets time aside to watch Samuel so that Stephanie can spend time with friends. She does the same for him.
- **Remember what it was like before you were a parent.** You'll be a better friend if you can put yourself in your friend's shoes.
- **Value friendships for the outlet that they are.** New parents need time away from their child and their families, and spending time with a valued friend can be a healthy break.

Your Health By 6 to 9 months postpartum, some women feel just great. Others are still suffering from the intensity of the last year and a half: they're tired, they're struggling to get back to their prepregnancy weight, they're depressed that they have no time for themselves. You can't put yourself last and expect to be a great mom. You need rest and pampering, but you also need stimulation—just as your baby does.

It's fine to take little breaks to do nice things for yourself. Have a cup of tea, take a bath, sneak a nap. Read a best-selling book, go to a museum,

Q & A
"How much exercise do I need?"

To determine how much exercise you need, decide what your goal is. If you're interested in staying generally healthy and fit, you should plan to be active for about 30 minutes a day at least four times a week. The intensity of the activity doesn't matter much; what's important is that you get moving—strolling the baby, working in the garden, folding clothes—every single day.

If you're trying to actually lose weight, your exercise needs to be more intense. Burning fat and increasing cardiovascular fitness require getting your heart rate up—and keeping it up—for at least 30 minutes three times a week.

find time to do the things you did before you had a baby. Women who think they're too exhausted to do more than plunk down in front of the TV are often invigorated by a short trip (sans baby) to the mall or by 20 minutes of exercise.

But how can you find time for exercise? The best way to carve out a little time for yourself is to make an inventory of your day. Look for 15- to 30-minute periods of time when you could squeeze in a brisk walk around the block between meetings or a few dozen sit-ups between feedings. Instead of driving to the corner market or to that lunch spot from work, hoof it. The time *is* there. You just have to find it—and use it.

Your Belly The belly roll is usually the last sign of pregnancy to make an exit, even if you've lost all of your pregnancy weight. These exercises created by Beth Rothenberg, who is a physical fitness instructor, focus specifically on that trouble spot.

Upright Crunches. Sit with your knees bent and feet flat on the floor. Place a telephone book on your shins. Hold onto the book with both hands. Tighten your abdominal muscles, lean back a little, and extend your legs. Bring your legs back into a bent position as you lean forward slightly. It can be a lot more fun if you replace the book with your baby. Face her toward you with her feet on your feet and hold her hands. She'll get a big kick out it.

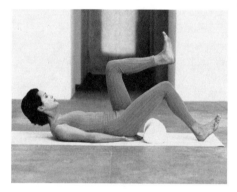

Leg Extensions. Lie on your back with a blanket or towel rolled up and placed under your thighs. Bend your knees and pull them in to your chest. Put your hands under your bottom to help keep your lower back flat. Slowly lower your right leg (keeping the knee bent) until your heel touches the floor. Repeat 10 to 20 times, all the while contracting your tummy muscles. Repeat with the other leg. After a while, you'll be able to do this with both legs at the same time.

Your Mind Yoga can be a great exercise for new moms because you can do it at home *and* it relieves stress. Try these classic yoga positions.

Child's Pose. Sit down on your knees with your weight on your heels. Bend forward until your forehead touches the floor. Your arms should be on either side of your head. Keep your bottom as close to your heels as possible. Hold for 15 seconds. Repeat several times.

Warrior. Stand with your legs 3 feet apart. Extend your arms at shoulder height. Turn your right foot out, about 90 degrees. Your left foot should stay facing forward. Exhale and slowly bend your right knee. Keep your back straight and abdominal muscles tight (don't lean over toward the bent knee). Hold for 20 seconds. Alternate legs and repeat twice on each side.

Downward-Facing Dog. 1. Get on your hands and knees. Your feet should be about a foot apart. Put your weight on your hands.

2. In one movement, lift your hips and knees off the floor and go up on the balls of your feet. Your body will form a triangle. Inhale and stretch your arms. Exhale while pressing your heels to the floor. Hold for three breaths and then return to your kneeling position. Repeat up to five times.

~ A MOTHER'S VIEW ~

"Exercise—You've Gotta Do It"

Before she got pregnant, Kathie Griffin had been running 3 to 5 miles a day, five days a week. She stopped exercising during her third month when she came home from a run and was bleeding.

Used to eating whatever she wanted, the mom-to-be from Federal Way, Washington, had a hard time adjusting her appetite to her lower level of activity. "I'm a vegetarian," she says, "but that doesn't mean I don't eat fattening things. I'm also a potato chip addict." In 9 months she went from 108 pounds to 156 pounds.

After baby Samantha was born, the thought of running wasn't very appealing to Kathie, but she forced herself to do it. "I knew the weight was not going to melt away on its own and that my stomach would look like a water bed if I didn't get off my tuchus and run," she says. At first she struggled to keep her feet moving for a half mile. "I was used to being in such good shape. But now I was a beginner again. It hurt. I couldn't breathe."

Kathie kept at it, however, and by month 10 was up to running 3 miles at a time—and down to 115 pounds. "I'm pretty content," she says, but occasionally she pulls out her old size 2 pants and sighs. How to develop a workout that works for you?

- **Try different kinds of exercise until you find what you really like.** Vary the activity from day to day if that helps you stay interested.
- **Get the support of your family.** Have your partner or a baby-sitter take over childcare while you exercise.
- **Explain the benefits.** Let everyone know that you'll be a better mother and saner person (and feel better about yourself) if you get the exercise you need.
- **Be flexible with your exercise schedule.** You don't want to set up a routine that's so rigid that if you can't exercise at a certain time you won't do it at all.

What's Happened to My Relationship?

When husband and wife become father and mother, there are bound to be some seismic shifts in their relationship. It's not only that you're changing diapers instead of going on hot dates; it's also that you may not be in the mood to carry on deep meaningful conversations, or to have sex.

Why You're Not Feeling Sexy

• **You've lost your sexual confidence.** Well, after 9 months of weight gain and 6 months of no sleep, it should come as no surprise that new mothers don't feel very sexually attractive (even when their partners beg to differ with them). It doesn't help that our society strips pregnant women of any sexuality and then bombards postpartum moms with impossible images of the ideal woman (skinny, gorgeous, bringing home the bacon and frying it up in a pan, love goddess). Yes, your husband still wants to make love to you, but there's many a new mom who thinks her husband is interested in her only because she's better than the alternative (no sex).

• **You've become your mother.** To complicate matters, many women get hung up on the old-fashioned notion of motherhood. Everyone knows that *their* mothers never had sex (except on holidays and to conceive them), so it's no wonder that your new status as a mother can throw your sexuality for a loop. There should be a "mothers do have sex and it's still great" club, where moms can reassure each other and share inspiring stories.

• **You feel invaded.** After carrying a baby for 9 months and then having him literally attached to you for months afterward—either to your breast or in your arms—you may not feel like being intimate with your husband. Once your baby is weaned or she can get around more on her own, you'll feel more open to the idea of sharing your body with your spouse.

• **You're embarrassed by your body.** It's hard to love your own body (or even feel comfortable with it) when no one has ever, anywhere, written about the seductive qualities of a postpartum tummy roll. And now that your baby is older, you may feel guilty that you don't fit into your pre-baby clothes. You may have forgotten that breasts aren't just for feeding. You may not like the fact that the geography of your vagina has been altered (your diaphragm, which used to go in and over a hill in your vagina, now just goes in).

You can't deliver a baby and not expect some physical changes. But your enjoyment of sex (and your partner's) shouldn't be affected by the changes, and Kegels will help you get your vaginal muscles back into shape (see "HOW TO: Kegels," page 172).

How to Get the Home Fires Burning In order for you and your husband to become more spiritually and sexually connected, you need to carve out time for yourselves. That's going to take planning. You need to plan date nights, plan sex, plan nights away. Many women find that they don't miss spontaneity all that much. It's pleasurable to spend a few days anticipating a planned time together, and if you're lucky, the warm glow will tide you over until the next time.

Don't hesitate to tell your husband that you need reassurance that you're still sexy and desirable (not just convenient). Although your partner may be experiencing the same new-parent overload that you are, he didn't go through the biological changes that you did (feel free to remind him of that).

And take some time to talk about how you feel about yourself and your relationship. You may need him to help you find the time to exercise, spend time with friends, or just get away by yourself occasionally. But he won't know that unless you tell him. There's nothing more important than keeping the lines of communication open.

It's also critical that neither partner confuses sex with love. Regardless of the intensity (or lack of it) in your sex life, it's important for you and your partner to still feel loved. Don't confuse quantity with quality. If you feel that your relationship with your partner, sexual or otherwise, is suffering to the point where you don't know how to fix it, consider talking to a sex therapist or couples counselor.

Fighting the Chore Wars Who's doing what around the house can turn into a big issue after you become parents—thanks to the avalanche of chores associated with a new baby. You may be tired of doing the lion's share of the chores—and amazed to find out that your partner thinks he's doing a lot.

According to folks who study such things, the chore breakdown for new parents typically looks like this: Dad does 13 hours/week; Mom does 44 hours/week. So where does your partner get the crazy idea that he's doing his fair share? Experts say that fathers often think they're pulling their weight because they're doing so much more housework and baby care than *their* dads did. Women tend to compare how much Dad is doing with how much *they* are doing.

Is there a solution to this problem, beyond hiring a full-time maid? Yes. One way is for new parents to write down and discuss their expectations. Workloads need to be figured out and distributed. You can avoid misunderstandings and resentment by spelling out who does what and why.

A MOTHER'S VIEW

"Our First Night Away from Baby"

It was Labor Day weekend and it was time to relax. Cristy Oliver's mother had volunteered to take care of 8-month-old Cristopher for a night so that Cristy and her husband could have some time alone together.

Cristopher and his parents spent Friday night with his grandmother so that the baby could get comfortable at her house. Then, on Saturday morning, the Austin, Texas, couple drove to a hotel in a nearby town.

Cristy was a little worried about her son, but they'd brought a pager with them in case there was a problem. "I wanted to call to see how he was doing, but David wouldn't let me," says Cristy. In spite of her anxiety, the couple enjoyed themselves. "We swam, went out for dinner, relaxed. We didn't do anything spectacular—just spent time together." The pager never went off, and "we slept like logs," says Cristy. "But we woke up at 6 A.M. because that's when Cristopher usually wakes up." She repressed the urge to rush home to the baby until after breakfast and another swim.

"I thought he'd be mad at us for leaving him. But he was fine," Cristy says. Since that first night away from the baby, Cristy and her husband have spent two more nights away. Her suggestions for those first nights away:

- **Plan ahead.** If you're breastfeeding, make sure that your baby has enough milk while you're away. Cristy started expressing and freezing milk two weeks before their night out.
- **Pack your baby's favorite comfort objects.** Baby Cristopher took along his Winnie-the-Pooh to Grandma's house.
- **Have a reliable means of being contacted, such as a pager.** Or leave an itinerary with phone numbers and locations.
- **Be realistic about your first night away.** Maybe it will be a hot romantic evening—or just a great opportunity to catch up on some sleep.

A FATHER'S VIEW

"What Chore Wars?"

"If I see a chore that needs doing, I get it done," says Michael Sexton, of Hawthorne, Nevada. What's more, he says, "I like to cook and clean up."

Michael isn't trying to win the model-husband award; he's just being practical. "With our hectic lifestyle, the chores need to get done by whoever can get to them." Michael is a full-time sergeant in the sheriff's office, where his wife, Heather, is the full-time dispatcher. They are parents to her 5-year-old daughter from a previous marriage, a 4-year-old foster child, and their newest additions: 9-month-old twin boys, Sean and Nicholas. There's just no time to argue over chores—and Michael and Heather never have.

"I wanted kids for a long time. Now that they're finally here, I'm glad to help out in whatever way I can," Michael says. "And since I was a bachelor for a long time, I'm used to chores."

Cooking and cleaning are split evenly between the two parents, "but Heather jumps on the laundry more than I do," Michael admits. He also finds that chores often seem endless: "I'll start folding clothes and just when I get done, here comes another load." How Michael avoids chore wars at his house:

- **Be prepared.** Know that with kids come more chores. "I remind myself that they're my kids, too," Michael says. That's the motto he lives by.
- **Do it yourself.** Tired of seeing the dishes piled up in the sink? Wash them. Want some clean underwear? Wash them. Instead of getting mad, Michael says, just tackle the chore yourself.
- **Cut your partner, and yourself, some slack.** "We don't get on each other's cases if a chore is left undone," Michael says.

The truth is, if you're now staying home full-time, your workday will probably include more chores than your husband's. If you and your partner are both working, nobody should come home and have to carry the bulk of the chores.

Look, Mom, no hands! It's a whole new world for the upright baby (and her parents).

CHAPTER 5

MONTHS TEN THROUGH TWELVE

To quote a Disney song, it really is "a whole new world" now that your baby can get up and go, go, go. Even the most careful and cautious babies are up and about and looking for trouble.

Parents often feel two steps behind their baby during the last part of his first year—and end up doing quite a bit of scrambling themselves: baby-proofing in places they never dreamed a baby could get to; realizing with a shock that their sweet child really does need discipline; and adjusting to the idea that in no time at all their munchkin will be 1 year old.

It's not as if your baby is about to leave home for college or even a stroll around the block, but the first birthday does inspire quite a mixed bag of feelings. You couldn't wait for each and every milestone, but where *did* the year go? It was just yesterday that your baby . . . was a baby. Now he's a regular little person with a real personality: strong-minded, mobile, in-your-face, adorable.

What else can you do as the whirlwind first year careens to a close but watch with pride as your baby takes his first steps away from you, and sigh with relief when he comes running back. Put that baby gate up on the stairs. Pat yourself on the back. Sing "Happy Birthday" with great gusto. And hope that every year is half as good as this one.

By the end of 12 months your baby will probably* . . .

- Have consumed 600 jars of baby food
- Have dirtied more diapers than you even want to think about

*Every baby is different and has his or her own developmental timetable.

- Have at least an itty-bitty display of hair
- Have gained 14 pounds and grown 10 inches
- Pulled the dog's or cat's tail 50 times in the past 3 months
- Have a clue that nighttime is for sleeping, a cup is for drinking, and these feet were made for walking
- Have outgrown 90 percent of the shower presents he received
- Actually need a first pair of shoes
- Be more than happy to stick her whole head and both fists in her cake

By the end of the first year, you will probably . . .

- Believe that time really does fly
- Have exaggerated your baby's abilities at least once to a friend or relative
- Have experienced your first power struggle with someone under 3 feet tall
- Think you have curvature of the spine from bending over to hold your little one's hands
- Have sung 100 lullabies
- Still wish that you had a baby owner's manual
- Be thrilled about turning the car seat to the forward-facing position (while keeping it in the middle of the backseat, if possible)
- Be a little teary-eyed about your baby's first birthday
- Have earned a big piece of cake for yourself—enjoy!

CARE AND FEEDING

Now you're in for it: wet Cheerios stuck to the kitchen floor was nothing compared to the food fun your baby will have in the next couple of months. A hint: remember the spaghetti-on-the-wall scene from the movie *Baby Boom*? Luckily, most babies love taking a bath at this age, so you'll have lots of giggles scrubbing the egg out of his hair. Cleaning the kitchen is less entertaining. So is weaning from the bottle.

Bring on the Finger Foods

Your baby still likes a variety of baby food but will be more excited about experimenting with new finger foods. Because of the choking hazard, many doctors recommend that first finger foods be no bigger than the chunk of fruit found in a typical fruit cocktail. And they should always be very soft.

Your finger-food menu might include:

- Ripe fruits, such as banana, melon, and pear

YOUR BABY'S WORLD

For 12 months your baby has used her senses to figure out her new world and how she fits in. Until now, you have pretty much controlled what she's seen and experienced. As she hurtles toward 1 year old, expect her to be both exhilarated and terrified about her newfound independence. On her brave days, her world is *sooooo* big and exciting, and she's in charge. On her "I'm still just a baby" days, all she wants is a world of cuddles and familiar faces.

What Your Baby Sees. Your baby's vision has gone from 20/200 at birth to 20/50 at 6 months and will be 20/20 by her first birthday. Now she can see as well as (or better than!) you can.

What Your Baby Remembers. All the hand motions to patty-cake. How a spinning toy works. Where you keep her favorite pacifier.

What Your Baby Feels. She's still fascinated with the different textures of food, fabrics, and the earth—all of which she continues to explore with her hands, feet, tongue. On the inside, she feels happy, mad, frustrated—sometimes within the span of just a minute or two.

What Your Baby Hears and Understands. She hears herself banging the lids of pots together and clapping her hands—and she knows what your reaction will be. She hears the dog yelp when she steps on her tail (and knows what the dog is saying). She laughs when she hears favorite songs and smiles excitedly when she hears you coming from another room. When she hears "Wave bye-bye, Susie," she knows just what to do, what bye-bye means, and who Susie is!

What Your Baby Likes. Your soon-to-be toddler enjoys toys that she can push around the room; she likes to swing and to play with balls. She adores being the center of attention. She thinks ice cream is a great treat. She may like playing on the floor even more than being held. But you're still her favorite toy.

What Your Baby Needs. She needs shoes for those traveling feet, hugs for those inevitable boo-boos, freedom to stretch her legs and practice her skills, and a feeling of security so she knows she's not braving the world on her own.

LIFE WITH ESTEBAN

Follow along with new mother Grege Lastra, in the final months of her diary of her first year of motherhood.

MONTH 10
This month Esteban stood alone for the first time. What a surprise for us—and for him! His little face looked sort of confused and sort of pleased as he stood there.

For several months now, he's loved to walk while holding either Steve's or my hands. The other day, as Esteban pulled away from me, I let him go to Steve, who was lying on the floor. He actually took a couple of steps before Steve caught him.

At the end of his first year, Esteban is more interested in walking—and kicking the ball—than he is in talking.

Even though he's mostly preoccupied with moving around—and he does move—he loves his toys. He'll put things in and dump them out of a box or pot for long stretches of time.

It's fun to watch Esteban look toward Steve or our dog when I say either's name, but he still doesn't utter any distinct words.

MONTH 11
I can't take my eyes off Esteban for one minute now. He's everywhere!

He started walking this month. At first he walked like Lurch in *The Addams Family*. To help him practice and gain confidence, Steve and I sat across from each other and passed him back and forth between us, always ready to steady him—or catch him. It wasn't long before he was pushing our hands away.

He says "Mama," "Dada," "ba" for his bottle, and "Caw" for Chaos, our dog. In fact, Chaos is his best friend. Esteban calls for him the moment he wakes up and feeds him all day long.

After all the drooling he's been doing for months, Esteban finally has two bottom teeth.

MONTH 12
Sometimes I look at Esteban and he seems so grown-up. He talks on the phone, waves hello and good-bye (even to people on the phone), and the minute we put music on, he heads to the middle of the room to dance. He's so curious and funny—and so much fun now, our little 1-year-old.

- Soft cooked vegetables, including peas, carrots, green beans, squash (be sure pieces are also small, but the biggest concern is that veggies are soft, not stringy)
- Tiny pieces of cooked pasta (not long noodles, but easy-to-grab shapes)
- Pieces of pancake or French toast (made without egg white)
- Scrambled eggs (made without egg white)
- Soft cheese cubes
- Small squares of cooked potato
- French fries (not too salty and cut into bite-sized pieces)
- Bite-sized pieces of cooked meat loaf or meatballs
- Cooked chicken liver
- Soft cheese pizza

Soft cooked vegetables are good finger foods for pint-size diners. Make sure the vegetables are very soft and not stringy.

When they were a year old, both of my daughters loved the breaded chicken pieces sold in fast-food kids' meals, but it was always a hassle to remove the breading and break the chicken into small enough pieces. If they got their hands on a full-sized nugget, invariably they'd stuff the whole thing into their mouths. This is a choking hazard that you should avoid. Better to serve chicken livers or meat loaf, which are sources of iron and protein that are far easier for a baby to chew.

How Much Does Your Baby Need to Eat?

By the time he's a year old, he'll be drinking 16 to 24 ounces of formula or breast milk each day. Many parents try to serve about half of the milk from a cup. After his birthday, ask your baby's pediatrician if you can switch to whole cow's milk from formula or breast milk.

To fulfill your baby's nutritional needs, each day he'll need two servings (about a tablespoon) each of cereal, fruit, vegetables, meat (protein), and ½ slice of bread or ¼ cup of soft pasta. (The best sources of vitamins A and C are deep orange or deep green vegetables, such as sweet potato and broccoli.) A good source of calcium, besides milk, is whole-fat yogurt. Juice should be limited to 4 ounces or less per day (see "The Truth About . . . Juice," page 254).

Q & A

"I'm worried that my 11-month-old is getting fat. Is it OK to give him skim milk instead of formula?"

No, it's not OK. If your baby isn't drinking breast milk, he should be drinking iron-fortified formula. If he's over a year old, he should be drinking whole cow's milk.

Until a baby is 1 year old, he needs the iron in a fortified formula (or an iron supplement or iron-fortified cereal, if the baby is exclusively breastfed). After 1, he needs the fat and calories in whole milk.

Dieting is *not* for babies. If you limit the amount of fat and cholesterol in your baby's diet, you risk affecting his physical and mental well-being. Both are essential for brain development, and cholesterol is believed to contribute to the formation of healthy nerve fibers.

At 2 years of age—not before—you can talk to your baby's pediatrician about weaning him from whole milk to 2 percent and then to skim.

The Messy Truth About . . . Self-Feeding

When my mother first saw her 11-month-old granddaughter feeding herself, she was appalled. Halley Rose would end up with more food smeared on her face than in her mouth. Crumbs and blobs of food would travel great distances from her plate. In an attempt to spoon food into her mouth, she would get much of it in her hair or ear (well, it is an opening).

It was a lot less messy when I was a child, my mom pointed out, because parents fed their children until they were 2 years old, and wiped up after every bite. That may be true, but we now know that allowing a child to feed herself is more practical and great practice for her fine motor skills—not to mention that self-feeding is a developmentally appropriate assertion of independence. Once my mother could see past the mess, she was impressed by how Halley actually succeeded in spooning some food into her mouth, and by her granddaughter's sense of accomplishment.

Your baby's interest in self-feeding is a sure sign of growing maturity. If you try to discourage it (or try to control the situation for neatness' sake) you could squelch her budding sense of independence and affect her interest in eating to the point where she's not getting what she needs to thrive. Who knows, if you give your baby a little control in how she eats, she may not be so likely to fight you for control in some other more important arena.

Although your baby will be interested in using utensils, she won't be proficient at it until she's over 18 months old. In the meantime, provide her with baby-sized silverware and let her take the lead. Many babies do well with the plastic spoons with loop handles. It gives them more to hold on to.

The Thumb-Sucking/Pacifier Debate

Some parents think that if they're weaning their baby from his bottle, they may as well go whole hog and wean him from his pacifier or thumb, too. That isn't necessarily a great idea. Pacifiers and thumbs both offer satisfying nonnutritive sucking. There's no reason to complicate bottle weaning with another traumatic

HOW TO
Deal with a Messy Eater

Babies are messy, especially when they're eating. It's best to focus on making the eating experience pleasant and fun, and not to obsess too much on making it neat. Still, there are a few ways to try to control the mess:

› **Be prepared.** Put a bib on Baby, an apron on you, and a plastic mat or newspaper under the high chair. Have a damp washcloth or wet wipe handy.
› **Provide distraction.** Meals that are family affairs are more fun for Baby. With any luck, she'll find "talking" with Mom and Dad more fun than throwing her food.
› **Call it quits.** If your baby is having one of those meals where she refuses to eat, remove her food from her tray and replace it with a book or toy. (She should be able to grasp that you want her to stay at the table for a while, even if she's not eating. This will also help her learn the importance of family dinnertime.)

As much as a baby enjoys feeding herself, it can also be frustrating. She'll let you know when she's ready for some help or to call it quits.

› **Keep dinnertime short.** Don't make her stay at the dinner table too long, though. A 1-year-old typically won't be able to happily stay in her high chair for longer than 15 to 30 minutes.
› **Nip food-throwing in the bud.** When a baby is tired of, or frustrated by, feeding herself, she may begin to toss it around. It's OK to say "Oh no, we don't throw food. I don't like it," but getting mad about it is useless. If the throwing continues, feed her yourself or conclude the meal.
› **Don't use breakable dishes.** To avoid having a whole plate of food go flying, put your baby's meal directly onto the clean tray of her high chair.

Q & A

"Why is it so important that my baby be weaned off the bottle by age 1?"

After hearing "every baby has his or her own timetable" 20 times during your child's first year, it's interesting that most experts agree that it's best for a baby to say bye-bye to the bottle by the time she's 1 year old.

Best in this case also means easiest. It may be less trouble to wean your baby from the bottle now rather than later. Expect her to become more—not less—willful and stubborn and attached to her comfort objects as she ages.

There are a few other reasons that the time is right. A 1-year-old should be getting the bulk of her nutritional needs from the solid foods she's eating, not from liquids. Juice and milk go down easier from a bottle. Too much, and your toddler won't be hungry for her vegetables. The American Academy of Pediatric Dentists gives you another good reason to ban the bottle: a higher risk of cavities (see "DEFINITION: Baby-Bottle Syndrome," 195).

One way to help your baby lose interest in the bottle is to make the experience very boring. If she can have a bottle only when she's sitting in her high chair, and then only if it's filled with water, it won't be long before she finds a cup of milk far more appealing.

WHAT IF . . . MY BABY GETS HEAD LICE

If your baby spends any part of her day with lots of other children, there's a chance that she'll be exposed to head lice. Lice pass from head to head in environments like childcare centers and school classrooms. They're no reflection on your hygiene or housekeeping, or of the center's, for that matter.

Head lice don't carry disease, but they are a gigantic nuisance for you and for the caregiver. Because they travel from child to child, if your baby has head lice she'll be sent home and not allowed to return until she's lice free (otherwise everyone will get a new batch). If your baby is under a year old, call your pediatrician to report the lice. He'll probably recommend an over-the-counter lice shampoo, which comes with a nit-removal comb. Nits are the little white eggs laid by the lice. Nits are easier to spot than the dark-colored lice. They often attach themselves to the hair at the nape of the head and around the ears. The only other symptom of head lice is an annoying itch, causing your child to constantly scratch.

To prevent a recurrence, it's wise to wash your child's clothes, sheets, and blankets, and to vacuum all rugs in your house. It's a good idea to bag up her stuffed animals for a week or so (to kill the nits), then clean them thoroughly in the washing machine.

change in a baby's life, especially when he may be seeking more comfort (instead of less) thanks to the onset of both separation and stranger anxiety.

Although a child's real need for sucking does diminish around the time he's 1 year old, most experts today agree that such sucking is a positive, soothing habit that you needn't worry about until a child's permanent teeth are coming in.

In any case, many children naturally lose interest in their pacifier around 8 to 10 months and never miss it. If your baby is very attached to his, wait until bottle weaning is over to get him thinking about giving it up. Because you're in charge of the pacifier (unlike his thumbs, which you can't

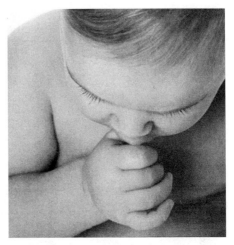

Some babies continue to find great comfort from sucking their thumbs. These days most doctors don't worry about thumb-sucking until a child's permanent teeth are coming in.

easily control), you can limit its use to naptimes and bedtimes. This is a good plan for many parents, who really don't mind that their baby uses a pacifier at home, but are embarrassed by it out in public. It's also a wise move because using a pacifier when he's asleep won't interfere with your baby's speech development.

Thumb-sucking is a whole other can of worms. Trying to wean a 1-year-old thumb-sucker from his favorite comfort crutch won't be easy. Explanatory books, videos, and discussions of future orthodontia problems may offer information for you, but they won't have any impact on your child. So what's a parent to do? Wait until it's a real problem to worry about it, say in another two or three years. The vast majority of 1-year-old thumb-suckers are not sucking their thumbs at age 2. Thumb-sucking is a perfectly normal way to self-soothe. And since it's not hurting anything right now, let it go.

SLEEPING

By 8 months of age, a healthy baby should be able to sleep an 8-to-10-hour stretch without a feeding. After he hits the 1-year mark, he may naturally move from a two-nap- to a one-nap-a-day schedule. Many parents find that this is when their baby finally eases into a normal sleeping schedule. By bedtime, he really *is* sleepy.

How Babies' Sleep Patterns Change

AGE	DAY SLEEP (HOURS)	NIGHT SLEEP (HOURS)	TOTAL SLEEP (HOURS)
1 week	8	8½	16½
1 month	7	8½	15½
3 months	5	10	15
6 months	3¼	11	14¼
9 months	3	11	14
12 months	2¼	11½	13¾

GOOD ADVICE
Nighttime Rituals

"We started a bedtime routine when our oldest son was ten months old. We would say to him, 'It's bedtime, so what are we going to do?' The response is, 'Brush our teeth, read a book, say prayers, and go to sleep.' Each step has a hand signal. It's kind of a game to the kids. The key is to keep it simple and stick with it."

—Mary Lewy, Lakeville, MN

A baby's sleep patterns can be disrupted if he has an ear infection or is teething. He also may wake up screaming for no apparent reason. Even a baby who could previously put himself to sleep may have difficulties now if he's suffering from severe separation anxiety. Make sure you're not skimping on his soothing bedtime rituals. He needs them more than ever now.

HEALTH AND SAFETY

A year ago you were walking into the pediatrician's office with a newborn. At her sixth well-baby checkup—at 12 months—it's more likely that your baby is walking *you* in. If you were lucky, you survived the first year with a collection of only minor colds, cuts, and bruises. Safety issues remain a top priority as your active toddler explores her newly expanded world.

The One-Year Checkup

Although it certainly seems momentous to you, the 12-month checkup is fairly routine. In addition to the usual well-baby examinations, the doctor may talk to you about your child's motor and verbal skills. You'll also discuss the transition to finger foods and cow's milk, and weaning from the bottle. If your baby hasn't already had the chicken pox, the pediatrician may discuss the vaccination with you. Some healthcare providers screen for iron deficiency sometime between 9 and 12 months. Your pediatrician may also give your baby a tuberculosis (TB) skin test.

Immunization: Looking Back, Looking Ahead

	DTP	HIB	HEP B	MMR	POLIO	TB TEST	VARICELLA
Birth			•				
2 months	•	•	•		•		
4 months	•	•			•		
6 months	•	•					
6–18 months	•	•	•		•		
12–15 months		•		•		•	•
12–18 months	•						
15–18 months							
4–6 years	•			•	•	*	
11–12 years			•				**
14–16 years	***						

*In some school districts
**Booster
***Tetanus only

Anatomy of . . . A Sinus Infection

I was surprised when my daughter Halley Rose was diagnosed with a sinus infection when she was around 10 months old. It seemed like such an adult malady, and it isn't that common in infants. But if your child has recurring ear infections, upper respiratory infections, or allergies, her sinuses may get zapped with an infection, too.

DEFINITION

Cellulitis

Cellulitis is a serious bacterial infection that spreads through a child's skin. If not treated, it can spread to the lymph glands, form an abscess, or enter the bloodstream.

A child with the condition may already be sick and feverish, and have an ear or sinus infection. Or you may just notice a reddish, hot spot on her skin, which is tender to the touch.

Immediate medical attention is needed to stop the spread of the bacteria. Usual treatment is antibiotics given orally, by injection, or intravenously. Sometimes a hospital stay is necessary.

The sinuses are cavities in the nose and behind the baby's cheekbones. If you've ever had an infection, you know how tender and sore these spots can become. The inside of the cavities swell and sometimes become blocked, preventing mucus from draining. That's when bacteria are likely to move in.

Signs of a sinus infection include a persistent cough or nasal discharge, bad breath (from the mucus draining down her throat), headache, and puffy eyes upon waking in the morning.

After months of ear and sinus infections, including one infection that turned into cellulitis (see "DEFINITION: Cellulitis," above), my 1-year-old had tubes put in her ears, her sinuses scraped, and her adenoids removed—all in one outpatient surgery. Although surgery can be scary, having antibiotic after antibiotic not work was pretty scary, too. After surgery, Halley Rose didn't have another ear or sinus infection until several years after her tubes fell out.

What You Need to Know About . . . Tonsils and Adenoids

Tonsils and adenoids have the same job—they help to keep infections away from a child's chest and lungs—but there the similarity ends. It wasn't until my daughter had her adenoids removed (but not her tonsils) that I understood the difference between the two.

Tonsils are located on each side of the back of the throat. When your baby opens her mouth wide, you may be able to see them way in the back. Tonsils grow from birth until about age 7, and then usually begin to shrink. Some children naturally have bigger tonsils than others, but if your baby's are swollen, you'll know it; sometimes they appear to be touching each other or seem to fill up the back of the mouth.

	Adenoids	Tonsils
Where located	Behind nasal passages near Eustachian tube	Back of mouth, either side of throat
Symptoms of a problem	Sore throat, green/yellow nasal secretions, mouth breathing, nasal-sounding or indistinct speech ("Mommy" may sound like "bobby"), chronic ear infections (swollen adenoids may be blocking ear drainage), recurring sinus infections	Sore throat, sore glands, fever of 101°F or higher, coating of pus on tonsils, difficulty breathing, lack of appetite, snoring or sleep apnea (stopping breathing while sleeping)
Treatments	Antibiotics	Antibiotics
When surgery may be considered	Four or more severe infections, recurring ear infections that don't clear up with antibiotics or tubes, possibility of facial deformity from constant mouth breathing	Four or more severe infections, tonsillitis that doesn't respond to antibiotics, serious obstruction of breathing or labored breathing that causes a restricted heartbeat

This is not intended to replace consultation with your pediatrician or otolaryngologist.

Problems arise when tonsils become so enlarged that they interfere with breathing or swallowing. Recurrent tonsillitis, in which the tonsils become infected and inflamed, can be painful. If your child's tonsils are enlarged, it's likely that her adenoids are, too. If the doctor decides to remove her tonsils, he may take out the adenoids as well. The combined surgery, from administering anesthesia to the recovery room, usually takes less than an hour.

Adenoids can't be seen by peeking inside your baby's mouth. They're hidden behind the nasal passages, beside the opening to the ear's Eustachian tube. Infected or swollen adenoids are often linked to ear infections. Adenoids are sometimes removed when ear tubes are inserted, as in my daughter's case. If your child's problem is adenoidal, it isn't usually necessary to remove her tonsils.

Q & A

"My baby's testicles still haven't descended. Should I call the doctor?"

It's not uncommon for a baby boy to be born with one or both testicles undescended. Often, the testicles will descend on their own by a baby's first birthday. If you're approaching that milestone and it hasn't happened, your pediatrician will probably recommend hormone therapy, surgery, or both.

Hormones to increase your baby's testosterone levels are injected on a twice-weekly schedule for several weeks. If that doesn't work, outpatient surgery will be performed to see if something is blocking the testicles' path to the scrotum. Sometimes a band of fibrous tissue physically prevents the testicles' descent.

Left untreated, undescended testicles can cause a number of problems in adulthood: an increased risk of testicular cancer, infertility, and, rarely, a testicle that becomes twisted and causes severe groin pain.

Surgery, of course, is always a last resort. Unless your child has a recurring problem or a complication from an infection in the tonsils or adenoids, surgery shouldn't be necessary. Her pediatrician will treat her infections with antibiotics or other medication.

What You Need to Know About . . . Allergies and Asthma

When I was a child, I couldn't have a pet, curtains on my windows, or a feather pillow. I wasn't allowed to jump in piles of leaves. My problem: allergies (animal dander, dust, feathers, mold) and mild asthma. After numerous respiratory infections and a bad case of pneumonia, I was put on a regimen of allergy shots. I had a few more episodes of nasty wheezing, which were accompanied by equally nasty

Q & A

"Should my baby get a flu shot?"

The vast majority of healthy babies don't really need an influenza shot. Most can recover from influenza without any serious complications. If your baby has a chronic medical condition or is in contact with a relative who has such a condition, your pediatrician may recommend the shot. For babies who have a severe allergy to eggs, the vaccination may not be given.

shots of adrenaline in my bottom (the old treatment for asthma), but for the most part I got by with only one case of bronchitis a year.

Asthma, which is a chronic inflammation of the bronchioles (small airways) in the lungs, can be aggravated or triggered by allergens. The number of children with the condition has tripled in the past 15 years, and today's treatments for the ailment are much more sophisticated and effective. Allergy shots are sometimes prescribed, but mild sufferers of asthma are more likely to be treated with inhaled medications.

By the time my babies were each 1 year old, they had had enough respiratory illnesses to warrant regular doses of albuterol, a bronchodilator that helps relax the muscles around the bronchioles. The medication is typically administered via a nebulizer, a machine that pumps a medicated mist into a face mask that attaches to the child. (Older children can use an inhaler.)

How do you know if your baby has asthma? Symptoms include shortness of breath, persistent coughing, and wheezing. Any of these symptoms should be reported to your baby's pediatrician; she doesn't have to be wheezing to have asthma.

There's some debate about whether or not children really outgrow asthma. Some seem to, but most continue to have symptoms into adolescence and beyond. Frequency and intensity of asthma episodes often become milder and milder as a child grows. My girls, for instance, now require a nebulizer treatment only once or twice a year during allergy season.

For More Help: Allergies and Asthma

- The Lung Line
  1-800-222-LUNG
  Offers information and resources to active members

- American Academy of Allergy, Asthma, and Immunology
  800-822-ASMA
  Has free brochures and referral lists of specialists

- American Lung Association
  800-LUNG-USA
  Provides information and referrals to support groups

- Asthma and Allergy Foundation of America
  800-7-ASTHMA
  Offers educational materials

Keeping Your Toddler Safe

More mobile toddlers sometimes seem like a disaster waiting to happen. Now is a good opportunity to deal with hazards that you may not have considered before. For instance, an upright baby can reach the stove, fall into the toilet, and run in front of a swing.

Burns Babies love examining the knobs on the stove and watching the steam rising from a boiling pot or teakettle. Now that your child can cruise over to the hot stove, it's even more important to turn pot and pan handles in while you're cooking. If the stove's knobs are in the front of the appliance, where your child can reach them, install a stove guard that provides a barrier between your baby and your stove's controls.

A crackling fire is magic to a child this age, but it can also be a magnetic draw. Never leave a child unattended in a house with a fire burning. Even screens and glass doors can be very hot.

More commonly, a child gets burned by hot liquid spilled from a coffee cup or soup bowl. Obviously it's best to keep such things away from your baby, but it also helps to tell her "Hot, ouch!" when you're serving hot food or drinks. To avoid scalds from too-hot bathwater, lower the temperature on your hot-water heater.

> ## HOW TO
> ## Treat a Minor Burn
>
> If your child is burned or scalded, the best thing to do is immerse the area in cold running water. Do this for at least 15 minutes.
>
> When the pain subsides, wrap the area in sterile gauze. *Don't* use an adhesive dressing that may stick to the wound or any sort of butter or grease. And don't burst any blisters.
>
> If the burn turns out to be more serious than you thought (on more than just a small part of her body, for instance, or on her hands or face), or if your child appears to be faint or in shock, seek medical help immediately.

Drowning Drowning remains the leading cause of accidental death among children ages 1 to 2. Eight percent of all toddler drownings (and 40 percent of all infant drownings) occur in the bathtub. Never, ever leave your child alone in the bathtub, even if he's in a tub chair. Since many 1-year-olds no longer fit into their bath chair but are still wobbly in the tub, they need you there for support and security.

When you're not using the bathroom, keep the door closed so that your curious child can't climb into the tub and turn on the water when you're not around. If he seems fascinated by the toilet, install a lid lock that will prevent him from lifting it and falling in.

Anything that's filled with water—including things you've probably never thought of—can be a drowning hazard. Besides being careful about toilets, keep a close eye on your baby when he's around buckets, pails, even ice chests with melted ice in them. A baby can drown in two minutes in just 2 inches of water—good reason not to

Warning: A baby can drown in just two minutes in only 2 inches of water

leave the mop and bucket unattended for even a second.

If you have a swimming pool, you know that it has to have a fence around its perimeter. The fence should have a self-closing, self-latching gate (one that's too high for your child to reach). In addition, it's smart to know CPR and to have lifesaving equipment, and a telephone, near the pool.

Playground Safety A baby who walks can get her hands on almost all of the playground equipment, not just the sandbox where you plopped her down while you read the paper. It's essential to keep the playground experience a safe one.

- Teach your child to walk a safe distance from swings, and only in front of them. This may be difficult for a 1-year-old to grasp, but it's wise to start this lesson as early as possible (and follow the rule yourself).
- Make sure your baby is wearing appropriate play clothes: no jackets or coats with strings, scarves, necklaces, or other dangly items that could catch on something and strangle her. Shoes should have treads, and her hat shouldn't obscure her peripheral vision.
- Check the playing surfaces of the playground. Surfaces several feet around and under each piece of equipment should be bouncy and absorb shocks (in case of a fall). Rubber tiles are good, as is a foot-deep layer of sand, wood chips, or other loose material. Concrete, grass, and dirt won't break a child's fall from a swing or climbing structure.

- Structures should be 15 feet away from each other for safe play.
- Check sandboxes and grassy areas for glass and animal droppings. Also, the sandbox should be well away from the structures designed for older children.
- Look for signs of neglect, such as peeling paint (which could be a lead-poisoning hazard if the playground is old), broken or cracked plastic parts, frayed ropes, wood that's rotten or splintering, metal that's rusty, equipment that's missing parts.
- Watch out for sharp edges or chains that could cut or pinch your child, and any pieces of equipment that clothing could wrap around or catch on.
- Some equipment has been deemed unsafe by the Consumer Product

Whee! Taking a swing can really bring on the giggles. Just make sure you check the age and safety of the equipment before giving Baby a ride.

Safety Commission. Don't let your child play on glider or animal-shaped swings or trapeze bars, which hang from ropes or metal chains. It's also wise to avoid merry-go-rounds until your child is old enough to hold on by herself.

MILESTONE

CAR SEAT TURNAROUND

If your baby is a year old and weighs more than 20 pounds, it's OK to turn her car seat around to the forward-facing position. The seat should still remain in the backseat, preferably in the middle. In the event of a collision from the side, your baby is safest in the middle.

Make sure that you reinstall the seat properly (see "What You Need to Know About . . . Car Seats," page 46). If you're buying a new seat for your toddler, remember that a seat with a five-point harness is considered the safest because it also restrains your child at the hips.

OTHER BIG DEALS

Who would have thought that climate control would be part of your parental job description? But it makes sense: if you're uncomfortable in hot or cold weather, imagine how your vulnerable baby will feel. Here's a primer for protecting your child from the elements.

Cold-Weather Care

Keeping a baby comfortable during cooler weather is a particular challenge. You want your child to be warm enough, but it's very easy to overbundle a baby and make him too hot. The trick is to dress him in layers, which trap air and add insulation. In the car or a warm store, you can strip off a few of the layers. Other tips:

- Pay special attention to your baby's head and feet, two vulnerable spots. A baby loses a lot of heat through his head, so make sure he's wearing a snug cap that covers his ears. Feet are first to get chilly, so warm socks and shoes are a must.
- If your baby is bundled up properly, it's fine to go out in weather that's above freezing for short periods of time—to take a walk or a roll in the snow. If it's windy, though, keep your jaunts very brief to avoid windburn. Wind also reduces the temperature dramatically.
- Sun protection is important in the winter as well as in the summer. Cover your baby's face or use a children's sunscreen if your baby is 6 months or older.
- Know the signs of frostbite: numb, stiff extremities with reddish or white patches.

Hot-Weather Care

While there's nothing wrong with having fun in the sun, it's crucial to take the proper precautions. Just one bad sunburn doubles your baby's chance of melanoma in later years. See chart, "Hot-Weather Hazards," pages 314–317, for more information.

Hot-Weather Hazards

PROBLEM/ SYMPTOMS	PREVENTION	TREATMENT	CALL THE DOCTOR IF . . .
Bee Stings Pain, itching	• All the precautions listed for bug bites (below) • Avoid flower beds and areas where bees gather; eating areas at zoos and other public places can be infested with bees • Have your child wear shoes	• Remove the stinger by scraping it with a credit card • Wash the area with soap and water • Apply cold compresses or ice • Apply anti-itch cream or a paste of baking soda and water • Go to the emergency room immediately if there's any unusual reaction	• Your child has had a reaction previously • You notice any of these reactions: hives, severe itching, severe swelling anywhere on the body, dizziness, thickened tongue, any wheezing or breathing difficulties, fainting, unconsciousness
Bug Bites Raised pink or white spot, sometimes with swelling and itching	• Cover your child when outdoors • Clothing should be light colored, not flowered or dark (which attract bees) • Don't use baby products with a fragrance • Stay away from standing water where insects like to breed • Consider using a bug repellent that contains less than 10 percent of DEET or is made of citronella oil • Apply repellent to child's clothing, not to her skin	• Clean with soap and water • Apply an anti-itch cream • Keep your child's nails short to avoid scratching (which can cause infection)	• The bite seems infected • Your child has any sort of allergic reaction; abnormal swelling, numbness, stiffness, convulsions

Dehydration
Cranky, dry eyes and mouth, dry wrinkly skin, fewer wet diapers or dark urine, sunken soft spot in skull

- Avoid getting sunburned or overheated
- Provide plenty of fluids

- Offer fluids and call your doctor immediately

- You notice any signs of dehydration; this a very serious problem that needs immediate attention

Heat Rash
Little pinprick-size pinkish dots in areas where moisture gets trapped (diaper skin folds) and around sweat glands (armpits, hairline, chest, neck, back)

- Dress in light, loose clothing
- Keep her cool
- Dry off sweaty spots every now and then
- Let her go bare indoors to dry sweaty areas

- Give child a lukewarm bath without soap
- Pat her dry
- Dress in light, loose clothing
- Avoid sunlight and heat

- The rash stays longer than two weeks
- The rash blisters or becomes inflamed
- Your child shows any signs of overheating or dehydration

Heat Stroke
Fever, crankiness, loss of consciousness, convulsions, diarrhea, weakness, sunken eyes

- Limit outdoor activities in hot weather
- Avoid direct sunlight
- Dress lightly
- Provide lots of fluids
- Limit time spent in a baby carrier or sling (where your body heat will make her even warmer)
- Keep a baby with a fever out of the sun

- Get child inside and to a cool spot ASAP
- Bring down her temperature with a cool, wet sponge or towel
- If symptoms are serious, include signs of dehydration, loss of consciousness, convulsions, or diarrhea, call your doctor or go to an emergency room

- Your child loses consciousness, has convulsions, diarrhea, or appears to be weak and listless
- She's feverish and cranky and doesn't respond to a good cooling off

(continued)

PROBLEM/ SYMPTOMS	PREVENTION	TREATMENT	CALL THE DOCTOR IF . . .
	• Don't leave your baby unattended in a parked car for even a short time. A closed-up car can quickly become like an oven		
Poison Oak, Ivy, Sumac	• Wear protective clothing	• If you know your child has	• The rash is extensive or
Red rash and tiny blisters within 24–48 hours after exposure (sooner if child is very allergic)	• Learn to identify poisonous plants and avoid them	wandered through a poisonous patch, douse the affected parts with water ASAP. Don't use soap, which will spread the poisonous oil	is on your child's face or genitals
		• Once a rash has broken out, apply cool compresses or have your child soak in cool water	• Your child experiences severe swelling
		• Apply an anti-itch cream	
		• Call the doctor if your child is very uncomfortable	
Sunburn	• Apply minimum SPF 15 sunscreen* 30 minutes before going out	• Bathe your child in cool water or apply cool compresses	• Your child has blisters or the sunburn is extensive and severe
Pinkish or reddish skin, hot, tender to touch	• Avoid midday sun (11 A.M. to 3 P.M.)	• Pat (don't rub) the skin dry	• Your baby has chills or fever
	• Protect face and scalp with a sun hat	• Use a water-based lotion to prevent peeling	• She is swelling up or seems to have an allergy to the sun (she may need an antihistamine)
	• Dress in light cotton clothing	• Give acetaminophen if your child is very uncomfortable or can't sleep	• Your baby shows signs of

heatstroke or dehydration (above)

- Your child shows symptoms of Rocky Mountain spotted fever: fever, headache, rash (especially on hands and soles of feet); this needs immediate treatment
- You notice symptoms of Lyme disease: flulike symptoms, such as body aches, stiffness, fatigue, fever, and headache
- Take the tick with you to the doctor or emergency room

(don't let child go bare)
- Sit in shade or under umbrella, at least part of the time
- Reapply sunscreen every hour or after water play

Ticks

If a tick is imbedded, it may at first resemble a hard little scab. As the tick feeds on blood, it gets larger, and the area around the tick may swell. Ticks can carry viruses and bacteria, which can make a child very sick, usually from 48 hours to a week after the tick bite (see "Call the Doctor If . . .")

- Wear protective clothing when in wooded areas
- Check your family and your pets frequently (pay special attention to children's hair)

- Remove tick carefully with tweezers if it's not too embedded
- If tick is in deep, don't squeeze it or it may break off.
- Light a match and blow it out; put the hot match tip to the end of the tick (if you can do this without harming your child)
- Keep the tick in a jar until you're sure your child is showing no signs of illness
- Go to the doctor if you can't remove the tick

*Babies under 6 months old shouldn't wear sunscreen; keep them covered up or out of the sun.

"When can my baby start swimming lessons?"

Most babies 6 months and older enjoy splashing around in a swimming pool with their parents, as long as the water isn't too cold. Never leave your child alone in the water, and make sure she has proper sun protection. Babies can become chilled very quickly, so it's wise to keep water play brief. Also, be aware that a baby who has had sunscreen applied can be very slippery. Also, water intoxication, which may lead to seizures, can result from water play in which the baby ingests too much water. Don't repeatedly dunk your baby.

As for swimming lessons, most experts suggest waiting until your baby is 3 or 4 years old and is comfortable going off on his own with other kids his age. At that time, he'll be able to follow the instructor's directions.

Before then, look for a water class that you and your baby can enjoy together.

Babies 6 months and older love to splash in the pool with Mom. Remember to apply sunscreen—and make sure the water isn't too cold.

What You Need to Know About . . . Carbon Monoxide Poisoning

When the weather gets cold, you and your family are at an increased risk of carbon monoxide (CO) poisoning. That's because appliances commonly used to heat a home—anything that burns wood, coal, propane, kerosene, oil, or gasoline, including a car running in the garage—can emit dangerous levels of CO. Typically, an appliance will give off a harmless amount of the gas, but if it's dirty or malfunctioning, or isn't properly vented, emissions can escalate.

More than 200 people die each year of CO poisoning, and more than 5,000 end up in the emergency room for treatment. A baby is particularly vulnerable to CO because of her fast metabolism and small size.

Because CO poisoning mimics the symptoms of less serious problems—sleepiness, dizziness, headache, nausea—it's difficult to diagnose. And the gas itself is colorless, odorless, and has no taste. That's why a growing number of people are installing CO detectors. Look for one that is approved by Underwriters Laboratories Standard 2034.

In addition to installing a detector, keep your chimney and flues clean and have them regularly inspected; use space heaters only in ventilated areas; and don't start your car with the garage door closed, where trapped fumes can build up or seep into your home.

YOUR GROWING BABY

Now, more than ever, your baby is learning from you. This instinctual drive to watch and imitate you is how he'll learn some important lessons and skills, including how to feed himself, how to carry on a give-and-take conversation, the importance of empathy and compassion, the love of books, and how to walk—to name just a few. As he moves into his second year, you'll continue to be the first place he turns for loving guidance.

Physical Growth

By the time she's 1 year old, your baby will have tripled her birthweight (usually a gain of about 14 pounds) and will have grown taller by 50 percent, about 10 inches, give or take a little. If your baby was big at birth, that doesn't mean she'll be a big 1-year-old, however. Birthweight is not a sure indicator of your baby's future size, and bigger babies are unlikely to triple their weight.

My first daughter was 8 pounds, 6 ounces at birth and *did* almost triple her weight by her first birthday. But by age 3, she had slimmed down to an average size. My second daughter was 9 pounds, 6 ounces at birth, but a little under 20 pounds at her first birthday. Because she's healthy and her growth (although slow and small) has been steady, her pediatricians have never worried about her. In both cases, my daughters' birthweights weren't harbingers of their future size.

Your doctor will track your baby's progress against national averages and chart her growth pattern from checkup to checkup. If her growth is very erratic or slows dramatically, she'll discuss with you the possible causes and treatments.

Motor Skills Babies this age move around in a variety of ways. Yours may be

Average Growth*				
TIME SPAN	0–3 MOS.	4–6 MOS.	7–9 MOS.	10–12 MOS.
Height	+2½ in.	+2½ in.	+2½ in.	+2½ in.
Weight	+3 lbs.	+4 lbs.	+4 lbs.	+ 3 lbs.

*There is a wide range of normal; every baby has her own growth timetable.

pulling herself to a stand, cruising, or walking. Even if she's spending most of her time upright, skirting the coffee table and walking from chair to chair, she may still drop to all fours if she's in a hurry. Crawling continues to be most babies' preferred mode of getting from here to there.

What if your baby isn't walking? It's probably nothing to worry about; the normal range for walking is between 8 and 18 months. Many things have to happen for a baby to be able to walk, in terms of muscle development, balance and coordination, and emotional maturity. If you think about it, it's a very big step for a baby to even *stand* alone. When she crawls, her center of gravity is just a couple of inches from the floor, midway between hands and knees. Once she's upright, it moves to a foot or more above the floor. No wonder it takes her so long to take a step.

You can't teach your baby to walk, but you can encourage her through play:

• Place some of her favorite toys on the coffee table so she's spending more time upright. (Make sure the coffee table has padded corners and isn't made of glass.)
• See to it that she has plenty of opportunities to safely cruise and lots of space to get around. This isn't the time to keep your baby in a playpen for long periods of time. She needs freedom and space.
• Walk her around holding her hands, if she seems to enjoy that.
• Stand a few feet away and encourage your standing baby to walk toward you, or between you and your partner.
• Stay close if she prefers it; give her space if that's what she wants. Some babies like the comfort of a parent close by; others would rather you just leave them alone, thank you very much.

If you're hovering or are overanxious about your baby walking, she'll certainly pick up on those feelings. If she senses your fear, she may even stay put. Likewise, she may even interpret your frustration over her not walking as a sort of criticism. Neither feeling is going to help her confidence much, so just relax.

To encourage walking, sit a few feet away from your baby and call to her. Make it fun and offer lots of praise.

Q & A

"Does my baby need shoes?"

Once your baby is taking her first steps, it's tempting to run out and buy her some fashionable footwear. She doesn't really need shoes, though, unless she's walking outside.

Inside, walking barefoot will help her develop balance and strengthen the muscles in her feet. Bare feet also get better traction. If her feet are cold, buy socks or slippers with treads for indoor walking. The treads are essential to prevent falls. Slippery socks and slippery floors have caused lots of bumps on noggins.

When you're in the market for baby shoes, keep the following tips in mind:

- New shoes are better than hand-me-downs, which may still retain the shape of the previous wearer's feet.
- Have a professional measure your baby's feet. If one foot is larger (and that's the case with most people), buy the size that fits the larger foot.
- Baby shoes should be shaped like a baby's foot, which is usually square, chubby, with very little arch. Avoid pointed shoes.
- Choose shoes made with flexible materials. The shoe should be bendable from heel to toe.
- Shoes made of plastic or rubber won't let feet breathe and will result in sweaty tootsies.
- Make sure the shoe salesperson pays special attention to how the heel fits. A shoe that slides off or pinches the heel can cause blisters.
- There should be about a half inch from the end of your child's foot to the end of the shoe. Don't buy large shoes and expect your child to grow into them; she'll trip over the toes. Do check the fit of her shoe every month—the American Orthopaedic Foot and Ankle Society reports that on average babies gain half a shoe size every month in their first year.
- High-top shoes provide a little extra ankle support; just make sure the top isn't so tight that it rubs your baby's ankle.

Once your baby is walking, you'll take a hard look at her posture and be amazed that she can walk at all. Many beginning walkers thrust their bellies out in front of them and lean back. This temporary swayback stance is fairly common (and may be her way of dealing with that changed center of gravity). Over time, your baby's legs will grow and her tummy muscles will strengthen. By the time she's 3 or 4, her balance and posture will be much improved.

Some other typical developments at this age:

CLIMBING Put up the barricades; it's climbing season. Your baby will probably make a beeline straight for any stairs you have, so beware. Keep basement

A Mother's View

"Slow Down, You Move Too Fast"

"You can't be walking yet. You're only ten months old." That's what Rosie Stevens said in shock when baby Amanda took her first steps. Her daughter's motor skills had been encouraged by her 2-year-old sister, Sanna, who delighted in pushing the baby's hands off the coffee table to see if she could stand by herself. She could.

Not normally one to squelch her children's development, Rosie was dismayed by Amanda's walking skills because they were living with a relative in Palm Beach, Florida, while looking for a house of their own. Baby-proofing for a mobile infant is more difficult when you're not in your own home.

"The house was a real safety challenge," Rosie admits. "There were little figurines all over the place and electrical outlets all over the floor." Rosie kept an eagle eye on Amanda. "Still, she would fall all the time, sweep everything off the low coffee table, and eat whatever she found on the floor."

By the time they moved into their own home a few months later, Rosie was a baby-safety expert:

- **Don't skimp on baby-proofing accessories.** It's worth the money to cover the outlets and use cabinet locks.
- **Remember that your standing baby is now right at stove height.** "One day Amanda ran in, turned on the stove, and ran out," said Rosie. If the knobs are within her reach, make sure they're kid-proof.
- **Pay special attention to drowning hazards.** Babies can drown in the toilet, in the bathtub, or in a bucket with only 2 inches of water. They're mesmerized by pools and streams. Rosie had to have her new landlord fence off a canal that ran by their backyard.
- **Don't count on safety equipment to keep your baby safe.** In spite of all of Rosie's efforts, she'd still find Amanda standing on top of a cabinet, with her sister egging her on.

doors closed. Gate the top and three steps up from the bottom of stairs so that your baby can go up only with your supervision.

Will she know how to go down? Some babies figure out how to go backward right away (which is the safest method). Others stubbornly insist on trying to plop down on their bottoms a step at a time. This is dangerous, especially given their limited ability to correct their actions if they plop too hard or far. Do your best to encourage your little one to crawl backward.

For an activity that's fun (and safer than stair climbing) for your baby, build an obstacle course of soft pillows and cardboard boxes. Your child will have a ball going under, over, around, and through the objects.

THE DIP AND PICKUP Here's something most adults wish they could do with the same ease they see their baby exhibiting: your standing baby will spy a toy at her feet, crouch down effortlessly (but carefully), scoop it up, and return to standing.

SCRIBBLE-SCRABBLE Give your baby a crayon or washable marker and watch her try to awkwardly hold it and put it to paper at the same time. The resulting swirls and scratches will be masterpieces and a sign of her growing dexterity.

THE STRIPTEASE By 12 months old, some babies are putting their pincer grasp to use by undressing themselves (including their shoes, if they have Velcro fasteners). Of course, your child will do this only when you *don't* want her to, like in the middle of the living room floor when you have the new neighbors over.

HANDEDNESS Although some parents begin to notice that their baby manipulates toys better with one hand than another, it's really too soon to determine whether your baby will be a lefty or a righty. Hand dominance doesn't usually stick until a child is 3 or 4.

An estimated 85 percent of the world's population is right-handed, so there's a good chance your baby will be a righty. It's thought that handedness is inherited, though, so if you're a lefty, there's a greater chance that your child will be.

Because lefties sometimes have a harder time learning to write and use scissors, some parents try to encourage the use of the right hand. That's not a good idea, experts say. If the child is a lefty, it will just confuse her and could cause developmental delays.

If you notice that your child *never* uses her right hand for anything, tell the pediatrician. It may be a sign of a problem.

Mental Development

One thing that greatly amuses parents is how their older baby appears to be thinking. A baby will stop playing, a thoughtful look comes over his face for a moment, and then he continues on. At 1 year old, my youngest daughter, Gracie, would interrupt her play for a minute by putting her forefinger up in the air in a sort of "Eureka" or "I'm going to stop and think a minute" position. At age 4, she still does this when she's answering a tough question or has had a brilliant idea.

This thoughtful pose isn't just an act. One-year-olds are really beginning to solve problems and make decisions. One mother I know came upon her 12-month-old baby furiously brandishing a broom (putting most of the items in the living room at great risk). When she tried to redirect her child to "sweep" in the kitchen, the baby erupted in frustrated crying and dragged the broom back to the living room. It was then that this mom realized he was trying to reach his favorite ball (under the couch) with the broom. Now that's brilliant.

Other typical mental developments at this age:

> ## MILESTONE
>
> ### "LET'S PLAY"
>
> "At the park, eleven-month-old twins Will and Libby love swinging on the swing set and playing in the sandbox. They roll balls back and forth and play peekaboo. I'm amazed by all the little games they make up. One of them will find something new and give the other a look, as if to say, 'Come and see what I've got.'"
>
> —*Valerie Dunay Corvin, Piedmont, CA*

Imitation Your baby will continue to enjoy any game that allows him to imitate you or mimic animal sounds. Instead of just making nonsense sounds, point to and label the parts of his body and have him repeat after you. When you sweep, give him a little broom so he can sweep, too.

More Complex Game Playing Babies are very busy at this age, trying to match and stack shapes. Nesting cups are great fun now as your child puts items into containers and takes them out again. Shape cubes will still be a big challenge, but he may enjoy trying to find the right opening for the triangle, square, and circle.

Look for toys that deliver lots of in-and-out or cause-and-effect punch. Four toys that were the biggest hits among 1-year-olds at my daughter's daycare: a child-sized mailbox with slots for coins and letters; a toy that changed colors when pushed hard on its top; a pint-sized plastic shopping cart; and a small plastic climbing structure that had lots of doors and windows to go in and out of.

Reading and Remembering Soon your baby will be able to turn a few pages of a book on her own: such power! Because her memory has improved, she'll really enjoy books that ask her to remember something ("Is Spot under the bed? No-o-o-o, there's an alligator under the bed . . ."). Expect to have to do daily repairs to favorite lift-the-flap books. Overzealous "readers" have been known to pull the flaps right out of the book—repeatedly.

Social Skills

The typical 1-year-old can say three to six words but understands lots more. Of course, it's not always easy to figure out exactly what your young babbler is saying. She'll have her own language of strung-together sounds. You can probably pick out "Mama" and "Dada" and "no" every now and then. Don't worry if you're not hearing distinct words. Her nonverbal methods of communicating are changing, too. You'll find that in addition to pointing at what she wants, she's using more gestures and facial expressions to get her meaning across and to show you how she's feeling.

Waving bye-bye is a cinch, and she attaches meanings to words. She'll look for the cat when you say "cat," look up when you say "airplane," and so on. She'll even understand simple sentences.

Other typical social developments at this age include:

Screaming Don't be surprised if your baby turns into a real screamer around the 1-year-old mark. Many babies get a big kick out of letting loose at the top of their lungs, especially if they know it gets a rise out of you. My niece would wait until she and her mom were at the checkout at the supermarket before screaming her head off just for the fun of it. It got so bad that my sister-in-law was afraid to take her out anywhere.

Most babies tire of the screaming game fairly quickly. In the meantime, don't return a scream with a scream of your own—that's the sort of reaction she's looking for. Instead, respond with a whisper (which may surprise

---

MILESTONE

"MY SOCIAL BUTTERFLY"

"I'd describe ten-month-old Noah as a happy flirt. He loves to chat and babble to people in the grocery store. He's always smiling. He goes and investigates something, then comes back and hugs me or maybe nurses, then he goes off again after he's had a minute with Mom."

—Jenny Doll,
New York City

her) or try to distract her with a game or song. And don't forget to compliment her when she speaks in a quiet voice. Reinforce her good behavior by saying, "Yes, inside is for quiet voices. You can be loud outside." Eventually, she'll catch on.

Separation and Stranger Awareness As discussed in Chapter 4, it's a natural development for babies this age to be frightened by their own independence. Yours may go exploring for a while and then scurry back to you. She may continue to have trouble sleeping because she's worried that you won't come back. Separation anxiety may last until a baby is 2.

In any case, the awareness of strangers should be viewed as a developmental milestone, not a character flaw. It's positive evidence that your baby is bonding to you and to her caregivers. Don't overreact.

Parallel Play Toddlers seem to enjoy being social and hanging around with others their age, but it's not likely that they're actually playing *with* these other babies. Instead, they play side by side, each doing his or her own thing.

Self-Care Your social baby will be attempting to feed herself, even to the point of mimicking you by trying to use a spoon and fork. When she's in a good

PLAYTIME

Baby Sign Language

At this age, your babbling baby may become frustrated when you can't immediately understand what he's saying. It might be helpful—and fun—to try a little sign language. Actually, your child already knows quite a few signs: bye-bye, sh-h-h-h, put me down, and pick me up. You can naturally build on that repertoire.

This communication aid is meant to be enjoyable, so don't overwhelm your baby with ten new signs right off the bat. Each day, do a sign for him while saying what it means. Then show him how to do it himself. Repeat the new sign and its meaning several times a day.

There's really no right or wrong way to sign. If you and your baby both know that when she pats her head she wants to drink from her cup, that's just fine. Signs can be whimsical, such as creating facial expressions and hand gestures for different animals, petting your hand to mean cat, for example. They can also be extremely empowering to your baby. Imagine how she'll feel when she can tell you she's sleepy (classic both-hands-on-one-side-of-tilted-head pose), sad (rubbing eyes), hungry (pointing to mouth), interested in reading (open palms like an open book), and so on. This won't inhibit her talking, but it may improve your communication.

⌁ A MOTHER'S VIEW ⌁

"My Baby Has Cerebral Palsy"

Savannah Diffenderfer has always been a happy, good-natured child, much like her two older sisters. But her mother, Stella, noticed that from an early age, Savannah was developing differently from the way her two sisters had. Savannah's motor skills lagged behind her sisters' at the same age, but weren't out of the range of normal. What really worried Stella, though, was that Savannah wasn't babbling. "Nobody agreed with me that there was a reason to worry," remembers the mom from Smyrna, Tennessee. "Maybe it was mother's intuition," she says, "but I just felt that she wasn't like my other kids."

At her 12-month well-baby visit, Savannah's pediatrician checked her hearing and found no problems. When she still wasn't walking or babbling at 14 months, her doctor referred her to a pediatric neurologist. His diagnosis: cerebral palsy.

Stella fought her fears—Would Savannah ever walk? Would she have to wear leg braces?—with action. By the time the baby was 15 months old she had started physical therapy, occupational therapy, and speech therapy.

Now, almost a year later, Savannah has caught up with her peers physically and can walk. She can say three words: "Mom," "Dad," and "Hi."

"When I first found out about her cerebral palsy, all I wanted to know is if she would walk," says Stella. "But every time she hits a milestone, I get impatient for her to hit the next one." Her lack of speech hasn't prevented Savannah from communicating her emotions, her mom says: "She's a very happy child and she's got seven different happy expressions to let you know it."

Stella's tips:

- **Go with your gut.** If you think your child has a developmental problem, talk to her pediatrician. Don't worry that other people will think you're pushy.
- **Fight for early intervention.** The Diffenderfers had to make waves with their insurance company and learn the ins and outs of available services before they could get Savannah the help she needed.
- **Get support.** It's very helpful to talk to other parents who are in a similar situation.

mood, she'll help you dress her by lying still. She's better at taking off her clothes than at putting them on (or at lying still!).

Although every baby develops differently, you should talk to your child's pediatrician if you're worried that yours is slow to develop or has a particular problem. The doctor may be able to put your worries to rest. If not, he can direct you to a specialist or order tests to diagnose if there really is any sort of developmental problem. The point is to trust your instincts. If you feel in your gut that something's not right with your baby, you won't feel better until you get some help or advice.

A Parent's Life

What will you remember at the end of your first year as a parent? Your aching back? Your limited social life? The kazillion diapers you changed? Your extreme fatigue?

Well, maybe. But more likely you'll look back with fondness on a year filled with new developments and challenges and growing love. And you'll look forward to another year of getting to know your baby, of forging a new relationship with your partner, and of being a family.

A Very Big Milestone

As a baby's first birthday approaches, parents are often exhilarated and, sometimes, just a little sad. They're proud that their baby is so big and strong and smart, but also a little shocked that the year went by so fast. Of course, they love their fast-developing toddler, but sometimes they miss their *baby*.

This is a perfectly normal feeling after the whirlwind year you've just had. A baby's and parents' first year is, after all, a perfect example of the quote "There is nothing permanent except change." In the midst of all these mixed feelings, many parents find comfort in celebrating the passage of their baby's first year with a traditional birthday party. It's a nice time to take a breath and remember what a year it's been.

Meaningful Celebrations Every year since I've been an adult away from home, my parents call on my birthday and sing "Happy Birthday." And then, like clockwork, my mother says, "It was _____ [fill in the blank] years ago today that you were born. We remember that day as if it were yesterday. We love you, and we're proud of you."

It's their way of saying "we remember" and "you're still our baby"—even though I'm miles away and decades away from infancy.

Milestone

CELEBRATING THE FIRST BIRTHDAY

"I remember the first time I saw Alessandra's face. Now she's already independent and I wonder, 'Where did the time go?' We had a party and everyone was wearing little hats and I let her dig into the cake with her hands. She had cake all over her face, and I think she knew it was her birthday. Of course, I miss that moment when a baby comes out of you and you see her for the first time, but now I'm enjoying watching her develop and seeing her character come out."

A first birthday party can be lots of fun. Just remember that baby may sleep through the event or be overstimulated by the fuss.

—*Candida Cappucio, Montréal, Quebec*

"The first birthday is sort of a catch-22. I'm excited that Arin's advancing and maturing, but I also feel really sad. That stage in her life will never be there again, and it went by so fast. In a way, it's like a loss—a grieving period—because she's the last infant in my life."

—*Alesia Adams, San Francisco, CA*

"I was so excited about Lauren's first birthday. I reflected back on how far she'd come in the past year. I remembered what our life was like a year ago, and what a difference she's made. I no longer carry a purse—I carry a diaper bag! We're on her schedule now. I was relieved she made it through the first year. When you're a new mom, you worry about everything, but she made it and so did we! On her birthday we looked at pictures of her to remind us how she has grown. She kept pointing to the balloons. She couldn't care less about the presents, but she loved the bows and gift bags."

—*Brenda McAden, Memphis, TN*

"I was sort of depressed around Anna's birthday. When people would ask how old she was, I could never say, 'One year.' I would say 'Eleven months' or 'Eleven and a half months.' It was an emotional day for my husband and me, but she didn't pick up on it too much. The day she turned one, I felt she became a new person—someone who's independent and who doesn't need us as much."

—*Aviva Goldberg, Riverdale, NY*

⌒ A MOTHER'S VIEW ⌒

"Happy Birthday to You"

"Let's do it simple," Stephanie Navalta remembers saying to her mother about her daughter Kelsi's first birthday celebration. "But it's part of my culture to have a big old-fashioned party for the first birthday," says the San Jose, California, mom.

So a big party was planned: There would be a roast pig for the adults and an inflatable jumper and piñata for the 25 kids invited. And there would be Winnie-the-Pooh decorations everywhere, including on the birthday girl's party dress.

The big day finally arrived, the party started at noon, and the party girl? Well, she slept until 2:30.

"I was disappointed," says Stephanie, "but I didn't want to wake her up and have her be crabby." Still, she made an appearance for the critical moments: "She woke up in time for cutting the cake and opening the presents," says Stephanie. Her tips for a first birthday:

- **Admit that the party may be for you.** Parents are more than happy to celebrate an exciting first year. But your 1-year-old won't really know what's going on and may be more confused than pleased by all the commotion.
- **Plan activities for adults and kids if it's a mixed party.** Stephanie focused on entertaining the kids while her mother dealt with the adults.
- **Be prepared for the best-laid plans to go awry.** Stephanie had scheduled the party at noon so Kelsi would be fresh from her morning nap. But the pre-party excitement knocked Kelsi's routines out of whack. "I could have been uptight that she missed most of it," says Stephanie, "but I told myself it's just a party."

In my own family, looking back is the key to a meaningful birthday celebration. I also start my daughters' birthdays by greeting them in the morning with "One year ago today," "Two years ago today," and so on. I want each one to know that I'll never forget the day that she was born. We make sure to spend as much time looking at their baby books (neither one completed, but special nonetheless) as we do opening presents and eating cake.

You'll probably plan to celebrate your child's first birthday in some special way (although your baby will be fairly oblivious), but it's also nice to mark the end of the first year in some way with your partner. (You know, your spouse, that other person who used to be so important in your life.) The first year of parenthood can be hard on parents, drawing you closer in some ways and pushing you apart in others. As a birthday gift to yourselves, vow to spend more time focusing on each other and on your relationship.

How You're Feeling

Fatigue—and miscellaneous aches and pains—tend to travel with you into your second year of parenthood. Some moms wonder if they'll *ever* catch up on their sleep. But most women just get used to feeling tired now and then, and try to snatch a nap when they can. If you're feeling seriously fatigued, or

Q & A

"I'm still exhausted and I'm wondering if something serious is wrong with me?"

Fatigue can do a real number on new parents, well beyond the first year. If your tiredness doesn't go away after a few good nights of sleep, or it's accompanied by painful joints and muscles, depression, flulike symptoms, weight loss, or the shakes, call your doctor.

You may be suffering from postpartum thyroid problems, which can sometimes disturb your metabolism and cause severe fatigue.

Chronic fatigue syndrome (CFS) is another ailment that has a variety of flulike symptoms, including extreme tiredness. Although the cause is unknown, one study suggests that it's a form of treatable low blood pressure. While more studies are being done, doctors usually treat CFS with anti-inflammatories for pain and antidepressants for the depression.

In any case, when you're tired you will need extra help. Line up caregivers and baby-sitters, cut back on work, turn the baby over to your spouse—and get some much-needed rest.

are tired along with other symptoms, see your doctor to rule out chronic fatigue syndrome, a thyroid dysfunction, or some other problem.

Some women get so keyed up from juggling all the demands of new motherhood that even when they're tired and have a chance to sleep, they can't. One mother I know keeps a journal by her bed and when she gets insomnia she writes down all the thoughts spinning around in her head. Often, writing down what's bothering her helps her relax enough to fall asleep. Other sleep-inducing tricks:

- Do yoga or deep-breathing exercises to get in touch with your body and to calm you.
- Drink a glass of warm milk.
- Take a warm, soothing bath.
- Make love.

HOW TO
Save Your Back

As your baby gets heavier, it's even more important to take care of your back.

Do

- Sleep correctly. The best position for your back is on your side with a pillow between your legs. Your pillow shouldn't be too fluffy.
- Alternate sides if you hold your baby on your hip. Look at yourself in the mirror while you're holding your child like this, and you'll see how you're twisting your spine.
- Lower the crib side before lifting your baby out.
- Bend at the knees whenever you're lifting anything heavy.
- Consider carrying your purse and baby items in a fanny pack instead of a too-heavy purse (which will drag down one shoulder).
- Encourage your child to walk.
- Stand up straight (but don't force shoulders back).

Don't

- Lift your baby out of the car seat from afar. Get in close to your child, with one foot in the car, if possible. Then bring him to your chest before backing out and standing up.
- Spend too much time bending over the bathtub. There aren't a lot of alternatives to this position (other than getting in with the baby), but do your best to sit upright. When you're lifting him out, bend at the knees.
- Give piggyback rides or shoulder rides. Why not? Because they hurt. And one of the worst things you can do is to lift weight *above* your shoulders.

ᶜᵉ⁓ A MOTHER'S VIEW ⁓ᵉᵒ

"I'm Still Not Getting Enough Sleep"

Cullen Murray began sleeping through the night at 10 months old. His mother, Amy, still can't. "Before he was born, I had no sleeping problems," says Amy. But waking up several times a night has become a habit that she can't seem to break—even 10 months later.

"I'm always listening for the baby because I know my husband won't hear him," says the DeKalb, Illinois, mom.

Amy has even been to the doctor for sleep advice. "He said I have to relax," she says, with a tired sigh. "I'm trying." And she is making progress, albeit slowly. She recently slept through the night three times. "It was amazing," she says. Here are some of the ways Amy has tried to get—or catch up on—sleep:

- **Exercise more.** Physical activity releases chemicals that can relax you.
- **Avoid caffeinated drinks.** Amy doesn't even drink water after 5 P.M. so that she won't wake up to use the bathroom in the middle of the night.
- **Reserve your bed for sleeping.** Amy had been doing her homework for nursing school in bed, but has set up a corner office in her bedroom instead.
- **Take short naps.** Nap during the day to catch up on lost zzzs, but not so much that you aren't tired at night.
- **Get help from relatives.** When Amy's husband is out of town, she and Cullen go to Grandma's house. Grandma will get up in the night to check on Cullen so Amy doesn't have to.

Your Aching Back Now that your baby is heavier, it can be a real strain on your back to pick him up and carry him around. It's more important than ever to lift the correct way, and to strengthen your back and abdominal muscles with exercise.

Stretching is a great way to limber up your back. And gentle sit-ups help build strong tummy muscles, which in turn provide better support for your back.

WHOLE BACK STRETCH
1. Get on your hands and knees.
2. Drop your head while tightening your tummy muscles and rounding up your back; exhale.
3. Inhale while raising your head.
4. Repeat ten times.

Whole Back Stretch, step 2.

LOWER BACK STRETCH
1. Lie on your back with your shoulders pressed to the floor and arms relaxed at your sides; feet are flat on floor, knees bent.
2. Bring both knees up to your chest (don't use arms).

Lower Back Stretch, step 1. *Lower Back Stretch, step 2.*

3. Rotate both knees to the left side and rest them on the floor for a count of three.
4. Return knees to the center; count to three.
5. Drop knees to the right side until they touch the floor; count to three.
6. Return to center and repeat each side three times.

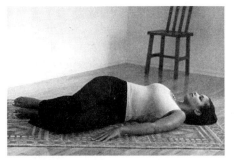

Lower Back Stretch, step 3.

TUMMY TIGHTENER
1. Lie on your back with feet flat on the floor and knees bent; arms at your sides.
2. Bring your left knee and your head up simultaneously while exhaling.
3. Hold and count to five.
4. Return head and feet to floor.
5. Repeat with other leg.
6. Do ten repetitions per leg.

Tummy Tightener, step 2.

We Are Family

You've been a family for a year now, but you still may have plenty of parenting issues to work out with your partner. A common conflict that arises at this stage of parenthood is the difference in child-rearing styles. During the first year, there wasn't much to disagree about (except the usual: sex, chores, and money). Few parents fight over how to change a diaper, for instance, or have strong feelings about the best way to heat a bottle.

All of that changes when your baby is eating at the table with you and getting more active. The early toddler years can be a real challenge to parents—even more so for parents who don't agree on how to guide their baby to good behavior.

Let's say you disagree on how you should deal with your toddler who has started hitting the dog. You believe he should be punished—put into a one-minute time-out on your lap, for instance. Your partner, however, just thinks it's funny. Then you feel like the bad guy. You think it's OK for your children to watch a half hour of educational TV now and then. Your partner believes it's lazy and inappropriate to let a TV be a baby-sitter, even for a minute. But you're the one who's home all day with the baby and, hey, a half hour is such a short amount of time.

Who's right? Who's wrong? You both are. To avoid constant conflicts and sending your child mixed signals, parents need to develop and then focus on common goals. Nobody wants a violent child, but maybe the dog just needs to be put outside or the child needs to be redirected instead of punished. You both want your baby to have a high-quality, enjoyable day, but maybe a half hour of TV is OK as long as you watch with him.

By setting common goals you'll feel that you're working together. Other tips:

- Avoid saying: "This is the way my parents did it" to your partner. The inevitable response will be: "So? That doesn't make it right." Your job is to create your own family rules together.
- Do discuss how you were raised, however, so that your partner has an idea of where you're coming from, and vice versa. If you were forced to sit at the table for two hours after everyone else was finished because you hated spinach, that goes a long way toward explaining your leniency when your baby tosses her food off her plate.
- Don't fall into the good guy/bad guy trap. Even if one parent is home more often, parents should be united on the discipline front. Never give your children a way to play you off each other. (Even toddlers will figure out how to do this.)
- Don't criticize your spouse, or argue, in front of your child. Even at this age, your child will be all ears. You're supposed to be building each other up, not cutting each other down. If you do argue in front of your little one, make sure she sees you kissing and making up, too.
- Think compromise. Then you both win.
- Be flexible. Know that there's more than one way to be "right."
- Disagree nicely and solve problems quickly. Don't let bad feelings fester, and don't act as if it's grounds for divorce every time you disagree about a time-out. Arguments have a way of escalating when such discussions start with "You always . . ." Stick to the issue at hand, not past grievances.

If you can't seem to find a common ground with your partner, consider couples counseling. It's not unusual for child-rearing to be the issue that sets couples adrift. A counselor can help you improve understanding and communication.

Growing Your Family First birthdays and the end of babyhood often inspire parents to start thinking about having another baby. And why not, since your first one is such a joy?

Of course, this is a decision that only you and your partner can make. If spacing (how many years between your children) is an issue, you may want to talk with other families about their experiences. You might also want to take a look at the size of your home and your budget. But most of all, check out the size of your heart. Many parents *can't imagine* ever loving another child as much as their first one. But hearts have an amazing way of growing—and all other obstacles pale in the face of parental love.

ILLUSTRATION CREDITS (by page number)

Thanks to Peg Perego for contributing the high chair used in the photo on page 188.

INDEX

Illustrations in the text are indicated by an italicized "i" next to the page number.

ABOUT THE AUTHOR

ANNE KRUEGER is past editor in chief of PARENTING magazine. She currently works as a freelance writer and editor specializing in family- and child-related publications. She lives in Knoxville, Tennessee, with her husband and two daughters, Halley Rose and Emily Grace.